Clarissa's Plots

University of Delaware Press
Manuscript Awards
for Eighteenth-Century Studies

The Moral Animus of David Hume (1987)
Donald T. Siebert

Literate Culture: Pope's Rhetorical Art (1989)
Ruben Quintero

Clarissa*'s Plots* (1992)
Lois E. Bueler

Clarissa's Plots

Lois E. Bueler

DELAWARE

Newark: University of Delaware Press
London and Toronto: Associated University Presses

Associated University Presses
440 Forsgate Drive
Cranbury, NJ 08512

Associated University Presses
25 Sicilian Avenue
London WC1A 2QH, England

Associated University Presses
P.O. Box 338, Port Credit
Mississauga, Ontario
Canada L5G 4L8

The paper used in this publication meets the requirements
of the American National Standard for Permanence of Paper
for Printed Library Materials Z39.48-1984.

Library of Congress Cataloging-in-Publication Data

Bueler, Lois E.
    Clarissa's plots / Lois E. Bueler.
      p.   cm.
    Includes bibliographical references and index.
    ISBN 0-87413-496-X (alk. paper)
    1. Richardson, Samuel, 1689–1761. Clarissa. 2. Epistolary
fiction, English—History and criticism. 3. Man-woman relationships
in literature. 4. Plots (Drama, novel, etc.) I. Title.
PR3664.C43B84   1994
823'.6—dc20   93-38743
                                              CIP

PRINTED IN THE UNITED STATES OF AMERICA

Contents

Preface 7

1. The Background 11
2. The Tested Woman Plot 22
3. Clarissa's Test 41
4. Clarissa's Trial 70
5. The Don Juan Plot 100
6. Prudence: The Plot of the Purposeful Life 117
7. Three into One: Plotting
   and Epistolary Technique 141

Notes 158
Works Cited 172
Index 177

Preface

In the broad sense this book is a source study, designed to describe the major received plots out of which *Clarissa* is constructed. As such it stems from my interest in Renaissance dramatic plots, especially in what I call the Tested Woman Plot. The book is also a structural study, making a particular argument about how dramatic plots work and treating Richardson's epistolary novel as in some important ways a dramatic construct. On the other hand, in no sense does this book attempt a complete critical reading of *Clarissa*. I have intended textual citations to be representative rather than comprehensive. Though I have acknowledged specific critical debts and have briefly situated my discussion in the context of Richardson criticism, I have focused on primary texts.[1] I have aimed, in short, for a slender book.

This aim has influenced some of my stylistic choices. For citations to the text of *Clarissa* I am using Angus Ross's 1986 edition, based on the first (1748) published edition of the novel. The attractions of Ross's text include its easy availability, its useful apparatus, its clear letter-numbering system, and the fact that it provides a base against which to identify the authorial explanations and elaborations of later editions. Since several other editions are in common use, however, my reference system is intended to allow all readers to find their places easily. Each textual citation includes Ross's letter number, the date as supplied by Richardson or (in brackets) as extrapolated, the initials or name of the recipient, and Ross's page number (e.g., L 522, to JB, 30 Sept., 1454). Where recipients of Lovelace's and Clarissa's letters are not indicated, Belford and Miss Howe, respectively, are to be understood. In discussing the plot characteristics of literary works other than Richardson's, most notably in chapter 2 with its survey of the Tested Woman Plot in Renaissance drama, I have restricted examples in the text to well-known plays, especially those of Shakespeare, and have used the endnotes lightly for illustrations from lesser known works.

I am pleased to acknowledge several specific professional debts. In

1989 when I was beginning to formulate my description of the Prudence
Plot, a National Endowment for the Humanities summer seminar in virtue
ethics at Harvard University guided me in reading both classical theory and
the modern debate. I am grateful to Professor Amélie O. Rorty for inviting
a student of literature to join her group of philosophers, and to the other
seminar participants for their helpful patience with a professional outsider.
I wish to thank the Special Collections librarians of the National Art Library
of the Victoria and Albert Museum for their hospitality in giving me access
to Richardson's correspondence. Correspondence from the Forster Collection is cited courtesy of the Trustees of the Victoria and Albert Museum.
Here at California State University, Chico, a helpfully timed sabbatical leave
in spring 1991 allowed me to complete the manuscript. My colleague
Gilbert Prince's graciously perceptive reading of the draft pushed me to
clarify my argument and chasten my style. My colleague Karen Hatch was
kind enough to scrutinize my translations from French and Italian. Finally
I am particularly grateful to Florian Stuber of the Fashion Institute of
Technology, SUNY, and reader for the University of Delaware Press, whose
commentary narrowed my focus, expanded my critical frame of reference,
and saved me from errors of fact.

My deeper debt cannot be encompassed by acknowledgment, for in a
real sense this book is a joint project. My colleague Victor Lams, himself at
work on a book about *Clarissa*, introduced me to the novel at a point at
which I was stymied in my attempts to extend my understanding of the
Tested Woman Plot beyond drama or beyond the Renaissance. Since then
he has abetted my enthusiasm, guided my critical and philosophical reading, welcomed my conversation, read untold pages of draft, and profoundly
influenced my understanding of the psychology of Richardson's characters
by means of his own fresh and wide-ranging work. No page of what follows
is without his presence. This book, then, is for him.

Clarissa's Plots

1

The Background

Despite Dr. Johnson's quip that if we were to read *Clarissa* for the story we would hang ourselves, the story is precisely what we do read it for. What happened, what is happening, what will happen, and to whom, are what hold us—or nothing does. Johnson's comment, made more than two decades after the novel appeared, may reflect the emphasis of fond familiarity: "Why, Sir, if you were to read Richardson for the story, your impatience would be so much fretted that you would hang yourself. But you must read him for the sentiment, and consider the story as only giving occasion to the sentiment."[1] Nevertheless, the evidence of Richardson's readers, then and now, belies him. What *is* happening among the Harlowes? Will Clarissa flee? Will Lovelace resort to rape? Will they marry? Will he repent? Must she die? These are plot questions, they are also very deep psychological questions, and *they* are what keep the pages turning, and have since Richardson initially tantalized his public with serial publication. When his first readers bombarded him with advice and inquiry about his all-too-slowly appearing story, these were the matters they harped on. When modern critics snarl at or condescend to each other or the text, these finally are the matters they are trying to come to terms with.[2] When Sarah Fielding marveled at the patience of friends reading *Sir Charles Grandison* and agreeing *not* to peep to see how it came out,[3] she was marveling at the capacity of Richardson to hold his readers by the unfolding of his story—which means, of course, with the evolving interactions among his characters—despite the pace at which he seems to move. All the more so is this true for *Clarissa*.

But we have to be reading the right story. The positions to which critics have often resorted, and the pressures for amending his design to which Richardson was subjected and which he refused, suggest how frequently readers have sought to read *Clarissa* as a courtship story. Doing so threatens to turn the novel into a vastly extended and frustrating version of the sexual foreplay of an overly fastidious Millamant and her unscrupulous

Mirabell. Will Lovelace ever combine, with the wit, grace and sexual energy which so clearly attract Clarissa, the steadiness that makes him acceptable marital material? And will Clarissa, estimable frost piece, admit the
sexual awakening that allows courtship, and develop the worldly flexibil-
ity that makes it possible for her to dwindle from paragon among virgins
into a wife? Can these two people make a contract? Why can't these two
people bring themselves to the point of contract? Surely Clarissa, Lovelace,
and Richardson himself are indulging a delicious but ultimately exhaust-
ing coyness bordering on the perverse.

Reading for that story will indeed frustrate us, and will deprive the
last third of the novel of any point beyond the merely sentimental. But
Clarissa is not a courtship story; it is not even, in any schematic sense, a
love story, though readers may be excused for thinking so. Miss Howe,
after all, thinks so. Yet none of the principals—not Lovelace, not Clarissa,
and emphatically not Richardson himself—act as though courtship is what
they are primarily about. They are committed to a different story, one
which has a moral struggle at its heart and moral judgment as its ultimate
purpose. That *Clarissa* has a homiletic flavor is no news. Nor is it any
longer news that Richardson's work has (perhaps enormously sophisticated) literary shape, that his characters are not merely gabbing their way
through an improvised set of conversations made up "to the moment." As
Jocelyn Harris says, "Richardson's novels depend upon ancient and modern books, not only locally but structurally" ("Richardson,"190). For all
the recent, much deserved attention to the literary, social and psychological intricacies of the novel, however, critical commentary has not thrown
much light on *why the story goes as it does.* Peter Brooks notes that "Plot is
so basic to our experience of reading, and indeed to our very articulation of
experience in general, that criticism has often passed it over in silence, as
too obvious to bear discussion" (*Reading for the Plot,* xi). If plot in *Clarissa*
were merely a matter of the obvious, it would bear discussion for its very
saliency. But I will argue that Richardson's technical innovations and his
indebtedness to a variety of narrative traditions render the novel's plot
structure far from obvious and thus additionally worth investigating.

This book is about why *Clarissa* goes as it does, and how seeing its
plot relationships is crucial to explaining its complexities. I argue that
Clarissa is constructed on an intricate web built from the interweaving of
three different plot structures. The first of these structures, the one that best
accounts for the main features of how the novel goes, has no name among

literary critics until we give it one. But it has a venerable history based squarely in the stage plays, homiletic texts, and Christian mythology that together constituted Richardson's chief literary background. I call this structure the Tested Woman Plot. The second plot which helps structure *Clarissa* does have a ready-made name. It is famous as the story of Don Juan and in the mid-eighteenth century it was at the height of its (almost exclusively dramatic) popularity. Unlike these two plots, whose antecedents are literary, the novel's third plot might best be described as meta-literary, though a version of it provides the narrative map for works like *The Pilgrim's Progress* to which we are happy to accord literary status. I call this the Prudence Plot, or the plot of the purposeful life, and find its antecedents in the combined classical and Christian virtue ethics tradition. Even before we know quite what these three plot structures are, it almost goes without saying that they vary from each other in significant and potentially radically incompatible ways. All three of them, however, contain to a rare degree what Angus Ross, characterizing the source of *Clarissa*'s greatest power, calls "the tensions of myth."[4] My purpose in describing them and their interworkings in the novel is to help account for those tensions, and in the process to help explain why *Clarissa* develops a power unavailable to Richardson's other two novels.

I have characterized the Tested Woman Plot as the plot most central to *Clarissa*'s narrative progression. I readily admit that "plot" may at first seem too confined and orderly a term for the events and characters that comprise it. Nevertheless, wherever it appears the Tested Woman Plot constitutes a fixed type identifiable chiefly by two features. One of these is its two-stage event sequence. The Tested Woman Plot first confronts the woman with a moral choice upon which she must act. Then, her choice made, the plot engages in an intensely communal judgment of that action. In addition to the two-stage choice/judgment sequence focused on the woman, the Tested Woman Plot also features a distinctive set of male character relationships and functions. The functions of Tempter, of Accuser, of Defender, and of Judge always occur in the plot, and although they may be combined in a single man, typically they are allotted for dramatic effect among a whole cast of male characters. Though highly complex and flexible, such an event structure and such character functions hold with remarkable consistency in all the literary genres in which the plot is found. The Tested Woman Plot is particularly pervasive in Renaissance and Restoration drama, however, which is the body of work that most influenced the more narrowly literary features of both *Clarissa* and its experimental predecessor *Pamela*.

Given the Tested Woman Plot's combination of histrionic and homiletic opportunities, Richardson found it compellingly attracting to his talents. His profound understanding of this plot, his taking for granted of the scheme within which he worked, is corroborated by his exasperation and his resort to increasingly didactic tinkering when his readers refused to see what he was up to as clearly as he himself did. Part of his problem was that the Tested Woman Plot had reached its high point as a quintessentially Renaissance construct whose brilliant practice on the Elizabethan and Jacobean stage had grown out of late medieval and Tudor psychomachic and homiletic theater. In using the plot Richardson was working with a tradition that had lost much of its literary power and social purpose. In retrospect we may say that he was attempting to find a new literary form in which to return that purpose to public notice, and that the form he found was obscured as well as enriched by the psychological complexity and sheer length of his novel.

The second plot with which Richardson was working in *Clarissa* is that of the Don Juan, again a plot identifiable both by its configuration of characters and by another two-stage structure. Elements of the Don Juan Plot were more immediately recognized by Richardson's readers, partly because it was essentially an Enlightenment construct rather than the soon-to-be-outmoded artifact of a previous age. Or perhaps we should say that readers were more readily prepared to identify the central figure of the plot, the libertine. Clarissa's readers were so attuned to the Don Juan figure himself, in fact, that Richardson worried obsessively about their finding one of Don Juan's expected features, his atheism, where that feature did not quite exist. But the libertine does not make the plot. It is important to understand, as Richardson understood, that no plot is identifiable merely by the presence of certain character types. The Don Juan Plot is not coterminous with the rake figure, any more than the Tested Woman Plot is identical with the figure of the abused woman. What distinguishes the Don Juan Plot, like any other plot, is its event sequence and its character groupings. In addition to the libertine, the necessary characters of this plot include his cohort of disciples, a succession of sexually attempted women from a variety of social backgrounds, and the avenging male who represents not just the family honor of one of those women, but the hand of Death itself. The event sequence requires an extended alternation of vauntings, seductions, and abandonments which find their only possible cessation in the libertine's self-sought encounter with Death.

The third, or Prudence, Plot, the plot of the wise, purposeful, and well-formed life, must be somewhat differently described because at root it is not a literary plot, but an ethical one. This means that the cases from which we extrapolate its structure are presented to us as historical rather than literary cases: they are examples of human beings from the world of lived experience, rather than examples of characters or personae from the world of the imagined experience of literary discourse. Not that the realms of the literary and the ethical will not overlap and commingle; that they *do* do so is part of the point of both. But the models from which the Prudence Plot is taken are finally held up as lived patterns, just as they are held up as frankly exemplary patterns, for they are intended to be models of what is both desirable and susceptible of human achievement. "Have you your Thomas à Kempis, sister?" Arabella's jibe situates us squarely in this third, this ethical, plot.

Yet I will argue that *Clarissa* is working to fashion this ethical plot into literary form. Now we know that in order to grant the Prudence Plot any sort of literary status we must be able to find in it also a stable set of characters or character functions and a predictable event sequence. The event sequence of the plot comes from its ethical requirement for the "formèdness" of the whole life, which gives it a moral teleology based in the classical and Christian tradition of character or virtue ethics. Its event sequence is that of the ages of man, involving at minimum the stages of youthful training, adult civic or social life, old age, the moment of death, and the posthumous reception or reading of the life. What gives these stages their sense of a plot is that they are all mediated by a coherent set of moral intentions or aspirations, an inner life that makes of the lead character not merely a patient submitting to the inevitable course of human existence, but the agent of the story of the consciously formed self. In this tradition, the characters are also prescribed. The agent or protagonist shapes and performs her life amid characters representing various kinds of virtues or their corresponding vices, shapes and performs it by the side of a special friend or soul mate who both mirrors and promotes the protagonist's excellence, shapes and performs it under the eyes of a judge who hands down the interpretation or reading of the whole life. This character cluster of exemplars, companion, and judge pertains whether the context is classical or Christian, though the specifically Christian version invests God rather

than the voice of history or of the *polis* with the role of judge, and sometimes positions Christ as both master exemplar and chief companion to the
striving believer.

This book argues that it is the interweaving of these three plot structures, with their different but in some ways potentially compatible systems, that creates the story of *Clarissa*. Subsequent chapters will explore
their literary and philosophical antecedents in some detail. Here the question is how Samuel Richardson came to know about them. The short but
finally most explanatory answer is that they were "in the air." Though it is
notoriously hard to trace Richardson's specific sources and influences, and
the less literary the material the harder,[5] nevertheless plot structures may
accurately and usefully be ascribed to a generalized cultural matrix in ways
that certain other features of his work cannot. So let us attend to what we
do know about Richardson's intellectual milieu, and let us start with Richardson's meager testimony about his own education and its relation to the
Prudence Plot. In his long letter of June 1753 to his Dutch correspondent
and translator Johannes Stinstra, Richardson famously draws a portrait of
his not-quite-eleven-year-old self getting in deserved trouble with his mother
for having penned a letter of moral admonition to a neighborwoman.[6] The
date of the episode is 1700 or thereabouts, for Richardson was born in
1689, and the verbally precocious young "Gravity" with his dame's school
education has already been both reading and listening. Within a few years
he will be writing letters mediating the delicate social and ethical complexities of family relationships, employment, and matrimony for young
women of his acquaintance.[7]

No writer, much less a juvenile writer, invents literate forms from
scratch. Students of Richardson are aware of his general familiarity with
the homiletic discourse of the age, from the sermons to the conduct books.[8]
I wish also to posit a specific influence suggestive for its currency, its
popularity, and its generic fit with Richardson's juvenilia. In 1690 John
Dunton and friends, among whom were men of letters including John Norris
as advisors and respondents, launched a journalistic experiment, the *Athenian Mercury,* that in one form or another held the attention of the public
for the next two decades. A weekly paper, the *Mercury* combined the various functions of our range of nationally syndicated advice columns. Its
"Athenians" responded to and admonished about the questions and per-
plexities submitted by their readers, on issues ranging from science to biblical exegesis to career counseling to cases of conscience. The *Mercury*

had an extraordinarily long run of seven years, and it spawned several imitators. It also yielded a "best of" collection, the *Athenian Oracle,* which appeared as a three-volume set in 1704, went into a subsequent edition in 1706, and created enough demand to make feasible a *Supplement to . . .* volume in 1710.[9] As one reads the questions and answers, one finds oneself among the social situations, ethical concerns, casts of characters, and language of Richardson's *Familiar Letters* and of his novels. "*Q.* Whether it is lawful to marry a person one cannot love, only in compliance to relations, and to get an estate?" (I, 31). "*Q.* Whether it is honourable for a lady to answer a gentleman's letters, when she intends not to entertain him?" (II, 272). "*Q.* I am a young woman that have been very dutiful to my parents, and have ever thought it my duty so to be; but now they have proposed a match for me whom I cannot love, therefore I humbly desire your advice, how I shall discharge my duty" (II, 227).

The importance of the *Athenian* material to my argument is that it bridges from the received virtue ethics tradition of Aristotle, Cicero, Aquinas, and seventeenth-century Anglican divines and philosophers to the daily social, moral, and literary interests of the printer's apprentice. For the Athenians are practicing Christian casuistry. "Put case," demands the practice of casuistry. "Given the generalized, theoretical precepts of Christian morality (or Stoic ethics, or English law), what should *this person* do *now,* faced as she is with this problem, this need, this set of circumstances?" Casuistry, in short, is dramatistic ethics, infused with the energies, idiosyncrasies and complications of the lives of particular agents but controlled or structured by the "plots" provided by well-enunciated ethical systems. To the query directed at theory—"Who is my neighbor?"—it responds with particulars of time, place, and human characteristics: "A certain man went down from Jerusalem to Jericho, . . ." In fact, as Albert Jonsen and Stephen Toulmin remind us in *The Abuse of Casuistry* (116), a case is at root a narrative. Casuistry tells particular stories. The casuistical tradition can even be said to "perform" those stories, for at its most fluent and compelling it gives voice to the characters themselves, who speak their positions and problems.[10]

Though Richardson was too young to have read the *Mercury* from its beginnings, he cannot but have known of it, and heard people read from it, at an early age. The paper was vastly popular among middle-class Londoners, including women, and it is tempting to imagine the youngster learning to read by making out some of its questions and answers for himself. At least we are safe to assume that by the time the compilation provided by the *Athenian Oracle* appeared in 1704, Richardson would have had wind of it. It was the kind of thing he himself had been practicing.

The tradition of virtue ethics behind the advice columns of the *Athenian Mercury* was directly available to every literate English man and woman by means of the plethora of casuistical treatises and conduct books (primarily seventeenth-century) of which *Holy Living and Holy Dying* and *The Whole Duty of Man* were the best known then and now. But the tradition was also formally debated and elucidated by philosophers of Richardson's own day such as John Norris the Athenian, who figures in *Clarissa,* and Bishop Joseph Butler, who had close family connections with Richardson's circle of intimates.[11] Though Richardson was not an educated man by the standards of his day, which really means that he had not undergone the male rite of passage that was Latin schooling,[12] he was thoroughly conversant with the bourgeois culture of his London. Such was a printer's business in an era when printers fulfilled the function of the modern publisher, and Richardson was conspicuously competent and successful at his trade.[13] If one follows the published and unpublished correspondence of the 1740s when he was writing his first two novels,[14] one can understand his business success. Scrupulously honest, unceasingly industrious, generously careful of the interests of all the people with whom he did business, he was also alert to authors, titles, and publishing trends. Over the period of years when he supplied his friends with free reading from his press and shelves one can catch him locating, recommending, commenting on or even providing summaries of everything from divinity tracts to scientific theory to political polemic to geographies and travelers' memoirs. Though he complained that he never read as much as he wished,[15] he appears to have skimmed, composed, proofed, priced, advertised, summarized, critiqued, or been alerted by his friends to a great deal of what was available to the reading public.

In addition to sermons, conduct books, cautionary tales, and casuistry, this included the drama of the late Renaissance and Restoration stage. That Richardson should be indebted to an entire 150 years of drama is not as surprising as it may seem. Unlike the repertory of the Elizabethan and Jacobean stage which was mostly composed new for the occasion, that of Richardson's day was primarily a repertory of revivals which included not just Restoration plays but, by the 1730s and 1740s, increasingly frequent performances of Shakespeare and of Jacobean drama. In addition to attending performances, at least as a young man, Richardson undoubtedly read some plays. Many more plays he learned about, presumably through the kind of conversation that figures in his novels, through scanning and skimming the works he printed, and through contact with the playwright Aaron Hill, his closest friend during the 1730s and 1740s, and with the other playwrights, actors and impresarios he came to know.[16]

But what did he know about such plays? Here we must rely primarily on the evidence of the novels. We may consult Pamela's discussion of Richard Steele's *Tender Husband* or Belford's condemnation of the heroine of Nicholas Rowe's *Fair Penitent* for extended pieces of moralistic criticism. But most significant is what the novels reveal about Richardson's way with characters and plot patterns. Although the bulk of the actual dramatic quotations in *Clarissa*, say, could have been culled from volumes like Edward Bysshe's *Art of English Poetry*, the plays from which they are taken—primarily those of Shakespeare, Lee, Otway, Dryden, and Rowe—were staples of the stage and reading repertory. What Richardson mostly knew of such plays, in addition to the purple passages that made their way into the compendia, was "how they went," what happened to the Claras and the Millwoods and the Roderigos and why, just as we know how prime-time television goes, and why. Popular drama, whether on the stage or in the soaps, is about standard character types and plots and moves, and these are matters which Richardson had absorbed.

But he also knew the stereotyped scenic structures and verbal and gestural language of the eighteenth-century stage, and in Lovelace he created a master actor and impresario. When Lovelace displays for Belford, as he does in virtually every letter, his style and his staging are almost inevitably histrionic. Frequently he recounts a dialogue, performing both sides of the agon with equal relish. We see such a sequence at its height in the face-off with Morden (L 442 & 443, 29 Aug., 1278ff.) where we watch the two gamecocks bluster and circle and perform their rhetorical body slams, while Lord M flutters to attract our attention to the dangerous moments, and reinforcements burst in to strengthen the dramatic build. At other times Lovelace set-designs, casts, and produces an entire scene. The dinner at Mrs. Sinclair's is intended to be a particularly effective example of this technique (L 161, CH to AH, 1 May, 542ff.). By contrast there are the episodes intended to display his virtuosity as an actor, even his quick-change mastery of styles and disguises: witness the "old rake" scene at Hampstead (L 233, RL to JB, 9 June, 767ff.). The stylized, theatrical body gestures with which Richardson is replete—the uplifted eyes and hands, the kneelings, raisings, flingings, wieldings of handkerchiefs—are found everywhere in *Clarissa*.[17] But they are especially thickly packed in Lovelace's text. The gestural equivalents of the appellations "charmer" and "angel," they represent the stock stage language of heightened passion. Where they come by repetition to call attention to their own theatricality, as in Lovelace's letters, they lead inevitably to the impression of passion both deliberately heightened and artificially conveyed. They betoken "acting" and therefore are rightly the special property of Richardson's most self-consciously histrionic character.

Drama, however, had more appeal for Richardson than its sheer popularity, or even its histrionic energy. Richardson lived for conversation, in person and on paper, and what he wanted to talk about was morality and ethics—the right behavior of people in society. Before the rise of that novel which Richardson helped create, plays were the literary genre in which different versions of social interaction got aired, argued for, jeered at, and wept over. This fact stems from more than the mere availability of plays; it is a matter of the genre's peculiar requirements. Then as now, plays put the burden of interpretation on the reader or spectator in a way demanded by no other literary mode. Playwrights try to control the interpretation of their work, it is true: Rowe's epilogue to *The Fair Penitent* tells us that husbands wouldn't be cuckolded if they didn't cheat on their wives, and two hundred years later Shaw insists upon explaining at far greater length why Freddy Eynesford-Hill will be a suitable husband for Eliza Doolittle. But such authorial intervention never works. It is the play itself—its characters, their acts, their evident intentions—that we must interpret for ourselves, just as we do the people around us, since neither author nor narrator is present to do it for us. Because Richardson lived for the act of social and ethical interpretation, drama was the literary genre that interested him most.

What we see in the novels, above all in *Clarissa,* is Richardson's struggle to find forms and structures that will both maximize and guide the need for interpretation—that will build the individual ethical case in its richest and most dramatistic form so as to involve the reader most fully in the effort of analysis and judgment. For in drama, we the readers or spectators become the casuists; it is we to whom the case keeps being put. Not surprisingly, then, the drama of his day supplied the stories that keep the readers turning Richardson's pages, and making what he hopes will be his judgments. The question then becomes: what is the origin of these plots and how are they built?

The case of the Don Juan Plot is fairly simple: the plot type is essentially a post-Renaissance artifact and the drama of the hundred years preceding *Clarissa* is the source. We can speculate with fair accuracy about whose play Richardson had chiefly in mind, and we can describe the type structure of the plot fairly easily. The case of the Tested Woman Plot is immensely more complicated. That plot type is as ancient as the major myths of Western culture; its prototypal tales are found in Greek myth, the Old Testament, Hellenistic romance, medieval hagiography; its prototypal women are the Susannas, Constances, Virginias, Lucretias, the virgin martyrs faced with the unholy urges of salacious Roman magistrates and the kings' daughters adrift among lascivious pirates. The tales appear sporadically among late medieval plays and become a fixture of Tudor homiletic drama, presumably as much for the inherently dramatistic nature of their conflict as for their didactic drive. The realistic or "literal" drama of the Elizabethan and Jacobean stage uses the plot compulsively and brilliantly in comedy, romance, tragedy, domestic drama. Astonishingly many of the greatest plays of the English Renaissance theater—*Othello* and *The Duchess of Malfi, Ralph Roister Doister* and *A Woman Killed with Kindness* and *Measure for Measure, The Changeling* and *The Broken Heart* and *The Winter's Tale* and many more—are Tested Woman plays. Thence to the heroic drama and "she tragedy" of Dryden and Otway, Lee and Rowe, precisely those works which Lovelace cites compulsively.

So of Richardson's knowledge of the Tested Woman Plot we can say this much: it *was* "in the air," it had permeated the English drama of the two hundred years preceding Richardson, and the evidence of his novels themselves points both to specific plays from which he borrowed its argument and design, and to general assumptions about character and structure that are typical of the plot type.

2

The Tested Woman Plot

The very notion of a moral test points to a fundamental feature of our Western ethical system. To say that one of the most elemental story types of Judeo-Christian culture describes the testing of a person's obedience to moral law is to say, first of all, that we construe morality legalistically. Not all cultures do so. Nor is a legalistic ethics the only ethics in the Western tradition, a fact we shall explore later. But it is unquestionably the dominant one, in which Hebraic and classical influences reinforce each other to conflate religious with civil morality and make law, whether sacred or secular, the controlling structure. When the legalistic tradition assumes narrative form in the story of moral demonstration, it focuses on obedience to the law. This legalistic bias imposes in turn upon the story's structure, and what it imposes is key structural features of the law itself.

To begin with, in our familiar Western story of the moral test, moral law is couched as prohibition. Theoretically, the Judeo-Christian ethical ideal can be summed up in positive terms: doing justice, loving mercy, and walking humbly with God represent the Jewish epitome, to which the Christian injunction to love God and one's neighbor constitutes a gloss rather than an extension. But in practice, in this legalistic tradition behavior tends to be scrutinized negatively, in terms of shalt-nots. The story of moral demonstration, then, has as its central issue the violation of a prohibition. Furthermore, the test tends to center on a single discrete action rather than on the sum of a character's intentions or behavior. It becomes a test of whether a character has violated a specific requirement rather than how well he or she has behaved in general. A third feature is that, since obedience to law means obedience to authority, the story of the moral test explores and sometimes questions the hierarchical relationships through which authority is expressed. Because in our tradition moral law is divine in its ultimate origins, even when expressed through human institutions, either overtly or

22

by implication the story of the moral test provides a mechanism for bringing into question the authority not just of man, but of God.

We can see these features starkly at work in the story of Adam and Eve. The Genesis story involves not the weighing of entire lives, but a single test of obedience. The issue is stated in the form of a prohibition which derives its force from the authority of its divine promulgator. Lest we have any doubt, Genesis validates this authority by framing the Garden narrative in the narrative of the Creation. In the story of the Edenic test, the Creator commands His creatures. There can be no stronger moral imperative.

But in the Edenic narrative we also see a seemingly unnecessary dramatic complication. The test requires only two participants, God and his creature, but we find a cast of four. The test might just as well have been directed by God, but instead it is directed by the serpent. It might just as well have targeted Adam, but instead it targets Eve. This multiplication of characters is motivated by the fact that moral tests occur only when moral authority is in disagreement or disarray—or at least appears to be so. The story of the Garden is constructed to demonstrate competing claims and allegiances. By putting the test on Eve, by placing her at the bottom of a hierarchy in which not just God but Adam and the serpent exercise authority, the Genesis story allows the playing off of one claim against another and opens the way to a questioning of the very concept of authority.

The multiplication of characters we see in the story of the Garden tells us something absolutely central about the tested woman: in plot terms she is a structural convenience, a device that makes possible the exploration of hierarchical relationships among authority figures. Like Adam, Eve is God's creature. But she is also Adam's wife and subject to Adam's marital authority. The serpent's approach, therefore, is made in part as though for Adam's benefit and Eve must weigh her obligation to Adam as well as to God. The approach is also made in terms which insinuate that the serpent himself is a superior being, superior in knowledge and by implication in authority and therefore worthy to be obeyed. Not Good against Evil, but one Good against another seeming Good—that is the stuff of the moral test, and that is what Eve is subjected to. Making Eve rather than Adam the object of the test is a simple way to introduce the competing claims which make a moral test possible. It gives dramatic form to the real issue: to what degree man, having been created in the image of God, has the right to share in His authority.

For exactly this dramatic reason, women are favorite objects of moral tests throughout Western literature. All manner of authority—civil and religious, parental and marital—can be exercised upon women by a variety of male figures, whether human or divine, for the ultimate purpose of establishing to whom that authority rightly belongs and how it is to be shared. Always these tests involve obedience. Usually they are focused on sexual behavior because in a patriarchal world it is a woman's sex that not only determines her hierarchical status but constitutes the very purpose for her existence. Sexual obedience or chastity, the appropriate reservation of her sexual and thus her reproductive services, is therefore her primary moral obligation because it is her primary social obligation: it is where her honor chiefly lies.

In the account I am giving, we see a telling conflation at work. The legalistic tradition out of which the story of the test arises, a tradition in which obedience to a prohibition is the moral key, comes to focus on a figure whose social identity is primarily defined in terms of her obedience to a prohibition. Unlike a man, a woman occupies her appropriate place in such a patriarchal society by means of, and only by means of, the fact that her sexual services are appropriately reserved or restricted in obedience to patriarchal prerogative. Her virtue—all her virtue—lies in what she does not do, what she refuses to do. In effect she becomes emblematic of an entire moral system based on prohibition. (Following the reductive logic of that system, we can see why it is no accident that modernly the word "virtue" refers primarily to women's chastity.) But when morality is based on prohibition and on prohibition alone, when the only virtue lies in refusal, then virtue can be demonstrated only under pressure. Without the occasion which allows its violation it is mere potential. Thus the prelapsarian Adam and Eve have no moral character; they just are. We have no basis for a moral estimate because there has been no opportunity for disobedience and therefore no moral choice. The same effect holds for the woman whose moral character is exclusively defined in terms of the passive virtue of chastity. Until she either violates or refuses to violate the prohibition which defines her, she has no moral character. Only a test which forces a choice can make her morality actual.[1]

Thus moral innocence really means moral ignorance, lack of knowledge of the test. Yet we must allow that in this moral system no woman after Eve totally lacks moral character. The moral genealogy is too potent, cultural expectations are too strong. For in the tradition with which we are dealing, a woman's sex also determines her psychological makeup, which is more passionate, more changeable, and more subject to temptation and vice than that of more rational males. Given the opportunity, women can be expected to err, as did Eve. "She is chaste whom no man hath solicited," sneers the bawd Dipsas in Ovid's *Amores* (I, 8). Only the extraordinary woman, supported by an unusual measure of divine grace, will be capable of virtuous behavior.

Interestingly, however, the great majority of stories about the testing of a woman work against the cultural expectation of female moral collapse. Though the fallen woman is a stock figure in Western literature, there is little to be said about her per se. It is the woman virtuous in the face of opportunity who is at the heart of the stock story. Perhaps this should not surprise us. The tale of the exercise of extraordinary virtue calls forth the dramatic power created by moral heroics and the reversal of audience expectations. Nevertheless, the testing plot has the same essential structure whether the woman stands or falls. The reason, which we shall explore shortly, is that its real dramatic and moral point lies not with the choice itself, but with the way authority interprets and responds to that choice. Further, occasions for choice may be repeated. And since once obedient does not mean always obedient, with each occasion the tested woman may fall, or the fallen woman may encounter new tests which allow her redemption. Thus the sequence may be played over and over, since the plot of the test, like the plot that is Christian life, ends definitively only with death.

The Tested Woman Plot is the literary formalization of the moral patterns and assumptions evident in the story of Adam and Eve. This formalization is always dramatic in the broad sense—that is, it consists of a narrative of human actions, employing human characters. And it is always centered on the test of a woman's obedience—usually her sexual obedience—to patriarchal authority. This brief survey of the plot's ethical background has alluded as a matter of course to archetypal features of Western patriarchy with which feminist cultural and literary criticism has made us thoroughly familiar. Among Richardson critics, both Carol Houlihan Flynn and Margaret Ann Doody give accounts of some of the ways this archetype found form in eighteenth-century literary convention and permeated Richardson's work.[2] Within this background, whose general familiarity I am assuming, my focus is the architectonics of the plot.

The two-stage event sequence typical of the Tested Woman Plot grows directly and naturally from the nature of the concept of obedience itself. The action of obedience requires at least two participants, the one who commands and the one who obeys. As a moral virtue, then, obedience has two components, fact and reputation. That is, it examines not just what the subordinate does, but what the superior thinks of it. This means that the plot which tests obedience contains a structural peculiarity: when exhibited in full it has two stages, a *fact* stage and a *reputation* stage. The first stage involves the occasion for disobedience itself, the point at which the woman takes or refuses an action of clear moral significance. To put the matter in terms both crude and familiar, it is the "will she or won't she?" point, the point at which her potential nature becomes actual. Schematically, the *moral issue* of this stage is *virtue* and its *essential dramatic action* is *choice*. To keep the terminology clear, I call this stage the *Test*. Although the Test may be spoken of as a temptation, it is significant that the woman faced with an occasion for sin may actually feel no desire to be unchaste or disobedient. The occasion for error does not necessarily induce the desire to err; the woman does not necessarily feel "tempted" in the ordinary sense of the word. On the other hand, she may experience a psychological struggle—a weighing of the appeals of competing claims or a desire to capitulate to worldly pressures.[3] In either case, the Test is the point at which she must choose to obey or disobey.

The second plot stage involves reputation—the opinion of others about the tested woman's action. It takes the form of an inquiry into the choice that occurred in the previous stage. In this second stage, the *moral issue* is *truth* and the *essential dramatic action* is *judgment*. I call this inquiry or demonstration the *Trial*, understanding that the trial is only sometimes formal or forensic. Once the woman's choice has been made, the Trial is a demonstration conducted by the authority figures to whom she owes obedience. If she has been disobedient, the Trial stage establishes that fact and metes out punishment. Even if she has been obedient, the Trial stage of the plot nevertheless goes on; in fact, most tested woman stories involve virtue upheld, if not always rewarded. During this Trial, the woman may simply be declared virtuous. Or she may face an honestly mistaken accusation based on genuinely misleading evidence against which she must be defended. Or she may be slandered by someone who wishes her downfall.[4] That the Trial goes on no matter what the woman's behavior underlines its fundamental purpose: it is conducted for the benefit, not of the woman, but of the men who command and judge her. The Genesis story is not for the edification of Eve. It is played out to educate the patriarchs Adam and Abraham and their seed forever, as *Paradise Lost* exhaustively establishes.

This two-stage event sequence invites richly productive literary variations without losing its essential shape. It may be entered at a number of different points, so that some of the required episodes occur before the story begins. Always, however, the antecedent portion of the plot is understood to have happened. Thus when *Othello* opens, the Test is already over. Desdemona has already made her choice—she has already left her father without his permission—and the entire first act is devoted to replaying that choice from a variety of perspectives. In the first act of *The Winter's Tale,* Hermione neither has been nor is being wooed illicitly, and thus has no sense of making a choice, so from one perspective the Test never occurs. But because Leontes in his madness thinks it has, the Tested Woman Plot is precipitated.

There is even greater variation in the way the Tested Woman Plot ends. The story cannot end until the truth has been demonstrated, it is true, but the Trial stage may be carried on largely or wholly without the woman's presence, even after her death.[5] Since the Trial concerns the woman's reputation rather than her ongoing actions, the record of her life is required for its conduct, but her physical presence is not. Some portion of the Trial typically is worked out without the woman present, whether her absence is caused by incarceration, casting away, sickness, madness, or actual death. A Tested Woman story is therefore open to striking variations of tone and mood depending on structural choices related to the timing of the Trial. The key manipulations involve how the truth about the woman emerges, when the male authority figures who surround her are able to come to a reconciliation among themselves, and whether she survives to see her vindication.

Many of these variations are exhibited by Shakespeare's four calumniated woman plays. The slandering of an innocent woman's chastity is the best-known variation on the Tested Woman Plot,[6] and Shakespeare uses it in *Much Ado About Nothing,* a comedy; *The Winter's Tale* and *Cymbeline,* both tragicomedies; and *Othello,* a tragedy. Thinking about these plays as a group clarifies the degree to which genre is a function of plot manipulation. In fact, seeing the variations at work in this one version of the Tested Woman Plot brings home a wider literary truth, the degree to which the manipulation of plot timing defines genre. The comic conclusions of reconciliation and joy are made possible because the plots buy time for the accused woman. The collapse of Hero and Hermione in the face of sudden, brutal, and seemingly unmotivated slander allows them to be hidden away as dead. Imogen's disguise and flight, along with the bloody sign which gives her out for dead, accomplishes the same thing. "Truth," says the Chorus of *The Winter's Tale*, "is the daughter of Time," and in the time bought by the women's absence change can be effected. *Othello*, on the other hand, allows no time. The claustrophobic physical and temporal concentration of its central three acts gives Desdemona no protection, Othello no possibility for reflection, and Desdemona's would-be defenders no working space to understand or to act. Iago uses this concentration as his chief tool, twisting and conflating dilatory time to his purposes. These variations suggest that if the woman can buy time for a fair trial—as the Duchess of Malfi tries to do, as Clarissa tries to do—she can hope that truth will out.

What time works toward is the face-to-face encounter among the men who surround the tested woman and whose competing claims have created the conflict to begin with. The Trial stage of the plot is constructed to seek the point at which the men will meet, examine the evidence about the woman, and know the truth. Iago's task is to prevent such an encounter, killing whoever might give evidence, sealing Othello off. Part of the tension of act 4, scene 1 arises because Cassio and Othello are together on stage yet inaccessible to each other: Cassio appears precisely when the swooning Othello is incapable of hearing him; Othello "oversees" Cassio's conversation with first Bianca and then Iago precisely without being able to hear them. In the comedies, the male encounters are timed beneficently. In the wonderful last scene of *Cymbeline*, father and husband and slanderer and faithful servant all meet, tell their fragments of the truth, and reach understanding and reconciliation before Imogen is reintroduced to them. In *The Winter's Tale* and *Much Ado*, the men meet and learn the truth, lay blame and take blame, perform acts of explanation and expiation, before Hermione and Hero can be reborn to them.

The genre variations in these versions of the Tested Woman Plot are owing, however, to something more than the timing within the separate plot lines that leads to the meeting and reconciliation of the competing men. They are also caused by the sequence in which the information reaches us. This feature is particularly clear in *Much Ado,* which is a romp because of the precise rhythm by which the Dogberry discovery action is interspersed with the Don John slander action. We first meet Dogberry within stage seconds after Don John has made his accusation against Hero. At the very moment that Conrade and Borachio boast about their part in the phony window scenario, we are hearing Dogberry and company overhearing. The arrival of Dogberry and crew to give evidence to the magistrate Leonato delays Leonato's departure for his daughter's wedding, where we know he will hear her slandered. Because we see these scenes in the order we do, we detect and rejoice in the providential workings of the plot. The mood established by the plot is a feature not just of the timing of the events in relation to each other, but the order and manner in which they are revealed to us. The powerful final scenes of *The Winter's Tale* and *Cymbeline* have very different flavors, although in terms of plot events they are rather similar. In one, the joyful surprise of the recovery of Hermione surprises us as well, while in the other our pleasure in the reconciliation of the men stems in part from our pleasure at sharing the event with Imogen herself. These variations remind us of what no merely formalist description of plot can convey: the power inherent in the manner and order of the telling.

In addition to its two-stage event sequence, the Tested Woman Plot is structured by a fixed set of characters or, more accurately, character functions. The woman herself is routinely categorized primarily by her familial position of Maid, Wife or Widow, more or less enriched by conventional expectations regarding female moral psychology. She is surrounded by a cluster of competing men, often far more vividly characterized,[7] who attempt to exercise authority over her. This exercise of authority is divided into four stereotyped functions—temptation, accusation, defense, and judgment—which to be dramatic must be carried out by characters who act as tempter, accuser, defender, or judge. Although for convenience I will refer to the tempter *figure,* it is crucial to recognize that function and character are not the same thing. In some stories the four authority functions are allotted to four characters, but in others they are combined so that a single man exercises more than one, or even all.

The *tempter* offers the woman the occasion for disobedience, thus serving as antagonist of the Test stage. His motives are various and may be mixed. As importunate lover or would-be rapist he may desire sexual or psychological possession of the woman. Or, since a test is the only way a woman can make her chastity active, he may offer the opportunity for disobedience in the hope that she will reject it. His motives may be confused or hidden, even from himself, so that he is genuinely uncertain which response he desires. Occasionally the opportunity for disobedience is offered by a male or female bawd, but the approach is always on behalf of a man who seeks illicit possession of the woman.[8] And usually the tempter knows whose patriarchal rights he seeks to violate. His real target, it is fair to say, is the man already in possession.

The *accuser* acts as antagonist of the Trial stage, bringing the woman's actual or supposed disobedience to public attention. He may be the injured party, the person in whom patriarchal ownership resides. He may be the tempter under a different guise who, having succeeded in his seduction, flaunts his possession or, having been rebuffed, revenges himself by a false accusation. Or the accuser may be a third party who brings a charge against the woman from a desire to protect or injure the possessor.[9]

In the Test stage, the *defender* may appear to strengthen the will of the woman against the blandishments of the tempter, though his presence is not required because it is she, finally, who must do the choosing. But because of its judicial or even forensic nature, the Trial stage does require a defender. He may be a new character. He may be the tempter or accuser who has repented his attempt or withdrawn his accusation. In frankly allegorical versions, the defender may even be God Himself who, in addition to strengthening the tested woman's will, converts tempter, accuser, or judge to a recognition of her virtue, appoints a human champion, or performs a retributive or revelatory miracle.[10]

The *judge* renders the decision in the Trial stage. Because he is the final arbiter, he is typically the highest-ranking character in the story, frequently an actual magistrate. Sometimes he is a neutral figure who reaches a frankly judicial decision. At least as often, he is not a disinterested party at all but the man in legal possession to whom the woman directly owes obedience. In this case he may have served as accuser, as defender, or even as tempter.[11] No matter who acts as judge, however, the crucial point of the Tested Woman Plot, the resolution toward which it moves, is the acceptance of that judgment by the man in duly constituted possession of the woman. It is this man—the husband, the father, or their surrogate—who must understand the truth about the woman. Judgment is rendered on his behalf, not hers.

Thus the plot's ultimate moral and social resolution is not primarily between the woman and the men to whom she owes obedience, though that is usually either cause or side effect. What is ultimately important is reconciliation among the male functions which have laid claim to her allegiance. Even when an abused woman is triumphantly vindicated, the real point is the reintegration of male authority. It is the comprehension of the misled men, the expiation of their guilt, the reconciliation with their friends, or the unified front against their common enemies that is the victory. The abused woman may be welcomed back from grave or exile, received back into a marriage, or made the rallying point of a political or military campaign,[12] but the health that is celebrated is that of the patriarchal establishment which has regained a hold upon itself. The plot uses the exemplary figure of the tested woman to educate and correct, not just its audience or the woman, but the male figures who comprise its own hierarchy.

The foregoing description of the character functions and event sequence of the Tested Woman Plot begins to help us account for the "tensions of myth" that Angus Ross finds at the heart of *Clarissa*. It establishes that some of the tensions are created by the interplay between the underlying structure and the form of the literary representation. In literature based on myth, for instance, we feel a conflict between our response to the characters as "people," folks like us, and our implicit understanding that they are in some sense the creatures of the mythic structure. We expect the characters, especially those in literal narrative, to be motivated by recognizably personal concerns, but we also detect and take comfort in the cosmic design of the plot, a design that seems to lie very deep in our collective expectations. Some light is thrown on this vexing and fruitful tension between what the character "is" and what the character "has to do in the story" by Vladimir Propp's study of the morphology of the folktale. Roughly speaking, the folktale is an intermediary form between the patterns of myth and the realizations of literal narrative. In his formalist analysis of this intermediary form, Propp demonstrates the extent to which the shape of the plot of a folktale, its morphology, is effectively the same thing as the stereotyped interactions of its character functions. The characters in a folktale do the things the tale type does; the folktale is the things they do.

Of course the relationship between events and characters in plays and novels is by no means so rigid. But the "rules" generated by Propp's analysis, because broadly applicable to the Tested Woman Plot, provide a possible explanation of its structural features. Propp maintains that in a given folktale the functions of characters serve as stable elements (as in the Tested Woman Plot there are always the functions of temptation, accusation, defense, and judgment). The number of character functions is limited (the Tested Woman Plot has four in addition to the testee), and their sequence is uniform (first temptation, then accusation and defense, and finally judgment). But functions are independent of the characters who fulfill them and may therefore be distributed among the characters in a variety of ways. (In the Tested Woman Plot a single character may take on a variety of functions; furthermore, a given social role like the family friend may be the tempter in one version, the accuser or defender in another.) This is why motivations "are the most inconstant and unstable elements of the tale." The overall morphology of a folktale hooks the functions together by means of one or more "moves," each proceeding from a choice among a stereotyped set of openings, through a series of intermediary functions, to one of several possible terminal functions.[13] Even this extremely brief description of Propp's work suggests its affinities with the above analysis of the Tested Woman Plot. Propp helps most by giving us tools for working against our modern expectations of psychologically realistic literary motivation, showing the degree to which the proto-literary structures of the folktale are motivated by impersonal forces. Instead of the language of human psychology—desire, fear, despair, hope—that of the motivations of Propp's tales is physical—balance, disruption, unity, stasis, the language of the cosmic dance of myth.

Yet the Tested Woman Plot is a potent literary artifact precisely because it carries moral significance, which means that human motivation—some version of human psychology—does matter crucially after all. There must be some connection between the character's social role, life purpose, even "personality," and the function she or he performs. The Test/Trial sequence of the Tested Woman Plot unquestionably has affinities with the simpler moves of Propp's folktale morphology. But this sequence also exhibits causal relationship, a teleological drive, the purpose of which is first to force and then to judge the characters' moral choices. Plot structure is inextricably bound to moral demonstration, constituting the most important difference between the Tested Woman Plot, a tightly constrained literary artifact, and the folktale types from which it sprang.

This brings us to the heart of the tension. To the degree that a literary plot displays moral dilemmas and drives toward a morally based conclusion, it must be centrally concerned with the deliberate acts of individual characters. Functions and motivations cannot be too arbitrary or unstable. They must be rationalized sufficiently so that behavior can be understood in terms of the currently available moral psychology; it is that rationalization which allows for conflict within the individual psyche. Given the architecture of this plot, we expect psychological complications distinctive to the two stages. In the Test or Fact stage, whose moral issue is virtue and whose dramatic action is choice, the psychological complication involves *intention*. In the Trial or Reputation stage, where the moral issue is truth and the dramatic action is judgment, the psychological complication involves *interpretation*.

Introducing *intention* and *interpretation* into the architectonic scheme introduces moral ambiguity or, more accurately, draws our attention to the ambiguity already present. Take the tempter and his intention. Like Angelo, the tempter may not be certain what he wants, whether he would have Isabella chaste or have her body his, whether it is not her very chastity that tempts him. So he can find himself faced with a psychological dilemma of his own making, in which desire struggles with duty. The tested woman, by contrast, may face a dilemma not of her own making that pits one obligation against another. Such a dilemma is most cruel, most unresolvable, when the two moral demands emanate from the same source of authority. Suppose that a woman is confronted with the moral requirement to maintain her chastity, which is her honor, in the patriarchal interests of her family. Suppose that the life of the head of that family can only be saved by the loss of that honor. Then we have Isabella's dilemma, which becomes Claudio's as well. What has this to do with intention? Angelo knows, and it is how he tempts. If this act is done to save your brother's life, are you not honoring your deepest obligations? Does not the virtue of your intention make the act possible? In fact, does not your very powerlessness excuse you? If your intention is vacated by my force, have I not eliminated your morality, and thus your dilemma, altogether? So argues Tarquin with his dagger at Lucretia's breast.

Even subtler forms of ambiguity are associated with the problem of intention. Because its authority is ultimately divinely based, the Judeo-Christian tradition internalizes authority as virtue and, particularly in the Protestant tradition, insists upon the primary moral authority of the individual conscience. One may imagine a Tested Woman story in which the woman's sense of her personal integrity is pitted against all sources of worldly authority. Then the problem of intentionality becomes stark: is the widowed Duchess who enters into a clandestine liaison unsanctioned by family, church, or social custom finally only a headstrong, self-indulgent, albeit charming, whore? How about the equally charming and headstrong young woman who has fled her father's house to secretly marry a foreigner unacceptable to her family by age, race, and social background? In these situations the Tested Woman Plot is raising the issue behind Mr. Harlowe's curse. Is the decision of the Duchess or Desdemona to place her confidence against the wishes of those in authority over her a sign of her wickedness? Or is it heroic virtue? Or is it something very much more psychologically ambiguous and morally strenuous than either? With these questions, the most interesting version of the Tested Woman Plot is afoot.

Whence come some of the more ambitious moral ambiguities possible to the Trial stage. In theory, the Tested Woman Plot operates to bring Reputation into harmony with Fact. The act of interpretation is supposed to be an act of truth-seeking. But what patriarchal authority finds convenient to recognize as truth is not necessarily consonant with what a given version of the plot has actually demonstrated or suggested. Authority figures may have to be painfully educated into the capacity to see and interpret accurately. The Tested Woman Plot, moreover, contains another hermeneutical layer involving the way readers or audience join in. All readers actively construct literary texts, but the readers or viewers of stories based on the Tested Woman Plot do more. They come to perform the actual plot functions. For instance, readers or viewers cannot regard the Duchess of Malfi as simply a headstrong, self-indulgent whore, though that is what her brothers call her. Her view of herself must count for something, and so must our view of her accusers. Thus we carry out the act of moral interpretation while it is going forward among the authority figures in the plot, as a reading of the criticism of Webster's play will demonstrate.[14] Although we were mere observers of the Test stage, by the very fact of that observation we become participants in the Trial. We too know a version of the facts; we too accuse, defend, and judge. This fact provides a literary explanation for why the plot has two stages and why the authority functions are distinguished and allotted as they are. In the Test stage, the Tempter operates without our participation, though not without our connivance. But Defender, Accuser, and Judge, the authority functions of the Trial stage, are our functions as well.

It is the Trial that implicates us most deeply in the Tested Woman Plot because it forces us to take parts. As my final chapter suggests, this part-taking is one reason for the nature of the critical debate about *Clarissa*. Yet I have implied that we connive at the Test as well. For one thing, the Test carries out the simple but titillating dramatic function of getting things underway, unbalancing and complicating so that in due time balance and clarity may be restored. In addition, the Test makes us voyeurs of a rich and disturbing phenomenon, the provocation of virtue. The provocation of virtue is what usually sets the Tested Woman Plot going, and to understand how it works, we turn to the plot's most seminal rendition, the story of Job.

The greatest test case in the Judeo-Christian tradition, the Book of Job schematically displays the two-stage structure and competing character functions of the Tested Woman Plot. In the brief opening, Yahweh provokes the test by praising the most virtuous of his creatures. Satan the Adversary, the functionary of the heavenly court who acts as Tempter, returns the challenge by arguing that untried virtue is no virtue at all: "Doth Job fear God for nought? / . . . But put forth thine hand now, and touch all that he hath, and he will curse thee to thy face" (1:8,10). Job's Test proceeds in the interest of forcing him to a choice, first by severing him from all external sources of happiness, then by tormenting his body. Having provoked and permitted the Test, God absents himself while Satan puts Job to the question. Will Job retain his faith in God or, given the overwhelming evidence of his rejection by the Creator, will he separate himself, curse God as his wife advises, and thereby find the only possible relief in death?[15] At the end of chapter 2, the conclusion of the Test stage, Job has made his choice. Though confusion and grief silence him temporarily, he does not curse God. What follows is the Trial, the examination of Job's case. Satan the Tempter disappears from the story, his function concluded. The friends step forward to act as Accuser and Defender, arguing on the one hand that Job must have brought this misery upon himself, on the other that however undeserved his lot he is obliged to accept the inscrutability of his suffering. In agony of spirit Job refuses both positions. He examines and confirms his sense of his own integrity, presents his own case, and while not questioning God's right to act as He wills, insists that only the Creator can weigh his life. Eventually ceasing to act the Tempter, God takes up His more appropriate functions of first Defender and then Judge, accepting Job's account and handing down an award of multiple damages.

The Book of Job, however, tests a man, not a woman. How can we call it a version of the Tested Woman Plot? Because it reminds us yet again that for this plot the woman is only a paradigmatic convenience in literal stories in which the authority figures are male human beings. Secular literature has an enormous problem in trying to render the story of Job or, for that matter, the story of Adam and Eve. The problem is God. A literature in the Judeo-Christian tradition which wishes to raise and examine the issue of authority without being frankly a theodicy must sublimate downward, substituting human power for divine. But in a literary form in which God may

be brought on stage—epic poems, miracle plays—the books of Genesis
and Job make prime plot material. The story of Job is one of the central
models of the Tested Woman Plot for the very reason that it demonstrates
what the plot is really about: the relationship between ultimate superior and
inferior. When God the ultimate authority can enter the story as a dramatic
character, a woman is not necessary. A man may be tested directly because
he can confront that authority directly.

The Book of Job does more than display the architecture of the plot,
however. It is also centrally informing about the origin of the Test, that
most difficult moment of all the plot to understand or rationalize. The story
has as its starting point Job's virtue: "There was a man in the land of Uz,
whose name was Job: and that man was perfect and upright, and one that
feared God and eschewed evil" (1:1). The fact of Job's virtue and his
prosperity once established, the tale is framed with an account of the heavenly court or debate, in which God makes a boast and Satan issues a challenge:

> Now there came a day when the sons of God came to present themselves
> before the Lord, and Satan came also among them.
>
> And the Lord said unto Satan, Hast thou considered my servant Job, that
> there is none like him in the earth, a perfect and an upright man, one that
> feareth God, and escheweth evil?
>
> Then Satan answered the Lord, and said, Doth Job fear God for nought?
>
> Hast not thou made an hedge about him, and about his house, and about
> all that he hath on every side? Thou hast blessed the work of his hands,
> and his substance is increased in the land.
>
> But put forth thine hand now, and touch all that he hath, and he will curse
> thee to thy face.
>
> And the Lord said unto Satan, Behold, all that he hath is in thy power;
> only upon himself put not forth thine hand. So Satan went forth from the
> presence of the Lord.

                                                          (1:6–12)

So the test begins.

In this exchange God does exactly what Posthumus does in *Cymbeline*.
God deliberately holds up for admiration the perfection of His servant Job,
the human partner who analogically stands to Him as the wife to her hus-

band. Like Iachimo, Satan immediately challenges the boast, and he and God together set the terms of the test. The boast/challenge pattern is so bold and its significance so central to the Tested Woman Plot as to demand examination. What provokes Satan to attempt to violate Job's perfection? What provokes God to test his servant? The interpretive clues are found in the terms of the wager and in traditional views of the nature of the participants. Satan's response is the easier to understand, for it is caused by envy. God's description—"there is none like him in the earth"—establishes Job as first among men. Although in the universal hierarchy he is God's inferior, within his own rank he is preeminent, responsible for the physical and spiritual well-being of a great clan (1: 2–5). Sketchily characterized in this story, Satan lacks such preeminence. One of the heavenly courtiers, he is distinguishable primarily for his busyness in going to and fro on the earth and in challenging God's estimate of His creature. Satan's power to harm Job is a power delegated and circumscribed by God. He is portrayed, in short, as the quintessential lieutenant.

In the face of this sketchiness, we are justified in appealing to the traditional elaboration of Satan's character which infuses Christian readings of the Book of Job. The envy implied in Satan's challenge is traditionally ascribed to his nature as a fallen angel, the once brightest son of God now reduced to a perpetually discontented instrument of temptation and chastisement. So strong is this tradition that when Milton's Satan makes his first testing approach to Christ in *Paradise Regained*, by denying envy as his motive he confirms the tradition:

> Envy they say excites me, thus to gain
> Companions of my misery and woe.

> (I, 397–98)

Christ, giving him the lie, naturally cites the experience of Job:

> What but thy malice mov'd thee to misdeem
> Of righteous Job, then cruelly to afflict him
> With all inflictions.

> (I, 424–26)

Since the terms in which God holds Job up for inspection imply a comparison of Job's righteousness with the blemishes of the tarnished Lucifer,

Satan's response is first to deny that Job is as perfect as he appears to be and then to seek to fulfill his own prophecy.

By raising the issue of Job's essence and his relationship with God, the boast has activated the issue of Satan's essence and his relationship with God. By rebellion Satan lost his position as God's most favored partner; with the creation of man he lost his position as heir. But he has lost none of his desire and only part of his capacity: that is the frustration. Coupled with his limitless aspiration to be powerful and perfect is a limited power to act. Having his attention called to God's servant Job is thus a triple affront: Job's relative perfection reminds Satan of his own imperfection, God's total power over his servant reminds Satan of his own limited power, and Job's most favored status with God reminds Satan of his own alienation from God. Satan's response is to attempt both to exercise power over Job and to reduce Job's status. Satan does not seek Job's death; he is indifferent to Job's existence as such. It is Job's virtue that he wishes both to own and to eliminate, for he wishes to make Job like himself. Here is the lure and the paradox of violation, which by transforming its victim at once possesses and destroys. Satan's power must operate on Job's will, though the means may be his goods, his family, or his flesh. In order for violation to occur, Job must be brought to curse God of his own free will. Job must destroy himself by taking evil into himself, thereby providing Satan with the ultimate thrill.

If Satan seeks to violate, God seeks to prove. God's situation is the opposite of Satan's because by definition He is the One in possession. He describes Job in the same words by which the narrative frame opens its account, and the implication is clear: God knows What Is; He knows that Job is a perfect and an upright man, one that fears Him, and eschews evil. Why then should God seek to establish what He already knows? Why should He seek to have what He already possesses? The wager gives us a partial clue. Satan's challenge provokes God's pride of possession; what He knows He must demonstrate to those who doubt. The creature Job reaches the height of his perfection and value only if acknowledged. The acknowledgment of the power and perfection of God's creation is the compulsion of the entire tale: that Satan acknowledge the perfection of God's servant Job, that Job acknowledge the mystery of God's creative power, that Job's friends acknowledge both Job's righteousness and the power and justice of God's dealings with him, that all God's creatures say of Him the thing that is right (42:7, 8). Proving, then, means demonstrating.

But proving also means testing, for God is stung by Satan's challenge into admitting a degree of uncertainty. In this ethical frame, virtue untried is no virtue at all, since true virtue lies in the refusal to do evil. Satan's prediction is that Job, if sufficiently tormented, will cut himself off from God as God has seemed to cut himself off from Job. Job's response to increasingly severe tests reinforces that uncertainty. Truly he has not feared God for nought, for he is first among his people in possessions, power and prestige. The initial test completed and Job's family and possessions stripped from him, it is also true that he finds consolation in his physical and spiritual integrity, his very reduction to his essential form: "Naked came I out of my mother's womb, and naked shall I return thither: the Lord gave, and the Lord hath taken away; blessed be the name of the Lord" (1:21). When the original wager is repeated and its boundaries extended to Job's body, he still insists upon his own integrity and justifies his own righteousness. Job does not curse God, as God would have known had He, in Jung's evocative phrase, consulted His own omniscience.[16] But Job does maintain his own case, he does stand on his own separateness, he does insist upon a response.

For God, then, the provocation of Job's virtue is that it is both His and not His, as Job is both His and not His. God may dictate the situations under which that virtue will be tested, but its essence is up to Job to create, its limits up to Job to define. To possess Job's virtue fully, God must find a way to ask for it. And Job must willingly give it. Thus, when the crisis comes, when Job ends his words at the end of chapter 31, stopping what has been a fruitless plea for dialogue, the test suddenly falls on Yahweh. It is He who must make it possible for Job to express the bond between creature and Creator.

This God does by an appeal to the ineffable majesty of His creation. But it is as much how He appeals as what He appeals to that matters. After all, Elihu has spent six chapters taking the same position, that God's power is beyond man to fathom and His ways beyond man to comprehend. But Elihu has *told* Job. God, when He responds to Job out of the whirlwind, *asks*. He takes the initiative for commencing what is to be a dialogue: "Gird up now thy loins like a man; for I will demand of thee, and answer thou me" (38:3). When Job in his humility refuses to answer (40:4–5), God repeats His proposition: "Gird up thy loins now like a man: I will demand of thee, and declare thou unto me" (40:7). The extraordinary sequence of statements and questions by means of which He describes His creation is not simply rhetorical. They demand interpretation. They demand that Job become aware by their means of the full import of the nature and power of the Godhead, an awareness out of which he may formulate the relationship between Creator and creature. This is what Job performs in his response. He humbles himself before God; he acknowledges God's omniscience and omnipotence as it is appropriate that he should. But the definition of God's power comes from Job. The servant defines the master.

The Book of Job gives us help with the commencement of the Test because it gives us a paradigm for the relationships and motives of the testers. Satan the dispossessed seeks by attacking the property and the body of Job to violate Job's spirit, transforming it by taking possession of it. God the possessor seeks by stimulating demonstration of Job's obedience to reassure Himself of His possession. In both cases the object of desire is the will of the virtuous man, for both parties desire the gift of virtue willingly bestowed. Satan clearly plays the Tempter. But equally clearly his behavior is sanctioned—even, by means of the boast, activated—by God. Though by right of pride, possession, and omniscience God should play Job's Defender, for the duration of the test He is symbiotically linked with the Tempter. In literary versions of the Tested Woman Plot not every man who feels the lure of violation is overtly sanctioned by the man in possession. But many are. For many more, as in *Clarissa*, the sanction is covert; the possessor and the man who longs for possession cooperate, through the force of their assumptions about authority, hierarchy, and the nature of women, to carry out the Test.

3

Clarissa's Test

In writing *Clarissa,* Richardson was energized by a coherent imaginative commitment which carried him through five years of unceasing labor. The intensity and directedness with which he composed and revised had clearly been prepared by his work on *Pamela.* In that novel he more or less stumbled into a highly episodic version of the Tested Woman Plot, seemingly learning about its literary potential and pitfalls only as he went along. When he turned to his second novel, he made two major changes in his use of the plot that vastly increased its dramatic potential. One change involves episode focus. *Pamela* is a beads-on-a-string story built on an repetition of the Test/Trial sequence, each episode involving a standard stage in a woman's life. Beginning with the tests of obedience inherent in the transfer of authority from father to husband, it goes on to the repeated tests of married life created by the unresolved contradictions within the husband. *Clarissa* is focused quite differently. Though it too gives us the story of a life, it does so in the course of enormously elaborating a single Test/Trial sequence, the episode of the attempted transfer of patriarchal authority from father to husband. Because in *Clarissa* patriarchal authority self-destructs, this transfer never gets made and the novel's social tragedy results. Putting the emphasis on this one episode, however, also provides the theological opening which it is Richardson's ultimate purpose to exploit.

The other dramatically potent change in Richardson's treatment of the plot involves how the woman chooses and how her choice is perceived. Pamela behaves virtuously in all the tests with which she is confronted. She has nothing to blame herself for, and neither, eventually, does anyone else except the critics. Employing our distinction about the moral issues and dramatic actions of Test and Trial, we can see that in each of her tests Pamela chooses virtue and that in each judgment or trial her virtue is acknowledged. There is no discrepancy, or at least never for very long, between the *facts* of her life and her *reputation. Clarissa,* of course, does not work this way. Here both aspects of the woman's virtue—both her actions and her reputation—are in genuine, and contradictory, question. On the one hand, Clarissa is in a sense disobedient: she fails a part of her test, though not all of it. On the other hand, Clarissa is calumniated: the facts of her case are misjudged or misconstrued, and she is slandered and abused. It is this contradiction between the two plot stages that puts the torque on Clarissa's story and makes possible the particular design of the novel.

Our task in this chapter is to understand the nature of Clarissa's test—as Lovelace engineers it and as Clarissa undergoes it. The fact that it is schematically a single test does not make it a simple one. It is carried forward in a series of waves or moves which commence before the novel begins with the entrance of Lovelace into the Harlowes' family affairs, and which end with the rape. These moves are Lovelace-engineered; but they are Richardson-controlled, and they have the effect of deepening and thickening the psychological and moral impact of the Test stage far beyond the point to which most renditions of the Tested Woman Plot take it. Since this is a very long novel rather than a short play, Richardson has the leisure to ask uncommonly interesting questions about Clarissa's test. Instead of emphasizing merely the time-honored *will she or won't she* question that Lovelace himself is obsessed with—"Will she fall; will she be disobedient?"—Richardson asks "What constitutes obedience? Wherein does this young woman's duty lie?" And he asks "What manner of person is this young woman? What stuff is she made of?" The story of the Test, from January to June, is the story of the stripping away of all of Clarissa's external support, down to her very sanity, in order to examine in increasing starkness the Joban issues of human essence and human integrity. Job is stripped layer by layer: first his goods, then his family, and then the health of his very body. So also is Clarissa.

All readers recognize the first stage of Clarissa's story as containing a test, specifically a test of sexual obedience to patriarchal authority. The novel quickly establishes two thematic clusters, one of which has to do with this patriarchal structure. Clarissa is the exemplary focus of the intensely patriarchal interests of the Harlowe family. As a well-brought-up young Christian woman, she knows her life purpose: to comply prettily in a marriage her family will approve and to become a fruitful and self-sacrificing mother on the model of Mrs. Harlowe. As a Harlowe, she has an additional purpose: to help carry out the Harlovian plan of economic consolidation and advancement begun by the grandfather's formidable energies and continued by her bachelor uncles' marital self-abnegation. Brother James is destined to be the chief entrepreneur and beneficiary of the clan, his sisters' marriages one of the agreed-upon means of continuing the ascent of the family's fortunes. In the early pages of the novel, no thread is more insistent than this theme of patriarchal concentration and control. For already, before the novel begins, patriarchal power has been both expressed and subverted by the grandfather's partiality toward his Clary. By his gift Clarissa has been made dangerously independent of her male relatives. Patriarchal hegemony has been threatened by the patriarchal hand from beyond the grave, and the second and third generation of Harlowe males are struggling to retain control.

In addition to patriarchy, Clarissa's exemplary status is the other salient theme in the opening pages of the novel. Clarissa is renowned throughout her world for her beauty, her charm, and her prudence. Whereas modern readers understand the seriousness and suitability of the theme of patriarchal power and family economy—understand, that is, how the Harlowes and Richardson and the eighteenth century could have cared about it—we have a great deal more trouble with Clarissa's exemplary status. Not with beauty, of course; nor with charm. Heroines require such graces, and the power they confer. But prudence? The word itself inspires resistance, which means that we need to do some translating. For this theme too needs to be confronted both matter-of-factly and seriously.

The letter from Miss Howe that opens the novel also opens the theme: "How must such a virtue suffer on every hand!—Yet it must be allowed that your present trial is but proportioned to your prudence!" (40). And what is prudence? We err if we think of it as a cautious virtue, as some form of narrow or crabbed self-interest. We seize its flavor better if we think of it in terms of the way Clarissa tries to live her life. Clarissa construes living virtuously as an exhaustingly active enterprise; she is as vigorous in pursuit of virtuous womanly behavior as is Lovelace in pursuit of women, their similar levels of energy being one of the things the two find interesting about each other. In the face of family problems (or needlework or neighborhood poverty) it is her nature to act. In her reflections upon her own and other people's actions, it is her nature to consider causes and consequences: why events have come about as they have, how they should rightly be regarded, what should best be done about them. Knowing how transitory life is, she tries to waste nothing: not goods, not time, not human goodwill. She attempts to live, not just joyfully, but wisely.

Wisdom, in fact, is the synonym for prudence, and how different a ring it has! Tellingly, in the texts of the Old Testament from which the Harlowe family and their creator primarily take their ethics, the two terms are exactly equivalent. The wisdom texts as translated in the King James Version operate by means of a paraphrastic poetic syntax in which *prudence* or its grammatical variants appears paired with or in the context of *wisdom*.[1] The scriptural frame for Uncle Antony's snarling opening in Letter 32.4 (154), where he proposes to search his niece's heart to the bottom, exemplifies the style: "The heart of the prudent getteth knowledge; and the ear of the wise seeketh knowledge" (Prov. 18:15). George Wither's *Collection of Emblemes* (1635), a text which helps us gloss Clarissa's coffin iconography, repeats this equivalency: *sapientia* and *prudentia* are the same both pictorially and verbally. Compare, for instance, the very similar paired-and-twisted-serpent illustrations 142 and 151, whose Latin mottos are *Rerum sapientia custos* and *Prudente simplicitate* respectively; or the circled-snake illustrations 74 and 109, with their mottos *Fato prudentia maior* and *Victrix fortunae sapientia* (see figs. 1–4). Emblem 142 (fig. 1) nicely demonstrates the typical verbal conflation, commencing with the *sapientia* motto and ending with a reference to *prudence:*

> But, you shall best preserve your *Honest-fame,*
> Your *Workes,* your *Hopes,* and *Honours* of your *Name*
> If you your selves be wise; and, so provide
> That *Prudence,* all your *Workes*, and *Speeches* guide.

For modern readers, understanding wisdom and prudence as the same virtue not only undermines our resistance, it helps us interpret Clarissa's prudential endeavor in terms of attitudes towards time and human responsibility.

The relationship of the virtue of prudence or wisdom to certain concepts of time and causation is part of a very long ethical and rhetorical tradition. Cicero tells us that the parts or divisions of Wisdom are based on time, that they are "memory, intelligence, and foresight. Memory is the faculty by which the mind recalls what has happened. Intelligence is the faculty by which it ascertains what is. Foresight is the faculty by which it is seen that something is going to occur before it occurs." This relation to time is what gives Wisdom the capacity to understand the moral character of events, says Cicero—"what is good, what is bad, and what is neither good nor bad."[2] It is why Renaissance iconographic and emblematic representations of Prudence stress its capacity to see the past and future in the

By Wisedome, *things which passe away,*
Are best preserved from decay.

ILLVSTR. VIII.   Book.3

THe *Laurell*, which is given for a Crowne
(To men deserving Glory, and renowne)
Is figur'd here, those noble deeds to show,
For which, the *Wreaths* of *Honour*, we bestow.
Two *Serpents* (WISDOME'S *Emblems*) twisted are
About this branch of *Laurell*, to declare,
That, *Wisdome* is the surest meanes to save
Our Names and Actions, from *Oblivion's* Grave.
The *Snakes* are two, perhaps, to signifie
That *Morall-wit*, and *Christian-policie*
(Vnited both together) doe contrive
The safest *guard*, and best *preservative*.
  Consider this, all yee, that trust your *Names*
To Marble Monuments ; or, mount your *Fames*
By those poore meanes, which Fooles and Knaves pursue ;
And, may effect as easily as you :
Nay, with more ease ; and, overtop you too,
When you have done the best, your wits can doe.
I say, consider this ; and, let the *Pen*
Of learned, wise, and understanding men,
Renowne your worths, and register the story
Of your deserved, and, well-gotten glory ;
Lest, else, it suffer close-imprisonments,
Within the walls of such poore *Monuments*,
As oft are built, to leave it quite forgotten,
Whose bones they cover'd, e're those bones be rotten.
But, you shall best preserve your *Honest-fame*,
Your *Workes*, your *Hopes*, and *Honours* of your *Name*,
  If you your selves be wise ; and, so provide
  That *Prudence*, all your *Workes*, and *Speeches* guide.
                                              Good

Page 142 of George Wither's *Collection of Emblemes* (1635); reproduced by permission of The Huntington Library, San Marino, California.

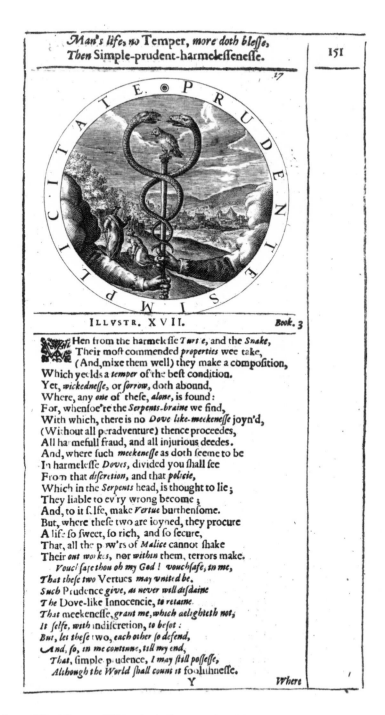

Man's life, no Temper, *more doth bleſſe,*
Then Simple-prudent-harmeleſſeneſſe.

151

SIMPLICITATE • PRUDENTES

ILLVSTR. XVII.   *Book.* 3

Hen from the harmeleſſe *Turte*, and the *Snake*,
Their moſt commended *properties* wee take,
(And, mixe them well) they make a compoſition,
Which yeelds a *temper* of the beſt condition.
Yet, *wickedneſſe*, or *ſorrow*, doth abound,
Where, any *one* of theſe, *alone*, is found:
For, whenſoe're the *Serpents-braine* we find,
With which, there is no *Dove like-meekeneſſe* joyn'd,
(Without all peradventure) thence proceedes,
All harmefull fraud, and all injurious deedes.
And, where ſuch *meekeneſſe* as doth ſeeme to be
In harmeleſſe *Doves*, divided you ſhall ſee
From that *diſcretion*, and that *policie*,
Which in the *Serpents* head, is thought to lie;
They liable to ev'ry wrong become ;
And, to it ſelfe, make *Vertue* burthenſome.
But, where theſe two are ioyned, they procure
A life ſo ſweet, ſo rich, and ſo ſecure,
That, all the p w'rs of *Malice* cannot ſhake
Their *outworkes*, nor *within* them, terrors make.
   Vouchſafe thou oh my God! vouchſafe, in me,
That theſe two Vertues *may vnited be.*
Such Prudence *give, as never will diſdaine*
The Dove-like Innocencie, *to retaine.*
That meekeneſſe, *grant me, which aelighteth not,*
It ſelfe, with indiſcretion, to beſot :
But, let theſe two, each other ſo defend,
And, ſo, in me continue, till my end,
   That, ſimple prudence, I may ſtill poſſeſſe,
   Although the World ſhall count it fooliſhneſſe.
                    Y   *Where*

Page 151 of George Wither's *Collection of Emblemes* **(1635); reproduced by permission of The Huntington Library, San Marino, California.**

Let none despaire of their Estate,
For, Prudence, *greater is, than* Fate.

ILLVSTR. XII.   Book. 2

BEe *merry* man, and let no causelesse feare
Of *Constellation,* fatall *Destinie,*
Or of those false *Decrees,* that publish'd are
By foolish braines, thy *Conscience* terrifie.
To thee, these *Figures* better Doctrines teach,
Than those blind *Stoikes,* who necessitate
Contingent things ; and, arrogantly teach
(For doubtlesse truths) their dreames of changelesse *Fate.*
Though true it bee, that those things which pertaine,
As *Ground-workes,* to *Gods* glorie, and our blisse,
Are fixt, for aye, unchanged to remaine;
All, is not such, that thereon builded is.
God, gives men power, to build on his *Foundation:*
And, if their *workes* bee thereunto agreeing,
No *Power-created,* brings that Variation,
Which can disturbe, the *Workmans* happy being.
Nor, of those *workings,* which required are,
Is any made unpossible, untill
Mans heart begins that *Counsell* to preferre,
Which is derived from a *crooked-will.*
  The *Starres,* and many other things, incline
Our nat'rall *Constitutions,* divers wayes;
But, in the Soule, *God* plac'd a *Power-divine,*
Which, all those *Inclinations,* overswayes.
Yea, *God,* that *Prudence,* hath infus'd, by *Grace,*
Which, till *Selfe-will,* and *Lust,* betrayes a man,
Will keepe him firmely, in that happy place,
From whence, no *Constellation* move him can.
  And, this is that, whereof I notice take,
From this great *Starre,* enclosed by a *Snake.*

                                              Their

Page 74 of George Wither's *Collection of Emblemes* **(1635); reproduced by permission of The Huntington Library, San Marino, California.**

Though Fortune, *hath a powerfull* Name,
Yet, Vertue *overcomes the fame.*

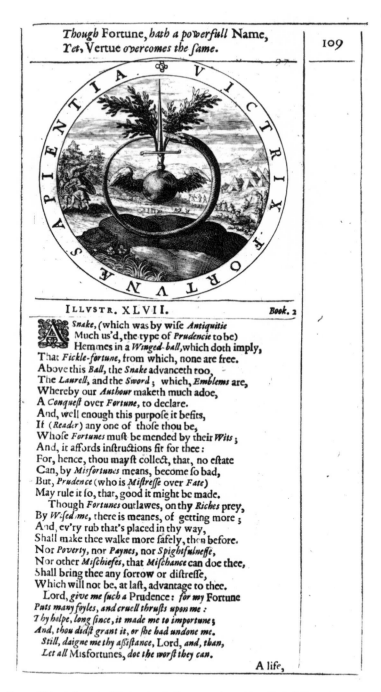

ILLVSTR. XLVII.   Book. 2

A Snake, (which was by wife *Antiquitie*
Much us'd, the type of *Prudencie* to be)
Hemmes in a *Winged-ball,* which doth imply,
That *Fickle-fortune,* from which, none are free.
Above this *Ball,* the *Snake* advanceth too,
The *Laurell,* and the *Sword* ; which, *Emblems* are,
Whereby our *Authour* maketh much adoe,
A *Conqueſt* over *Fortune,* to declare.
And, well enough this purpoſe it befits,
If (*Reader*) any one of thoſe thou be,
Whoſe *Fortunes* muſt be mended by their *Wits* ;
And, it affords inſtructions fit for thee :
For, hence, thou mayſt collect, that, no eſtate
Can, by *Misfortunes* means, become ſo bad,
But, *Prudence* (who is *Miſtreſſe* over *Fate*)
May rule it ſo, that, good it might be made.
    Though *Fortunes* outlawes, on thy *Riches* prey,
By *Wiſedome,* there is meanes, of getting more ;
And, ev'ry rub that's placed in thy way,
Shall make thee walke more ſafely, then before.
Nor *Poverty,* nor *Paynes,* nor *Spightfulneſſe,*
Nor other *Miſchiefes,* that *Miſchance* can doe thee,
Shall bring thee any ſorrow or diſtreſſe,
Which will not be, at laſt, advantage to thee.
    Lord, *give me ſuch a* Prudence : *for my* Fortune
Puts many foyles, and cruell thruſts upon me :
Thy helpe, long ſince, it made me to importune ;
And, thou didſt grant it, or ſhe had undone me.
  Still, daigne me thy aſſiſtance, Lord, *and, than,*
  Let all Misfortunes, *doe the worſt they can.*

A life,

Page 109 of George Wither's *Collection of Emblemes* (1635); reproduced by permission of The Huntington Library, San Marino, California.

PRVDENZA.

nel Vangelo *Prudentiores sunt filij huius saeculi filijs lucis* . Ne uien diftinta la
qualità dell'attione, dalla diuerfità de fini, quando fieno infieme ordinati,
come è la felicità politica, con la quale ordinatamente viuendo, fi può fare fcala per falire alla felicità preparataci in cielo; la quale è più, & meno
conofciuta, fecondo che minori, ò maggiori fono i doni della natura, ò del
la gratia.

Per dichiaratione delli vifi , bafterà quello che fi è detto auanti.

L'Elmo dorato, che tiene in capo, fignifica l'ingegno dell'huomo prudente, & accorto, armato di faggi configli , che facilmente fi difende da
ciò, che fia per fargli male , & tutto rifplende nelle belle , & degne opere
che fà .

La ghirlanda delle foglie del moro , che circonda l'elmo, dinota, che
l'huomo fauio, & prudente non deue fare le cofe inanzi tempo, ma ordi-
narle con giuditio; & però l'Alciato diffe.

                                                                    Non

Prudenza (Prudence) from Cesare Ripa's *Iconologia* (1611); reproduced by
permission of The Folger Shakespeare Library.

loro operatione alla fine fi fcopre piena di mortifero veleno, & fi dice effer Gerione, perche regnando coftui preffo à l'Ifole Baleari, con benigno volto, con parole carezzeuoli, e con ogni familiarità, era vfo à riceuere i viandanti, e li amici, poi fotto color di quella cortefia, quando dormitano l'vccideua, come raccontano molti fcrittori antichi, e fra' moderni il Boccaccio nella geneologia de i Dei.

F R A V D E.

DOnna con due faccie, vna di giouane bella, l'altra di vecchia brutta, farà nuda fino alle mammelle, farà veftita di giallolino fin'à meza gamba, hauià i piedi fimili all'aquila, e la coda di fcorpione, vedendofi al par de'le gambe, nella deftra mano terrà due cuori, & vna mafchera con la finiftra.

Fraude è vitio che vuole inferire mancamento del debito offitio del bene, & abondanza d'inuentioni nel male, fingendo fempre il bene, & s'effeguifce col penfiero, con le parole, & con l'opere fotto diuerfi inganneuoli

A a 2   colori

instant. We see this time focus in Cesare Ripa's *Iconologia*, which became a kind of European instruction manual for the verbal and visual rendering of personifications. Ripa's figure of Prudenza is a "Janus-like" woman with two faces who achieves her "true understanding" of the present precisely from this combined capacity to interpret the past and predict the future (see fig. 5). "The excellence of this virtue, and the reason it is so important, comes from the ability to remember the past, shape the present, and anticipate the future," he glosses. Citing Aristotle, Ripa tells us that Prudence is an active virtue, which is why she holds an arrow entwined by a remora or lamprey denoting her capacity to move ahead swiftly in the cause of good at the same time that she puts a brake on hasty decisions. In her other hand she holds a mirror into which she gazes, for "in order to control his actions, a prudent person must examine and correct his defects, something he cannot do without knowledge of himself." In some visual representations the mirror is replaced by a death's-head, which according to Ripa signifies the importance of considering how matters will come out in the end.[3]

George Wither's treatment of prudence takes a different form from Ripa's because he is writing a collection of verse meditations rather than a handbook of personifications. But his influential representation of the English emblem tradition confirms that prudence is identical with wisdom and reiterates the characteristics that Ripa has delineated. In addition, Wither's treatment of prudence is intriguingly linked to the emblem which Clarissa eventually chooses for her coffin. Representations of Prudence, as Ripa notes and Wither confirms, often cite the biblical injunction to "be wise like the serpent" and therefore depict this virtue as a snake. Of the four emblems in Wither's collection that are devoted to prudence or wisdom, two picture a pair of snakes entwined around a staff or tree and the other two depict a single snake encircling a symbol for fate—one a winged ball, the other a star. The snake encircling the star (fig. 3) holds its tail in its mouth, and its motto reads "Fato prudentia maior: Let none despaire of their Estate, For Prudence greater is than Fate." The verse which follows elaborates on the notion of man's responsibility for his actions and maintains that, unless he is betrayed by lust and self-will, prudence infused with grace will keep him on track. We know that the ouroboros or snake-with-its-tail-in-its-mouth, especially a snake encircling the ephemeral lily, is a traditional symbol of the passage through death to eternity. Thus Clarissa's choice of such an emblem for her coffin contributes to our sense of her spiritual progress during her preparations for death.[4] Clearly, however, this symbol of a hopeful death is also related to the symbol of a prudent life.

These traditional emblematic features of Prudence help us understand how its demands are related to the Test/Trial sequence of the Tested Woman Plot. We have seen that prudence includes the attempt to act wisely in the light of events past, present, and to come. It is not mere rule-following, because prediction is a part of its job. But since the causal factors with which it is concerned deal with human life, they cannot be predicted algorithmically. They never lead inevitably to predetermined ends but are always complicated by human interactions. And they always involve particular cases, cases in which the prudent person must choose the virtuous action. But we also see that prudence involves the effort to interpret accurately: hermeneutics, as well as action, is its sphere. Prudence reads the past, present, and future in order to attempt to see it whole, seize its causal relationships, and understand its significance. Nothing suggests that the prudent person always acts or interprets rightly. Human beings are fallible. Wisdom is something we seek, and attempt to exercise. What Prudence does is set the agenda. That agenda mirrors the double agenda of the Tested Woman Plot: to choose virtuously; to judge truly.

In the context of the Harlowes' patriarchal interests and her own prudential designs, what is Clarissa's purpose during the first part of the novel? What does she attempt to do? Despite the upheavals caused by first her grandfather's, and then Lovelace's, intervention into the family order, her purpose remains what it has always been: to live so as to carry out her obligations as a good Christian, a good daughter, and eventually a good wife. The correspondence of January through early April unfolds the complexities of that attempt, primarily from Clarissa's vantage point. Duty entails continuing to play the role of beloved youngest daughter, for her mere existence has been the chief pleasure of her parents' lives. Unfortunately, playing the family darling comes to be seen as seeking selfish advantage. Duty entails being sociable, which for a young, unmarried woman means being discreetly open to courtship. However, when Lovelace comes seemingly to court Arabella and then turns his attentions to her, she provokes her sister's jealousy. Duty entails being peacemaker. But when she attempts to buffer the ill feeling between Lovelace and her family, she risks being seen as his tool.

All this complication is a direct result of the active character of Clarissa's virtue, her unceasing efforts to behave wisely and well—which is to say, prudently. And it leads to the first point at which she makes an unequivocal choice. Whatever her growing inclinations regarding Lovelace—and she cannot know what they are, for she does not yet know him—she knows that she cannot marry Solmes, that to do so would violate both the letter and the spirit of her obligation to be a good wife. Solmes is morally and physically repulsive to her, so that she *cannot* honor and therefore obey and love him, cannot transfer to him, even at her father's command, the duty she willingly owes her father. Since she cannot be a good wife to Solmes, duty demands that she remain a good daughter by refusing to be a bad wife, which is exactly what she seeks when she begs her father to allow her to remain unmarried. Beyond that point of certainty, she is confused—not about what Virtue is in the abstract, but about how she should respond virtuously to the contradictory and self-defeating demands of the males around her.

How, then, does Lovelace the Tempter tempt? He tempts in two ways that correspond to the two thematic clusters we have noticed. On the one hand he recognizes and exacerbates the patriarchal conflicts already at work among the Harlowe males. On the other hand he seeks to undermine the operation of Clarissa's prudential faculty by reinforcing male assumptions about the nature of women—all women. The heart of Lovelace's attitude towards women is his assumption that none of them can resist him, that he can seduce at will. If he can be in Clarissa's presence, can reach her even by letter, he believes that sooner or later she will be his simply because she is a woman. It is inconceivable to him that, coming to know him, she might accept or reject him on his merits. Now the Harlowes assume precisely the same thing—that if Lovelace pursues Clarissa, he will take her. So they justify her incarceration by arguing the need to protect her, unwilling to admit that the decision must be hers and that she can make it wisely only by knowing with whom she deals. By denying her access to knowledge, Lovelace (and her family) tempt with half-knowledge.

But Lovelace also tempts by exploiting the tensions among the Harlowe males to the point where unified patriarchal authority is lost. His chief tool is ambitious, hot-tempered, self-centered Brother James, whose unseemly challenge and subsequent humiliation allow Lovelace to be construed as a physical threat, whose sexual sadism makes the prospect of Solmes press upon Clarissa to the point of terror, whose fear of Clarissa's persuasiveness cuts off her access to her father. The result of this unholy alliance, which Lovelace manages with a zestful appreciation for its ironies, is the systematic subversion of all the patterns of authority that have given stability to Clarissa's life. Spreading exceedingly fast, the disease invades every corner of Harlowe family life. The maidservant Betty Barnes is set to torment and spy upon Clarissa, James's manservant Joseph Leman is corrupted to work against his master, all pretense to moral authority is withdrawn from Mrs. Harlowe, the extended family councils become occasions for envy and recrimination between generations and sexes, valued old friends are suspect, public worship is denied to Clarissa and becomes a tainted ordeal for her family. Above all, Mr. Harlowe's power is usurped by his son. Retaining ultimate authority over the family, Mr. Harlowe nevertheless abrogates its exercise: he refuses to inform himself directly, to judge equitably and openly, or to carry out his will in his own person. Familial power and authority once split, Clarissa has no source of direction other than reflection and self-scrutiny. Further, she lives in terror that her existence will become an excuse for the bloodshed her father seems helpless to prevent. Having with ample assistance provoked domestic chaos, Lovelace presents himself as heir to the Harlowes' now-lost familial purpose.

The stripping of Clarissa has begun, and in her case, unlike Job's, it begins with family, for family is to Clarissa what possessions are to Job, the source of her position in the world. The deprivation will quickly proceed to possessions, though, to the daily, petty, grinding humiliation—the more petty the more grinding—of being dependent upon Lovelace for her food, her travel, her accommodation, her clothing, the services of those who wait upon her. And finally she will be stripped of the control and integrity of her body. But family first. For Lovelace imagines that Clarissa is powerful, and therefore resistant to him, only because she lives in the economic, social and psychological matrix of the Harlowe family. Smash that matrix, or crack it merely, and Clarissa will lose her moorings. Thus lost, she will be forced to turn to him.

Given the usual configuration of the Test, given the struggle as the Harlowe family sees it, Clarissa's flight of 10 April seems her choice, and her Fall. She has disobeyed her father, not willfully or willingly but of her own free will, and has placed herself in the company of Lovelace, who pretends to authority over her. In her ongoing examination of her own condition, Clarissa never ceases to agree with this assessment. The disobedience of her flight (and of the clandestine correspondence that leads directly to it) is the fault she suffers under and seeks ever after to repair. Her agonized analysis of her act throughout the rest of the novel returns always to the fact that she has lost her position as her father's daughter. Her attempts to repair, rejected one after another, are attempts to heal that breach: to establish contact, to tell her story, to be forgiven, when forgiveness is beyond possibility merely to be blessed in an act which acknowledges that Mr. Harlowe is her father and she his child.[5] The Test would seem to be over.

Yet Lovelace claims, right at this point, that it is beginning. His extended letter to Belford of 13 April (L 108–10, 423ff.) announces with more than the usual number of italics, exclamation points, and rhetorical questions The Testing of Miss Clarissa Harlowe, Paragon of Virtue! Though it speaks not at all to plot structure, the letter is a veritable catalogue of the themes of the Tested Woman Plot. Its heart is the pretense that the test is actually in Clarissa's interest, as it was in Job's:

> Satan, whom thou mayest, if thou wilt, in this case call my instigator, put the good man of old upon the severest trials. To his behaviour under these trials, that good man owed his honour and his future rewards. An innocent person, if doubted, must wish to be brought to a fair and candid trial. (430)

A delightfully Lovelacean rendition of the traditional rationale of the Tempter, this letter captures the ironic nature of an argument which purports to glorify virtue but remains permeated with Dipsas's sneer. If the only chaste women are those who have never been solicited, it is clearly the obligation as well as the pleasure of Lovelace and his brethren to unmask hypocrisy by bringing that morally disappointing but sexually gratifying truth to light. If by some unlikelihood this woman should turn out to be chaste, why, what has she to complain of? She will bask in a glory unattainable without his help.

The timing of this letter exemplifies Richardson's by now exceedingly sophisticated understanding of the Tested Woman Plot structure. The letter's placement is dramatically astute because it brings the test to our full consciousness at precisely the moment when a stock rendition of the plot, in the hands of a less innovative writer, would indeed be declaring the testing action all but finished. In Richardson's version, however, the woman and her tempter are just now beginning to recognize the depth and irrevocability of their conflict, because just now have they been brought face to face, no longer buffered by the patriarchal community out of which that conflict grows. To the impersonal operations of the ancient plot structure Richardson has thus added, for the first time ever, an extended examination of the moral psychology of the chief parties to the test. He announces this examination by interrupting our expectations about the plot's progress.

We must remember how the world, and we, are interpreting events. By her flight, Clarissa has rejected her father's authority and put herself in the company of Lovelace. Has she thereby put herself under Lovelace's authority? Has she given herself to him? The Harlowes assume so. Miss Howe assumes so too, and assumes that Clarissa had best make the transfer legal as swiftly as possible, for that is how her flight will be interpreted. In most Tested Woman stories, and certainly in dramatic ones where time is at a premium, the woman's rejection of one man's authority is simultaneous with her commitment to the authority of another. But not here, where "taking myself from" is not the same as "giving myself to." Clarissa knows in what state she fled, knows that that temporary derangement of body and mind in no way represented her intention. And Lovelace knows it too, whatever he pretends. The Harlowes have lost possession but Lovelace has not gained it—and cannot gain it except from Clarissa herself. Whereas before Clarissa's flight his major effort was directed at the family, he now turns his full attention to her. The letter to Belford is his version of the Test as game, part self-justification, part an enhancement of his pleasure through contemplation of the difficulty of the pursuit and the rarity of the prey. As he presents it, it is a game he will win. He *will have* Clarissa, whatever her response to his terms, for he presumes that she can be brought to either concubinage or marriage. By means of the exceptional circumstances of the flight, Richardson has taken a bold step into the dark heart of the Test, in which the woman will face her danger absolutely alone, without even the psychological comfort of a clear conscience.

Lovelace's announcement, a kind of Tempter's Manifesto, helps clarify both the Test's usual assumptions and Richardson's particular psychological concerns. As elsewhere in his discussions and justifications, Lovelace maintains that the central target of the Test, generically speaking, is the woman's will:

> *Importunity* and *opportunity* no woman is proof against, especially from
> a persevering lover, who knows how to suit temptations to inclinations.
> This, thou knowest, is a prime article of the rake's creed. (L 110, 426)

Catechizing himself in mock surprise at including in such generic company "this most admirable of women," he goes on to list the ways Clarissa's will has already proved faulty (427) and to catalogue the signs of amorous interest, perhaps even love, her behavior has already exhibited (428). Her circumstances have been abnormally complex and difficult, he admits, but what can only be described as her affectation, even her pride, causes her to present herself as above such excuses:

> What though the provocations were such as would justify any other woman; yet was a CLARISSA to be susceptible to provocations which she thinks *herself* highly censurable for being so much moved by? (428)

And if already faulty,

> may she not *further* fail?—Fail in the *greatest* point, to which all the other points in which she has failed, have but a natural tendency? (429)

According to this description, Clarissa has already clearly been susceptible to a failure of will, a failure to carry out the duties she as clearly has understood and subscribed to. Her own sense of failure and guilt stands as corroboration.

But although an attack on the will—by means of *importunity* and *opportunity*—is what Lovelace claims to be engaged in, that is not in actual fact how he behaves. His prime target is never Clarissa's will; rather, it is her understanding. Though he claims to desire confrontation between his male ardor and her female reserve, claims to be testing whether the strength of his desire will not finally overcome her artificial, socially constructed resistance, he in fact always misrepresents his intentions. He actually conducts the Test as though his purpose were, not to move Clarissa, but to confuse her, and the more we read of his correspondence the more we understand that such is indeed his deliberate intention, and the salient feature of his characterization as Tempter. This feature is authorially deliberate as well, for Richardson is dramatizing the fact that behind the problem of the will is the deeper problem of knowledge. Where knowledge is hidden or prevented, wisdom is stymied because it cannot link past and present to predict the future coherently, and the will is therefore misdirected. That Clarissa feels guilty, that she feels she has already failed, does not indicate a failure of her will but of her understanding. She knows now that she has erred, has been mistaken, but it is something she can truly understand only after the fact. The irony inherent in the unchanging human pattern is terrible and inescapable: if Eve truly knew, if she already had the living and particular knowledge of Good and Evil of which only the Tree can be the source, then she would know not to eat of that tree.

Now people characteristically arrive at their knowledge of each other, and therefore their capacity to respond wisely to each other, by gauging each other's intentions. It is when intention meets intention that the will is engaged. When Harriet Byron, the heroine of Richardson's *Sir Charles Grandison,* is abducted by Sir Hargrave Pollexfen, the clarity and accuracy with which he signals his intention—to force marriage upon her—makes possible the manner of her response. Because she will not be married to him, she screams, she struggles, she eventually is heard and rescued. Her behavior may be faulty—she blames herself for wearing the provocative masquerade dress by which Pollexfen pretends she is a runaway wife—but her will is not. Likewise Clarissa faced with the prospect of Solmes: since she knows his intentions, she can refuse marriage to him and nothing can reach her will to resist. Uncle Antony's letter to Mrs. Howe (L 197.1, 15 May, 624) may be the reductive epitome of the declaration of intentions, and Anna gets a great deal of comic mileage from the fact, but it marks one boundary of the range of intelligible courtship. But Lovelace, unlike Pollexfen and Solmes and Uncle Antony, does not present himself accurately. At the point of the testing letter, and for some time after, Clarissa believes he is wooing her to marriage. Though his behavior as viewed from that perspective is often baffling, she does not know, given her experience she could not know, that his aim is "the greatest point, to which all the other points in which she has failed, have but a natural tendency." Given the goals Lovelace professes, there is nothing natural about such an aim, for why, as she subsequently asks, would a man in his right mind bring dishonor upon the woman he seeks to marry? The letter from Cousin Morden that might help educate her about this man's intentions, written this very day of 13 April, will not reach her for weeks.

Were he candid, here in this testing letter where he pretends to that quality, Lovelace would admit that he fears the firmness of Clarissa's will too much to engage it directly. Belford has a practiced sense of the discrepancy between Lovelace's claims and his conduct and helps us critique Lovelace's version of the Test by starkly delineating the choices. Once having met Clarissa, he is less inclined to enjoy the spirited wit of Lovelace's testing argument. But he understands that there are essentially two ways to proceed, both of which he names:

> Lovelace, I conjure thee, if thou art a *man,* let not the specious devils thou hast brought her among, be suffered to triumph over her; nor make her the victim of unmanly artifices. If she yield to *fair seduction,* if I may so express myself; if thou canst raise a weakness in her by love, or by arts not inhuman; I shall the less pity her. (L173, 4 May, 560)

Fair seduction. Or unmanly artifices. By May we can believe the possibility of artifice. We should have figured out Lovelace's role in Joseph Leman's play-acting in the garden, the presence of the edifying books at Mrs. Sinclair's, or the pretense regarding Hannah's reemployment. Artifice aside, however, has Lovelace even been bent upon seduction, fair or not? Has he attempted to "raise a weakness" in Clarissa "by love"? Not much. Not in the usual sense. We can hardly help being struck by Lovelace's curious lack of ardor or erotic depth. When he sparks, when he flames up or gets carried away, it is in response to the game. What he typically attends to, during his encounters with Clarissa, is the way he plays his role and the effect it has on her. Like any fine actor, he loses himself only when being overcome can serve his ends. His romantic language both about and to Clarissa is not merely exaggerated and, as she points out, over-voluble, it is flattering, formulaic, detached, and inaccurate. "Goddess, charmer, angel, dear creature," he gushes, to the point where Clarissa longs for relief, punctilious Clarissa who objects to being called "lady" because strictly speaking she isn't one. Not all his language about her gushes. He can describe her accurately as well as admiringly, as he does to Belford shortly after their arrival in London:

> She knows nothing of the town, and has seen less of its diversions than ever woman of her taste, her fortune, her endowments, did see. She has indeed a natural politeness which transcends all acquirement. The most capable of anyone I ever knew of judging what a *hundred* things are, by seeing *one* of a like nature. Indeed she took so much pleasure in her own chosen amusements till persecuted out of them, that she had neither leisure nor inclination for the town diversions. (L 154, 25 April, 523)

This remark strikes Clarissa off well. It is the kind of absorbed appreciation that might seem to prelude real human contact. But it too turns out to be part of the campaign: "I hope in a while to get her with me to the public entertainments"; "these diversions will amuse," and amusement leads to "susceptibility."

What is missing from Lovelace's temptation is the powerful invitation of genuine sexual passion. At no point does he woo Clarissa to pleasure, either hers or his, whether the pleasure of flirtation, of companionship, or of lovemaking. His campaign is compulsive, but it does not seem compelled by any longing to enjoy this woman, much less to cultivate a longing in her. The absence of this tone of passion has nothing to do either with the age or with Richardson's capacities as a writer. Richardson's Mr. B is genuinely passionate in plenty, clumsy though he may also be; it is the power of his emotion that woos Pamela. For a style of passion more compatible with the image Lovelace pretends to project we can turn to *The Fair Penitent,* the tested woman play in which Lothario provides the eighteenth-century model for the seduction of a "haughty, insolent" virgin. Having with "prevailing, youthful ardor" won her to "ecstasies too fierce to last forever" (1.1.139; 157; 161), Lothario seeks to resume his affair with a Calista now married to his rival:

> Weep not, my fair, but let the god of love
> Laugh in thy eyes and revel in thy heart,
> Kindle again his torch and hold it high
> To light us to new joys; nor let a thought
> Of discord or disquiet past, molest thee;
> But to a long oblivion give thy care,
> And let us melt the present hour in bliss.

(4.1. 20–26)

This is, at times, what Lovelace pretends he wants. But quite apart from the fact that Clarissa is no Calista, neither is Lovelace a Lothario. Reveling and kindled torches, joys and laughter, softness and fondness and melting bliss—not only can Lovelace not bring Clarissa to this state, he does not seek to do so. He may term her a frost piece, but his dominant tropes of temptation tell us that there is nothing of the melting agent in him. He does not want her warmth, nor her pleasure. He wants submission—as an end, not merely a means. He wants, not seduction, but enforcement.

From mid-April to mid-June, between the flight and the rape, Lovelace's is the active role and Clarissa's the passive one. If we study the ebb and flow of the Test by cataloguing the elaborately staged events by which Lovelace controls the action during this period, we see that, in addition to the flight itself (10 April), the most important of these events are Clarissa's incarceration at Mrs. Sinclair's (26 April), the dinner for his friends (1 May), the ipecacuanha illness (26 May), the Captain Tomlinson campaign (begun 27 May), the fire plot (8 June), the invention of the fake Montague relatives (12 June), and finally the rape itself (13 June). Some of these events operate primarily on the personal, even explicitly sexual, level, intended as they are primarily to increase Lovelace's physical and emotional proximity to Clarissa. Other of the events operate socially, being designed to substitute a cast of puppets for Clarissa's family and friends. The two kinds of events alternate, generating first one kind of pressure on Clarissa, then the other. What we might call proximity control is a function of the flight, by means of which Lovelace forces daily contact; the incarceration at Mrs. Sinclair's, by which he prevents Clarissa's leaving him; the self-poisoning, by which he probes her heart; the fire plot, by which he fondles her body; and the physically penetrating rape itself. Social control proceeds from the flight, by means of which Clarissa is severed from her family; through the dinner, at which she is introduced to a new public; to the Tomlinson charade, which invents a Harlowe connection; to the fake-Lady-Betty scenes, which fraudulently recreate the Montague connection; and again finally to the would-be socially defining relationship of the rape.

Although the predatory psychology of these event strings is continuous, their dates show a period of interruption. Between the dinner of 1 May and the ipecacuanha-induced illness of 26 May, Lovelace launches no major campaign. Various of his activities are ongoing, of course—the intrusion into Clarissa's correspondence, the pretenses about alternate accommodations, the attempts to exploit the diversions of the town, the interdiction of her physical freedom, the gestures toward wedding preparations, the calculated changes of emotional temperature during their interviews—but no major new enterprises emerge because Lovelace cannot imagine them necessary. Once Clarissa is trapped at Mrs. Sinclair's, presented as his wife, and forced into daily contact with his insinuating presence, she should crumble. When at the end of May the stalemate can no longer be denied, he lunges forward on both fronts at once, moving both to assure himself of her personal interest by means of his illness and to reengage her familial hopes by means of the pretense of contact with Uncle John.

Seeing the various campaigns from flight to rape as organized along these two different fronts helps us make some necessary distinctions about Clarissa's behavior under the most extreme pressures of the Test. The physical liberties Lovelace takes during the fire plot so thoroughly arouse her fear of sexual violation that she is catapulted into flight, and from that point on the prospect of finding herself unprotected in his presence terrifies her. The physical side of Lovelace's campaign is thus at an end; on the personal front he has no weapon left but force. On the social front, however, Clarissa still has hopes—that Uncle Harlowe will serve as go-between with her family, that Lovelace's family will take her under their protection, that Miss Howe can arrange a safe haven—so that on this front Lovelace still has a range of weapons. Ironically, her flight to Hampstead gives him a more generous space in which to deploy them, as well as to indulge his histrionic bent. To understand how the Test operates, it is essential to assess accurately what Clarissa attempts once he tracks her down at Hampstead. All too attuned to her physical danger but still hopeful of the social connections that may salvage some version of her hoped-for future, she plays for time with every human contact within her reach. She buffers herself with the far-from-impregnable Hampstead women: Richardson's sophisticated use of the dramatic conventions of the Tested Woman Plot is nowhere displayed more subtly and wittily than in his characterization of the conventional triad of the maidenly Miss Rawlins, the matronly and matter-of-fact Mrs. Moore, and the salacious young Widow Bevis—all prey to Lovelace's equally conventional assessments and manipulations. Still believing herself to have social resources beyond the goodwill of strangers, Clarissa also insists upon waiting for letters from Miss Howe. She willingly entertains Captain Tomlinson and rejoices in his messages of family concern and possible reconciliation. She embraces contact with Lovelace's family, both to protect herself and to defend her family against violence. Lovelace knows exactly how to exploit the social considerations which weigh upon her, as we see in the last joint operation with Tomlinson when he jerks every string almost to the breaking point:

> I pleaded my own sake; the captain his dear friend her uncle's; and *both* the prevention of future mischief; and the peace and happiness of the two families.
>
> She owned herself unequal to the conflict. She sighed, she sobbed, she wept, she wrung her hands. (L 245, 10 June, 844)

The exploitation of his own family, unexpectedly cynical and fraudulent even for him, gives Lovelace his opportunity to carry Clarissa back to London under the color of their physical and social protection. Agreeing to a day trip to Sinclair's to collect her belongings, she intends to be preparing a reentry into a social world from which she will be able to treat with Lovelace with whatever dignity and value remain to her. The news that the supposed cousins have left Sinclair's house, then that they have been detained by illness, rightly appalls her, for with their absence she has no protection left. She need not know them to be frauds to know her hopes of salvage destroyed.

It is an understatement to reiterate that, rather than "fairly seducing" Clarissa by enhancing his attractiveness and her desire, Lovelace's "unmanly artifices" seek to reduce her options and increase his power. His master trope of the ensnared, confined, reduced, and reeducated linnet, presented as a version of harmless boyish play, actually demonstrates his totalitarian fixation. In this regard his campaign elaborately parallels the Harlowe-driven Solmes action, where Richardson has explored a more blatant power play. That parallel in turn constitutes the most horrific feature of Clarissa's plight between April and June: having fled her family in terror of overt enforcement, she finds herself subject to a far more dangerous, because more veiled, subtle, and premeditated, control.

But why is it that Clarissa, so attuned to gradations of physical intrusion, can be socially imposed upon so successfully? Or, to state the question from its opposite side, if Lovelace's campaign is one of enforcement or enslavement, how can we call it temptation? Because, to succeed, it baits its trap with Virtue. Lovelace does not pursue genuine sexual temptation less because it would not succeed with Clarissa than because he does not really desire it himself. In fact, however, he knows that the pleasure of obligation is the temptation to which Clarissa is most susceptible. She cannot, it may be, resist virtue. Her family know this too, which is the importance of the Solmes parallel. There, where Clarissa is tempted to violate her own psychological, social, and physical integrity, family members repeatedly evoke the pleasure, the sheer satisfaction, of being dutiful. Everyone takes that line—everyone including her cousin Morden. In the first week of May, long after Clarissa has fled and regretted and struggled to resume contact with her family, she opens the trunks of clothes and books sent by them and finds his letter from Florence. Dated 13 April (the date of Lovelace's "testing" letter to Belford), Morden's letter sets out the

character of the rake Lovelace in terms that Clarissa, in the light of her
present experience, cannot but recognize. Then Morden sounds the pleasures of obligation, the more strenuous the more pleasurable. Notice how
he invites Clarissa to find her greatest satisfaction in taming and mortifying
her will:

> Weigh all these things, which I might insist upon to more advantage,
> did I think it needful to one of your prudence: weigh them well, my
> beloved cousin; and if it be not the will of your parents that you should
> continue single, resolve to oblige them; and let it not be said that the
> powers of fancy shall (as in many others of your sex) be too hard for your
> duty and your prudence. **The less agreeable the man, the more obliging
> the compliance....**
> You have an opportunity offered you to give the highest instance that
> can be given of filial duty—Embrace it; it is worthy *of* you; it is expected
> *from* you; .... Let it be said that you have been able to lay an obligation
> upon your parents (a proud word, my cousin!) which you could not do,
> **were it not laid *against* your inclination!** ...
> I hope I shall soon, in person, congratulate you upon this your meri-
> torious compliance. (L 173.1, 564; my emphasis in bold)

To a woman of Clarissa's strength and character, here is temptation indeed:
the temptation to be greatly good, please those she loves most, and thereby
live happy in her own extraordinary merit. Only her prudence—her ability
to project the pathological future with Solmes that her present disinclina-
tion presages—has saved her from the pleasures of self-sacrifice. Having
disobliged in the matter of Solmes, however, she is that much more anx-
ious about her duty.

So Lovelace sets about to make Clarissa feel obligated to cooperate in
his schemes. Remember Clarissa's double commitment to virtuous action
and virtuous reputation, and her determination to maintain their congruity.
Seduction works from the action end of the equation: "Come live with me
and be my love. . . ." It lures the woman with the implied argument that
reputation can be controlled by hiding the action, manipulating its public
reception, or at least putting off thinking about it ("To a long oblivion give
thy care," woos Lothario). Enforcement works from the other, the reputation, end. It sets up a public perspective and pressures the woman to bring
her actions into harmony with that account. So the Solmes action, for in-

stance, argues that since Clarissa wishes to be dutiful, and since duty is equated by family and friends with marrying Solmes, she should bring her behavior into congruity with that public perception. In a variety of far more subtle ways, Lovelace also works primarily from the reputation end. Repeatedly he manipulates the appearances and expectations connected with Clarissa and then exploits her virtue by pressuring her to bring her private actions into correspondence with those perceptions.

As Clarissa notices, presumption is a large part of Lovelace's method. He simply presumes to authority over her one piece at a time, substitutes a familial structure of his own invention for that from which he has almost succeeded in detaching her, and dares her to dislodge him. Always he attempts to exercise authoritative functions, purporting to defend her in the flight from the garden or in the fire scene, accusing and chastising her when she seeks to slip through Mrs. Sinclair's door, granting or withholding permission when she wishes to go to church. For the benefit of the outside world he bolsters these authoritative functions by also play-acting a series of authoritative roles, passing himself off as Clarissa's brother at St. Albans, as the supposed cousin of his supposed female relatives at Hampstead, as her husband at Mrs. Sinclair's. The role of husband is the most important, of course. Not only is Clarissa held captive by the lie that she is Lovelace's wife, but her life at Mother Sinclair's parodies the introduction of a bride into her husband's family's house, where she is to be taught, and is duty-bound to accept, the ways of what is now her family. The battle against this presumptive encroachment upon the authority that is still her father's is one of the battles that harries and wearies Clarissa. Her cry against the women of the brothel is not that they are evil or debased (though of course they are), but that they have no authority over her. For it is authority that creates obligation.

Lovelace's purpose in this encroachment and this role-playing is partly legal. He is mindful of the threat of an action for abduction or rape and wishes public evidence of Clarissa's compliance, as his party invitation to Belford makes clear: "here are—let me see—how many persons are there who, after Monday night, will be able to swear, that she has gone by my name, answered to my name, had no other view in leaving her friends, but to go by my name?" Why, "no less than four worthy gentlemen of fortune and family," in addition to Sinclair and her crew. But the narrow legal point is far from the whole purpose of the dinner. Lovelace is set upon increasing

Clarissa's sense of obligation by luring her to submerge her serious social embarrassment at the irregularity of her position in the smirking levity of customary post-nuptial celebration. Imagine

> everyone complimenting and congratulating her upon her nuptials; and that she received such their compliments and congratulations with no other visible displeasure or repugnance than such as a young bride, full of blushes and pretty confusion, might be supposed to express upon such contemplative revolvings as those compliments would naturally inspire. (L 158.1, [29 April], 539)

Having allowed herself to be so represented, can Clarissa publicly recriminate? Is she not obliged, in fact, to be grateful for Lovelace's solicitude for her reputation? Far from publicly vaunting himself upon her abduction, is he not generously attempting to present her in the best possible light? His pretense is still to courtship, his explanations are plausible in their particulars if not always in their totality, and she is one to give the benefit of the doubt. Further, she is heartily disinclined to make a public fuss on her own behalf. Lovelace rightly calls her "delicate. " Her delicacy is not weakness but *pudeur,* a desire for privacy, fitness, and a refined accuracy of physical and verbal expression. It is the exact opposite of his impudence, in fact, and thus a trait easy for him to turn to his advantage. For her, the temptation is to keep on trying to be the decent, discreet, civil human being she has always tried to be, which means behaving graciously in at least some particulars as a woman accompanied by and in fact beholden to Lovelace.

And if in these particulars, he presumes to hope, eventually in all. For Clarissa's letter to Anna immediately after the dinner expresses the "debasement" she feels at the position it placed her in (L 161, 1 May, 546). Bringing this sense of debasement home to Clarissa is itself part of the temptation. Precisely because she is exact in her morals, strict in her demands on herself, and guilt-ridden over her flight, Clarissa may be prey to the all-or-nothing effect, she may be seized by despair at the least crack in her defenses. Seeing herself in some one particular as Lovelace's creature, she may, whatever her momentary self-loathing, even perhaps because of that self-loathing, become altogether his. Some version of this precipitous slide lies behind the histories of Sally Martin and Polly Horton; perhaps it can be made to operate on Clarissa.

As the stalemate at Sinclair's lengthens, Clarissa's total capitulation comes to seems less and less likely. Far and away the greater temptation is for her to settle piece by piece for what she can get, and here Lovelace's best ally, had he the wit to know it, is Anna Howe. Lively, worldly Miss Howe speaks, we remember, for the reputation side of the action—and reputation reflects an undeniable social reality. Miss Howe says what all of us, including Clarissa, know—that in their world an unmarried woman cut off from family and friends is powerless and therefore prey. Any man who even claims to attach her thereby owns her—owns her in actuality, because by public expectation. The only form of such ownership that gives her any public rights whatever is marriage. Having left her family in the company of Lovelace, Clarissa is in all eyes his possession, however she regards herself. Miss Howe knows that she had best salvage what rights and position she can. She had best marry, the quicker the better.

Now we know that Lovelace's masquerade at Sinclair's does not aim at marriage, whatever he may periodically claim, because he does not *act* as though it does. He both admits and acts as though it is intended as the means to the complete subjugation of Clarissa's mind and body, the temporary enjoyment of her reduced and reeducated husk, and her eventual discarding. Courtship is a stalking horse. Though not the *novel*'s plot, it has been Lovelace's primary "plot" throughout. But for a long while Clarissa is not sure of this, and for that while she is willing to consider the possibility of marriage. During this middle period, up until the Fire Plot and the flight to Hampstead, she attempts to arrive at an honorable contract. She is hideously handicapped by her situation, of course. Stripping her of her family and of her means of independent living has stripped her of a decorous setting for negotiation and deprived her of any power but the negative power of her own resistance. Nevertheless, though familial reconciliation remains her primary goal, she believes for a while that if Lovelace were to behave honorably, she might negotiate a contract to honor him, and either arrange the reconciliation that would ease her pain or, if need be, learn to live without it.

As the novel proceeds, Clarissa's decreasing willingness to entertain marriage is precisely balanced by Lovelace's increasing dependence upon marriage as the ultimate tool of enforcement. The Fire Plot is a critical turning point in Clarissa's estimation of Lovelace's intentions and therefore of her desire to forward the off-again, on-again negotiations that have in some particulars mimicked courtship, for now she fears that an honorable contract with Lovelace may not be possible. As for Lovelace, it is impossible to say at exactly what point he ceases to regard marriage as the unnecessary alternative to concubinage and comes to see it as the only way to attach Clarissa. His inclinations fluctuate wildly during the summer of the novel; truly he does not know his own mind. But without question the rape, whatever its other motives and effects, is designed to bring the weapon of marriage definitively into Lovelace's arsenal.

It is crucial to understand why the rape makes marriage possible for Lovelace. Because Lovelace wants to subjugate and control, marriage can be entertained if, but only if, it maximally debases the woman while empowering him. Hence the rape, which we must understand as a mere setup for the ultimate violation, a means to his goal rather than the end itself. By forcing Clarissa's body, Lovelace intends to force her hand. Knowing his plot, he knows that a virgin raped by an unmarried man has two choices, either one of which will continue the game on his terms. Considering herself definitively ruined, she can accept her state, enjoying its pleasures with the excuse that, having been forced, she is not ultimately at fault. Or the raped woman can demand the rectification of marriage, submitting to the extortion of being made thereby an honest woman.[6] Marriage is what Lovelace expects Clarissa to attempt, and what he professes himself willing, now, to tolerate. The rape will bind Clarissa once and for all, for the strength of her virtue will establish his power. He will not be forced into marriage; she will. It is she who will beg, he who will grant.

Readers who see Richardson's novel as a courtship plot resulting in either sexual frustration or fulfillment expect some version of this denouement as well. Appalled as they may be by the rape, they expect it to break the stalemate, forcing the protagonists into new negotiating positions from which they must reach an accommodation. Such readers (among whom we find Richardson's own correspondents) long for reconciliation and a happy marriage, but would be willing to entertain a sequence of recrimination and separation, of punishment and even death. Let Clarissa die, but allow Lovelace to make an honest woman of her first. Or let her refuse him, if only she will acknowledge the compelling force of his passion and her attraction. Or make this deed the means to his reformation so that she and we may have the satisfaction of knowing that her unwilling sacrifice has salvaged a Christian soul.

Such readers are mistaken in their expectations about the rape, as Lovelace is mistaken in his. It is equally crucial to understand why the rape makes marriage impossible for Clarissa. Instead of binding Clarissa to Lovelace, the rape frees her from the Test stage of the plot by allowing her to make the last part of her required choice clearly and unequivocally. She erred in leaving her father's house. But after the rape she no longer entertains the possibility of submitting to Lovelace's authority. Lovelace has not had her, for her will was absent during the rape. He will not have her, because she cannot honorably contract herself to a man essentially dishonorable. The rape shows him definitively for what he is; it gives her knowledge.

4

Clarissa's Trial

For readers of *Clarissa*, recognizing the Test stage of the Tested Woman Plot is comparatively easy because the characters themselves know so much about it. Lovelace consciously plays the Tempter. Clarissa understands that she is being tested. Richardson keeps his readers up to test speed by means of the conversation among the Harlowes about female obligation, by Clarissa's discussion of her behavior with Miss Howe, and by Lovelace's "testing of Clarissa" correspondence with Belford. Recognizing the Trial, however, is a different matter. Seeing it is a problem for readers partly because the events that preceded it were so complex, lengthy, and morally equivocal. Furthermore, during the Trial stage Clarissa is less readily available as our guide: her active role becomes more private, her correspondence dwindles, and her voice eventually is still. But the chief source of the problem is that recognizing the Trial is difficult for the characters themselves. That difficulty of recognition, in fact, becomes part of Richardson's story. The result is several radical and therefore disorienting plot variations which it is the purpose of this chapter to describe and explain.

First, an overview. One radical variation involves Lovelace. We know that as a result of the rape Lovelace loses his function as Tempter, with its task of conducting the Test. Richardson's twist is that Lovelace himself does not recognize that loss, and because he does not, he keeps trying in increasing frustration to make the old promise-and-presumption mechanism operate when it does not pertain. For the Harlowes also, everything should change with the rape, but in fact it does not. To the degree that they respond to it at all, their response is unsurprised and unreflective: "We told you so." An even more radical variation occurs with Clarissa. At first the rape disorients her completely. She understands that it has changed everything, but for some weeks she does not know what comes next, does not know that the Test was merely preparation for a Trial which she must learn to recognize. And not just recognize but, finally, conduct. Here in fact is Richardson's most radical move. For the second half of the novel gradually brings home to Clarissa the immensely painful evidence of the collapse of her patriarchal world. And it involves its readers in the growing recognition that she must therefore be responsible for her own Trial. Thus we discover with Clarissa the extent of Lovelace's perfidy. We see her acknowledge her family's limitations. With her we come increasingly to doubt Lovelace's capacity for change at the same time that we watch Belford's metamorphosis into the recording agent of truth. Above all we grow to appreciate, with Clarissa herself, her increasing need and capacity to interpret her own acts.

In addition to the characters' radically atypical responses to plot events, there is another reason for some of the disorienting features of the Trial stage. Thanks to Lovelace's deliberate machinations and the Harlowes' unwitting but synchronized cooperation, a kind of false trial has been underway for months before the rape, during which erroneous or partial versions of facts and intentions have become fossilized. Even before her flight from Harlowe Place, Clarissa was attempting in the face of every conceivable frustration to describe accurately to herself and others what was actually happening and what were actually her intentions. But by its nature a forensic action is about the past; possibilities have to be closed off before judgment can be reliably handed down. Therefore Clarissa cannot compose a complete and accurate account before the Test comes to a close. In part this is because the absence of full knowledge of Lovelace gives her hope in him and thus gives him a hold over her. In part it is because she cannot make herself believed by her family. Before their certain knowledge of the rape, Clarissa's every explanation is viewed by her family as "rhetorical," as attempting to shift events in the direction of Clarissa's designs. If her will or desire is corrupt, as the Harlowes come uniformly to believe, then her language must also be corrupt. Nothing she can say will stand as true description; all has to be special pleading. With the rape, however, not only does she gain knowledge of Lovelace, but she is freed from her family's misinterpretations because she has no more to lose. The Harlowes can say "We told you so" and she can say "I was both foolish and culpable not to believe you." That clears the way for her to compose a complete version of events. Since nothing in her life will now change as a result of her account of it, she will be able to tell it and be heard.

The Trial stage of the plot is also disorienting because so many characters launch so many competing versions of it, so many "possible narratives" out of whose "concatenation" (Castle, *Clarissa's Ciphers,* 27) the

novel is constructed. Lovelace sets up the "penknife" scene as a trial designed
to seduce and punish Clarissa. But there was also the trial at Harlowe Place
at which Clarissa was not allowed to be present, and the one at which she
was, and the one at which she would have been had she not fled with Lovelace. Then, after Lady Betty receives Clarissa's letter, Lovelace's family
subjects him to an examination which he calls his trial. Having discovered
Clarissa's successful flight from Mrs. Sinclair's, Belford serenely takes
down evidence ("like a Middlesex Justice," says Mowbray to Lovelace—
L 292, 28 June, 963) for some eventual trial. Clarissa is taken up in the
street and carried off to the bailiff's as part of an actual legal process. Her
various friends urge a prosecution for rape. When she has become convinced that her family will not hear her, she gathers at the Smiths' a jury of
her moral peers and gives in the complete evidence of her case.

So not only must we recognize that there is a Trial, but both we and the
characters must find the right version of it. To this end, Richardson provides a number of literary and homiletic exempla that are designed to direct
our attention and mold our interpretation. One of the most extended is
Nicholas Rowe's *Fair Penitent*, which Belford critiques in a key letter to
Lovelace (L 413, 17 Aug., 1204). Richardson would have expected his
readers to know about this play. First performed in 1703, *The Fair Penitent*
was a staple of the eighteenth-century London stage[1] and had been brilliantly revived at Covent Garden during the winter of 1746–47.[2] In terms of
understanding *Clarissa*, the importance of Rowe's play is that it contains
an exaggeratedly schematic working out of the function relationships of
the Trial stage of the plot,[3] for which Rowe gains room by getting the Test
stage over before the play begins. Calista had to choose whether to obey
her father's command that she marry Altamont despite her preference for
Lothario; she also had to choose whether to accept Lothario's sexual
advances. When the play opens we immediately discover that she has both
agreed to the marriage and yielded to Lothario, so that she is contracting
herself under false pretenses. Thus the play moves straight to the Trial
stage, and the relationships among its four male authority functions. The
Tempter Lothario is so archetypal a figure as to have given his name to the
character type. The Accuser Horatio, Altamont's friend and brother-in-
law, insists that Calista is not what she seems. Altamont, her Defender, is
furious at the accusation against his bride. As Judge, Sciolto the father
sternly warns Calista against sexual impurity before her marriage and sto-
ically prepares to execute her when her disobedience is revealed. Rowe's

event sequence demonstrates how schematically the plot carries out these four functions: Calista marries, the friend accuses her of impurity to the husband, the husband quarrels with the friend, the husband becomes convinced of her impurity, the husband kills the lover, the father seeks to kill her but is restrained by the husband, the husband is reconciled with the friend, Calista kills herself, the father is reconciled with both the husband and the friend, and both father and husband die, essentially from the strain of it all.

A couple of features of Rowe's play are especially notable. To begin with, character functions correspond to social duties: a friend should be solicitous of his friend's honor; a husband should trust and defend his wife; a father should warn his daughter against unchastity and punish her if she transgresses; and a rake who is also an enemy of the family should attempt its women if he can hope for success. In Rowe, these functions are very stable. The husband Altamont is the only man who changes his mind, and therefore his function. Even so, Altamont performs exactly as the plot requires, first defending his wife against the charge of unchastity, then, convinced of its truth, taking revenge against her seducer and reestablishing friendship with her accuser. Also notable is the extreme clarity of the unity/rupture/unity progression among the men. The point of Calista's marriage with Altamont was the cementing of the male triad. The discovery of Lothario's seduction violates that cohesion. The entire purpose of the play's ending is the reconciliation among father, husband and friend made possible by a common interpretation of Calista's behavior and the elimination of the interloper.

Presumably Richardson brings *The Fair Penitent* in at such length because he has a variety of these features on his mind. But for Belford, the point of the critique is to describe the course Clarissa has not taken and must not take. His contrastive argument is that Calista, whose "devil is as much *within* her as *without* her," is, unlike Clarissa, no true penitent at all. Belford's scorn is lavished on Calista's post-Test behavior and the havoc it wreaks on the men around her—the flagrant pretense with which she consummates her marriage, her exacerbation of the breach between Altamont and Horatio, her responsibility for the deaths of Lothario and her father, her suicide:

> Calista is a desiring luscious wench, and her penitence is nothing else but rage, insolence, and scorn. . . . Her character is made up of deceit and disguise. She has no virtue; is all pride; and her devil is as much *within*

her as *without* her. . . . Knowing her own guilt, she calls for Altamont's vengeance on his best friend, as if he had traduced her; yields to marry Altamont, though criminal with another; and actually beds that whining puppy, when she had given up herself body and soul to Lothario. . . . Her penitence, when begun, she justly styles *the frenzy of her soul;* and as I said, after having as long as she could most audaciously brazened out her crime, and done all the mischief she could do (occasioning the death of Lothario, of her father, and others) she stabs herself. And can this be an act of penitence? (1205–6)

Belford is contemptuous, in short, of the way Calista conducts her Trial. She fractures rather than seeking to bind and heal. She takes her life rather than taking it up for the purpose of examination and reformation. She despairs.

Clarissa on the other hand, says Belford, is "a penitent indeed! I think, if I am not guilty of a contradiction in terms, a penitent without a fault" (1205). Belford builds his case for Clarissa's being the true penitent not just on the greater perfidy of her seducer's behavior towards her, but on the charity of her response even though she was more truly wronged. Not only will she not entertain suicide, but

as much a stranger to revenge as despair, [she] is able to forgive the author of her ruin; wishes his repentance, and that she may be the last victim of his barbarous perfidy: and is solicitous for nothing so much in this life as to prevent vindictive mischief *to* and *from* the man who has used her so basely. . . . Whatever the ill-usage of this excellent lady is from her relations, [she] breaks not out into excesses; she strives on the contrary to find reason to justify them at her own expense; and seems more concerned for their cruelty to her for their sakes hereafter, when she shall be no more, than for her own. (1206)

Clarissa's true penitence, Belford is saying, lies not in guilt or in accusation, but in hope. The virtuous woman's obligation is to assist in the reestablishment of the social configurations which have been ruptured by the strains of the Test. By striving to explain and to heal, Clarissa is truly fulfilling her penitential obligation.

Now by this letter of mid-August Belford is Clarissa's partisan, so much so that his postscript announcing her cousin's arrival in England admits to his pang of jealousy that he might be replaced in his executorship. This skillfully placed admission emphasizes the degree to which the introduction of Rowe's play serves the same plot purpose as the arrival of Morden and the whole August portion of the Lovelace/Belford correspondence, to scrutinize and reconfigure the male relationships. We are not surprised that Lovelace resists the lesson (L 415, 20 Aug., 1208): "What an unmerciful fellow art thou! . . . But if Nick Rowe wrote a play that answers not his title, am I to be reflected upon for that?" The answer, however, is yes. Belford has used Calista's trial as a means to explain, contrastively, his growing understanding of the nature of Clarissa's trial. The effect the Tested Woman's behavior has on the men who compete over her depends upon their knowing the truth about her virtue, which means knowing the nature and motivation of her choice. The entire burden of the plot structure is that if truth can be arrived at, truth itself will reform the guilty and solace the innocent, thereby reweaving the patriarchal fabric. If Rowe's heroine had been a true penitent, says Belford, she would have aided the pursuit of truth and healing, at whatever cost to herself. Calista's family is destroyed less because she was unchaste than because she did not fulfill that obligation. Clarissa's costly pursuit of truth and of healing is therefore a sign of her true penitence, though she has comparatively little to be penitent about.

But as Lovelace fears, Rowe's play also provides contrastive commentary about male responses in Richardson's novel. If the woman's trial is to have its desired effect, the men who surround her must seek, accept and act upon the truth about her behavior. As in the play, their character functions should correspond to their social duties. In *Clarissa*, whereas the woman fulfills her obligations to the fullest extent of her extraordinary strength of character, the men prove incapable of fulfilling theirs. Mr. Harlowe, for instance, should seek out his daughter, search her heart and her behavior, and reconstruct his family in the light of her evidence. Lovelace, if he is the penitent he claims to be, should admit that he deliberately caused Clarissa's catastrophe, should witness to her virtue in all her dealings with him, and should cease his threats against her family. The failures of the men are not necessarily morally incriminating, it is true. Morden is delayed abroad, and Dr. Lewen is enfeebled by age and sickness. Nor are the men the only ones who fail; the Harlowe women must be held accountable as well. But for whatever reason, none of the men responsible by patriarchal right or pretense for Clarissa's physical, social or spiritual well-being behave with full responsibility toward her. The only even partially effective family member is the distant cousin. The men who show best—like Belford, the despised Hickman, even the doctor[4]—are men who step in from outside, however late or quietly, to adopt Clarissa's cause as their own. The Trial stage of the novel, in truth, exhaustively details the bankruptcy of the patriarchal structure on which Clarissa's life is built.

One of the ways Richardson both demonstrates and explains this collapse is by means of his manipulation of the authority functions of the Tested Woman Plot. Unlike those of Rowe's males, the character functions of Richardson's men are neither stable nor appropriately responsive to their social obligations. Richardson's male characters try those functions on, pass them about, struggle over them, refuse them. In fact, we can chart all of the major male pathologies in functional terms. And because the functions are so unstable, we can follow the permutations best by proceeding from the character end rather than the function end, watching how each man attempts to come to terms with his patriarchal obligations.

Though Lovelace never puts his formidable energies to the service of the truth about either Clarissa or himself, he aspires to all four functions, which is one way of explaining his disease. His prime function in the Testing stage is that of Tempter, of course, and when the Test is over, that function disappears. But Lovelace is literarily the most witting character in the novel; he names the other functions of the Tested Woman Plot and plays at performing them all. In his letters to Belford he is ever elaborating the presumptions he practices on Clarissa: accusing her, defending her, judging her, taking on all available functions in sheer delight at his virtuoso performance of them, a performance that continues, though with increasing anxiety, even after the rape. The mad necrophiliac letter (L 497, 9 Sept.) that follows her death presents a distillation of his presumptive powers in a monopolistic fantasy: "She has no father nor mother, no sister, no · brother; no relations but me" (1385). He excuses his offenses against her, accuses himself of offenses against her, promises revenge against others on her behalf, demands control of her body, her will, her name, her reputation. The madness has the method of a contorted, concentrated post-view of male authority functions: Lovelace had wished to monopolize Clarissa absolutely; here are the naked terms in which he understands that monopoly.

As in so many particulars, James Harlowe mimics Lovelace in his desire to control Clarissa and his incapacity to describe his own behavior truthfully. During the first part of the Test he noisily monopolizes the function of Defender, though with neither goodwill nor good effect. Having committed passion and prestige to forcing the marriage with Solmes, poisoned as he is by the assumption he shares with Lovelace that if Clarissa is tempted she will fall, James is both confirmed and undermined by Clarissa's flight. Unable to abandon his rivalry with the apparently victorious Lovelace or to forgive his sister's challenge to the patriarchal power he has usurped, he seizes the function of Accuser as the only way to justify his behavior and maintain his hold on the family. The prospect of the grandfather's inheritance corrupts James, it is true, but the frustrated will to power corrupts more. Ironically but not surprisingly, the gathering evidence that his sister has stood firm against Lovelace's sexual advances—has suffered a genuine rape rather than conniving in a seduction—merely hardens the brother's position, for with this evidence he has now been proved wrong at every turn and lacks even the balm of cheap moralistic superiority. James is the Accuser as loser, festering with social and sexual envy; we remember the failure of his courtship of Miss Howe. Though he lacks the stature of the great accusers of the Tested Woman Plot, the Iachimos and the Iagos, he palely reflects the type. What he cannot control, he will spoil.

Once James has turned definitively to accusation, the function of Defender is vacant. Lovelace pretends to it, for that is what the seduction away from Harlowe Place claims to be about. Clarissa's instincts attempt to fill it elsewhere, if not with father or brother or uncles then with the agonizingly awaited cousin Morden. When the vacancy is finally filled, however, it is with Belford. Belford's intrusion into the intimate patriarchal configuration is particularly striking if we compare his initial role with the superficially similar role of Miss Howe. As the novel gets underway with its contrastive sets of letters, Belford is Lovelace's confidant as Anna Howe is Clarissa's. As we will see in chapter 6, the additional dimension of the Aristotelian friendship of the *phronemoi,* or equal partners in virtue, which is the essence of the women's relationship, is not present between the men. Belford is Lovelace's disciple or gang member, not really his soul partner because not at all his equal. Nevertheless, in terms of standard dramatic roles Belford and Anna Howe are nicely comparable confidants. They have the personalities typical of this role—plainer, earthier, more practical than their principals, and above all responsive to the opinions and crises of the friends to whom they are foils. Miss Howe continues in this vein, though her importance diminishes. Belford, however, becomes something first subtly then definitively different. Even before the rape has brought the Test to a close, his attention has increasingly turned from Lovelace to Clarissa, and his arguments, rather than responding to and shaping those of his principal, as they once did and as Miss Howe's continue to do, take on a direction of their own. From being the Tempter's mirror and admirer, he is metamorphosed into Clarissa's Defender.

It is important to keep in mind what the function of Defender entails. In the essentially psychomachic structure of the Tested Woman Plot, in which contradictory impulses struggle for control of the male psyche, the Defender does not necessarily swoop down to rescue the lady. Late in the novel, it is true, Lovelace attempts to bolster his spirits by blaming Belford for not having saved Clarissa (L 516, 26 Sept.), thereby corroborating the degree to which both he and Richardson are consciously exploring the properties of the Tested Woman Plot:

> Thou sayest thou wouldst have saved the lady from the ruin she met with. Thou art a pretty fellow for this: for *how* wouldst thou have saved her? What methods didst thou *take* to save her?
>
> Thou knewst my designs all along. Hadst thou a mind to make thyself a good title to the merit to which thou now pretendest to lay claim, thou shouldest, like a true knight-errant, have sought to set the lady free from her enchanted castle. Thou shouldst have apprised her of her danger; have stolen in when the giant was out of the way; or hadst thou the true spirit of chivalry upon thee, and nothing else would have done, have killed the giant; and then something wouldst thou have had to brag of. (1440)

But Lovelace's berating of Belford, like his other function manipulations, misses the plot point. Giant-killing is not the Defender's primary task. The Defender primarily represents the function of male authority that speaks for the woman's virtue—argues against the Test, or argues that it has been virtuously undergone. The rape accomplished, the Trial underway, Belford comes to speak thus for Clarissa, describing her actions, conveying her desires, and executing her will. His executorship involves carrying out the terms of her legal deposition. More compellingly, it involves making the book *Clarissa*, serving as a collector of the letters, hers and others', which will tell the full story.[5] The sense of fullness is essential to Belford's task. Although he is Clarissa's increasingly fervent advocate, his speaking-for is never partial, however quickly it ceases to be impartial. Belford wishes, because Clarissa wishes, that all parties speak as fully and passionately in the book as they have seen fit to speak in life. All correspondence is contained and ordered within this record; Lovelace as well as Clarissa, Uncle Antony and Mrs. Norton and Elias Brand as well as Miss Howe and Belford himself, all testify here.[6] Advocacy of Clarissa is accomplished by the demonstration of Truth itself.

Where then does Morden fit? The Test over and Morden once in England, Clarissa turns to him for help. He does help, menacing Lovelace with his obvious capacity to revenge, strengthening Belford's power to execute Clarissa's will, facing down James's attempt to break that will. To a degree he is the physical, social, and familial defender as Belford is the psychological and moral defender—and Belford, we noticed, is momentarily jealous of sharing that function with him. Again we see the interconnectedness among the male characters so typical of the plot: as Belford the Defender is also Lovelace's confidant, so Morden the Defender is a member of the family whose treatment has driven Clarissa to her present straits. Further, Morden is frankly Lovelace's counterpart in social standing, military prowess, intelligence, and sexual experience, a fact that both men acknowledge and that Lovelace attempts to take comfort in. "Colonel Morden, thou hast heard me say, is a man of honour and bravery—but Colonel Morden has had his girls as well as you and I," he reminds Belford (L 415, 20 Aug., 1209). In recounting the interview with Morden at Lord M's, he finds common cause not just in the other's spirited worldliness but in his disgust at the Reverend Mr. Brand: "I cannot say, Jack, but I am greatly taken with Colonel Morden. He is brave and generous, and knows the world; and then his contempt of the parsons is a certain sign that he is one of *us*" (L 443, 29 Aug., 1291). The similarity between the two men, though it does not extend as far as Lovelace would like to believe, means that when we read Morden's letter telling Clarissa what Lovelace is, we recognize in his words, as we never did in those of James, a portrait of the man.[7] But the awkward fact remains that as a defender Morden seems behindhand and superfluous. During the Test, when Clarissa could most have used him, he was absent; now, the Trial underway, Belford's witnessing is more to the point. For the Tested Woman Plot is not a revenge tragedy. Clarissa even forbids revenge. So Morden seems only partially compatible with the Tested Woman Plot; he is more intelligible as a figure from the novel's Don Juan Plot where, as we will see in chapter 5, he is essential.

For Clarissa does not need justice performed upon Lovelace; she needs judgment performed upon her. And who should judge? We know it must be the father if familial reintegration is to take place. Clarissa seeks unceasingly to recover her relationship with her father because it is he whose authority she acknowledges and whom she has disobeyed. No amount of consultation among family or friends can substitute for the father's decision. But Mr. Harlowe, in one of the most significant and unsettling features of the novel, absents himself. He lives, and yet he continually withdraws from Clarissa's presence and ours, disappearing through doors ahead of us, conveying his wishes by means of lieutenants, never answering letters though always in some fashion originator of the responses. Only let me speak to you, Clarissa cries; let me tell you. Give me an answer, any answer, but let it be from you. Mr. Harlowe turns away.

This is an extraordinary absence, given the period, the persons, the purposes of the novel. It is the opposite response from the one the plot itself has prepared us to expect. In their biography, Eaves and Kimpel argue that the father is not realized novelistically because of a failure of Richardson's imagination:

> [Mr. Harlowe] was necessary to the plot, but Richardson had not created him as a character, had not imagined him. His motives may be explained, but they do not exist so far as the novel is concerned. . . . The father is the only character in *Clarissa* who is entirely inadequate for the role he has to play, and the fact that he is present largely in name leaves a serious gap in the first two volumes. (*Biography,* 251)

And in the rest of the novel, we must add. Eaves and Kimpel have got at part of an important truth here: Mr. Harlowe's absence controls this version of the Tested Woman Plot as much as his presence would control it if he existed in more than name. The gap created by his absence causes problems all the way through the novel, among other things accounting in considerable part for its length. That is, what the nonrealization of Mr. Harlowe does is to proliferate the competing loci of authority against which Clarissa must struggle. But such is the Tested Woman Plot's inherent logic, a logic which Richardson is allowing to explore and exploit itself. If Mr. Harlowe's absence causes Richardson trouble, it also provides some of the novel's greatest opportunities—not just the burgeoning number of characters who get to meddle in Clarissa's business, but the whole point of the denouement. As always, we can count on Clarissa eventually to understand and explain. On her deathbed she tells Morden and Belford *exactly* what the moral point, and thus the plot point, of that absence is:

All I wished was pardon and blessing from my dear parents. Easy as my departure seems to promise to be, it would have been still easier had I had that pleasure. BUT GOD ALMIGHTY WOULD NOT LET ME DEPEND FOR COMFORT UPON ANY BUT HIMSELF. (Richardson's emphasis; L 475, JB to RL, 7 Sept., 1356)

In describing to Lovelace the heartrendingly tardy arrival of her family's letters of reconciliation Belford repeats the rationale, *that God would not let her depend for comfort upon any but Himself*" (L 482, [8 Sept.], 1364).

Mr. Harlowe is absent from the novel, then, and in a sense we can say that he is novelistically unimagined. But not from Richardson's inability to imagine him. Our evidence is not just the plethora of marvelous characterizations of middle-aged males, from Lord M to Uncles John and Antony, that Richardson does give us. It is Clarissa's evidence, and the evidence of the novel's Trial stage altogether, that this is an essential plot move on Richardson's part. The absence of the father or his legitimate surrogate might be merely incidental or peculiar in another plot, but in the Tested Woman Plot judgment is crucial; the plot cannot end without it. The judge must be the patriarchal figure in legitimate possession, and to judge he must have knowledge. If Mr. Harlowe is to fulfill this role, it is his obligation to gather and weigh evidence, listening to the competing claims about this woman and her deed, seeking Truth as far as he is capable of doing so. That Clarissa has offended against him makes his obligation all the stronger. His final offense against her is that he refuses. But his effective novelistic absence from the opening moments of the book sends the strongest signal, though a signal not intelligible until much later, that Mr. Harlowe is not the patriarchal figure in ultimate possession. God is. Given the demands of a literal social novel, this plot feature is very difficult for Richardson to manage, it is true. But he will not give it up, for it is the heart of what he has to say.

In these mirroring phenomena of patriarchal social collapse and patriarchal religious affirmation, we see yet another aspect of Richardson's unsettling originality. In *Clarissa* he seems at once the most radical and the most conservative of writers. This effect results from his profound moral seriousness and courage, and it should not surprise us, though it keeps doing so.[8] That Richardson is capable of scathing social opinions is evident when we look closely at the famous "attack on the drama" passage of *The Apprentice's Vade Mecum*. What really fuels that attack is a very vigorous class critique. At root Richardson is indignant that malleable young men of the business and artisan class—the class he regards as the heart, brain, and sinews of English society—should waste their money, time, and emulation on a vehicle primarily devoted to celebrating the socially destructive follies of the upper classes.[9] As a child of the working-class slums and a craftsman and self-made businessman of impeccable integrity Richardson had no use for the idle and self-important rich. Naturally the upper classes were capable of reciprocating his distaste. The most common attack on his work in his lifetime took the form of a sneer at the inaccuracy of his depiction of upper-class manners.[10] The mistakes he made in small matters were the readiest counterirritant, we cannot help but notice, to an all-too-accurate larger picture.

But Richardson's social critique is not, finally, a class critique. Like his heroine Clarissa, he believes that the much-to-be-desired health of the hierarchical structure into which he was born lies in the appropriate reciprocity between power and obligation. If he critiques upper-class irresponsibility, it is for the very reason that extraordinary power confers extraordinary obligation. When in his novels he chooses increasingly to portray the socially and economically fortunate and powerful, it is because Mr. B, Lovelace, the Harlowes, and Sir Charles Grandison carry greater and more subtle responsibilities and face more complicated sources of temptation than does Goodman Andrews. When he exposes the bankruptcy of the men in authority over Clarissa, his grounds are precisely the degree to which they insist upon that authority. If they demand of a loving and sheltered girl absolute loyalty in exchange for absolute protection, then they had better be able to deliver on their pretensions. To do less is to expose themselves as hollow, or worse. The worse takes the form of an internecine power struggle which, while it wounds its hierarchical subordinates, damages its own members even more.

So major a permutation of the Tested Woman Plot helps account rather precisely for much of the novel's closing. Mr. Harlowe's absence fatally prevents any real resolution of the male competition which tore his family apart. Hence the ending, so uncharacteristic of the Tested Woman Plot, which focuses on the death of the interloper Lovelace rather than on the fortunes or attitudes of the family. Further, the moral bankruptcy of the human authority in whose terms she has sought to live forces Clarissa to conduct her trial herself preparatory to placing the record of her life before her ultimate judge, who is God. Such a self-trial is not unique in renderings of the plot; it occurs embryonically, for instance, in *The Duchess of Malfi*.

Having technically violated patriarchal authority in the interest of social
and sexual health by contracting a secret marriage against the wishes of her
politically and sexually possessive brothers, the Duchess at their hands
suffers betrayal, arrest, and various forms of torture: isolation and deprivation, the apparent murder of her husband and children, and a visitation by
madmen. Herself momentarily unhinged, she regains her mental stability
in a meditation sequence permeated with the language of Deuteronomy
and Job, insists upon the integrity of her life and acts, makes her will, and
welcomes her murderers with composure. In the Duchess's world, given
the corruption of her brothers, there can be no earthly justice because there
is no one both entitled to and capable of weighing her intentions and her
acts. So too with Clarissa. But the immediacy and extension of Richardson's
epistolary form gives Clarissa's self-trial a psychological complexity altogether beyond the reach of drama.

The realization that the Trial exists and that she must conduct it herself
comes to Clarissa only slowly.[11] The Test endured, her choices made, at
first she simply suffers and, given the woman she is, she suffers in her
intellect. In chapter 6 we will see what it means in terms of the Prudence
Plot to be "the woman she is," and why her suffering will necessarily
involve her intellect. Here it is enough to remind ourselves that the opium
overdose, coupled with her gradual comprehension of what Lovelace has
done and what therefore he is, makes her mad. In the two weeks following
her rape she is not devoid of intermittent "method and good sense," as
Lovelace says about her papers (L 261, 16 June, 894), but she lacks consistency and control. His violation of her body tempts Clarissa to embrace a
definitive rupture between her past and her present self, a temptation the
course of which is charted by her letters to Miss Howe. That of 28 June
captures Clarissa's first flush of incoherent despair and misery:

> Oh, my dearest Miss Howe! Once more have I escaped—but, alas! *I,* my
> *best self,* have not escaped! . . . But no more of myself! my *lost* self.... O!
> my best, my dearest, my *only* friend! What a tale have I to unfold!—But
> still upon *self,* this vile, this hated *self!*—I will shake it off, if possible;
> and why should I not, since I think, except one wretch, I hate nothing so
> much!—Self, then, be banished from *self* one moment (for I doubt it *will*
> for no longer) to inquire after a *dearer* object, my beloved Anna Howe!—
> whose mind, all robed in spotless white, charms and irradiates—but what
> would I say?—. . ." (L 295, 974)

This is the language of fragmentation. Clarissa is threatened here with disintegration because she longs for disintegration. Lovelace has contaminated her present self, which she loathes and would escape, while her former self seems definitively lost.

The calm intelligibility of Clarissa's letter of 20 July likewise stresses the difference between past and present, as well as between friend and friend. Purged of self-hatred, however, it speaks not of fragmentation but of radical metamorphosis:

> Think not of me, my only friend, but as we were in times past: and suppose me gone a great, great way off!—a long journey!—. . . Love me still, however. But let it be with a weaning love. I am not what I was when we were *inseparable* lovers, as I may say—Our *views* must now be different— . . . . (L 343, 1088)

"I am not what I was." If by this declaration Clarissa were to mean that she could not carry forward into present and future her psychological and moral identity, then she would be lost and Lovelace would have won, for he sought to separate her from that identity. If, however, rising from the tortures of betrayal and its resultant madness, she can, like the Duchess of Malfi, be herself still, Lovelace is superfluous to the work that lies ahead. He is no longer a threat but merely a nuisance whom she will flee because she is too busy for him. "So, pray, sir, don't disturb or interrupt me—I beseech you don't—" (L421.1, 22 Aug., 1233).

Reachieving that integrity is no simple task. Clarissa's return to full sanity delivers her to a potentially destructive depression: since she no longer is what she was, she no longer knows what the person she has become must do. Her first work is to learn that not only is her life not finished but it has a very specific shape to come which, once understood, will focus her energy. She is restored to herself by recognizing that the Test is not the end but the means; that it leads to her conversation, speaking by means of the conduct of her life, with those to whom she owes life. Clarissa comes to know this partly by attempting to carry out that conversation with her family. As her expectation of her father's participation wanes, she also discovers models for her gradual recognition that it is a conversation which can be held only with God.

One such model is Mrs. Norton's letter of 1 July, which supplies the history of a woman stripped of family and means but not of integrity or hope, a woman whose appeal to Providence is an appeal to the design and the purposefulness of life. The letter in turn prepares Clarissa for her recourse to the Book of Job, the primary material of her meditations. The Book of Job serves as her model not just because it is a tale of tribulation but because, as we saw in chapter 2, it displays the two-stage structure and competing functions of the Tested Woman Plot. And because in it the final threat and the final agony lie in the seeming absence of the father. In that respect especially, Job's story is a version of Clarissa's story.

We know that the Test portion of the Book of Job has as its starting point Job's virtue, and that the Test is undertaken as the result of a conflict within Yahweh himself. We also know that Satan argues for the Test on precisely the grounds advanced by Lovelace, that untried virtue is no virtue at all: "What may not both men and women be brought to do in a mortified state? What mind is superior to calamity?" (L110, [13 April], 426–27). Job's Test proceeds, like Clarissa's, in two waves. In the first, Satan receives the Lord's permission to sever Job from all his external sources of happiness, and in the second, to touch Job's "bone and his flesh" (Job 2:5). Now comes the question: In the face of God's seeming rejection of him, will Job choose to separate himself from God? Will he despair and, because despairing, die? At the conclusion of the Test stage, Job has made his choice. He does not "sin with his lips" (2:10); he holds firm. But he too is disoriented, and his friends find him silenced: "So they sat down with him upon the ground seven days and seven nights, and none spake a word unto him: for they saw that his grief was very great" (2:13). During the ensuing Trial, Job examines his own sense of self, rejects the interpretations of his friends, and presents his case to God. That case consists finally of his insistence that the Creator may do whatever he will with his creature—except absent Himself. Job rests his case on the expectation of God's response. And he is not denied. When God speaks to Job out of the whirlwind, He opens a dialogue. It is this conversation itself, the face-to-face assurance that God has listened, has known, has not absented himself, that Job craves and in which he finds humility, repentance, and peace.

It is in this last regard especially that the Book of Job serves as Clarissa's chief model for her Trial. It is true that Job's story helps reinforce her native commitment to the muscular examination of her own integrity. It also helps confirm her sense of her distinctiveness, which is one of the sources of her will power, for the story of Job, like Mrs. Norton's letter, in reminding that she will be required to bear in proportion to her strength, reminds her that she is strong. But most significantly, Job helps her confront the absence of Mr. Harlowe and the necessity of turning directly to an invisible God. Daunting as her Trial may be, the knowledge that it is part of the pattern to be performed gives her the power to perform it.

Quite extraordinary corroboration regarding Clarissa's uses of the Book of Job is provided by one of the novel's subterranean texts. We know that the novel itself contains five of Clarissa's "Meditations," biblical excerpts compiled in reference to her own situation; three of them are transcribed by Belford, one is stitched in black silk onto a letter Clarissa sends to her Uncle John, and one is purloined by Lovelace in his raid on the Smiths'. But Clarissa wrote many others, says the novel, gathered into a collection of which upon her death her mother received the original and Mrs. Norton and Mrs. Lovick received copies. Though we hear no more about them in the novel, they were written in fact; late in 1749 Richardson printed the entire set of thirty-six in a volume which he distributed to friends, though he never sold it. In a splendidly useful article entitled "Richardson's *Meditations:* Clarissa's *Clarissa*," Tom Keymer describes the entire set, of which the "extent" five, those appearing in the novel, stand as numbers VIII, XII, XIII, XVII, and XVIII. For our purposes, the most important feature of *Meditations*[12] as a whole is that it confirms Clarissa's sense of the life pattern to be performed. "From the earliest meditations," says Keymer, "a narrative begins to emerge, in which her suffering ceases to be arbitrary, and takes on the character of a divinely sanctioned trial. . . ." In the passages she selects and shapes, "the random and inexplicable cruelty of her antagonists can appear in a new light, as part of the pattern of a Christian ordeal. In consequence, the cry of despair becomes increasingly a defense: that she has been selected for the distinction of trial" (96–97). And thus, "the meaning of her life becomes fixed by analogy: reinterpreted and rewritten according to the model of Job's trial, it takes on a new and arresting significance. She is a latter-day Job, tested by adversity; Lovelace is the Satan sent to try her; the Harlowes become the comforters, compounding her sufferings by reading them, maliciously, as retribution" (98–99).

In addition to a sense of purpose and shape, the Book of Job helps give Clarissa language, and an attitude toward the importance of language. If her Papers record the dangers of despair in the language of fragmentation, her Meditations practice various forms of the language of integrity and therefore of hope. And the focusing texts of the Meditations, of which the novel's five are a mere indicator, come from the Book of Job. In the sepa-

rate volume called *Meditations,* says Keymer, Clarissa ends her preface
"with an apology for having 'taken the liberty of substituting the word *her*
for *him,* and to make other such-like little changes of words,' a liberty she
hopes 'will be thought pardonable' (p. viii). Her little changes, however,
carry the deepest implications: by adopting and redeploying Job's words,
she also adopts the precedent of his life, which hers now appears to reiterate" (97). The Book of Job confirms, in fact, that her task is the examination and recording of her own life, a literal recording, the making of a book.
Job's sense that the colloquy between him and his accusers stands as a
record of his life is very strong, and though it takes place in oral exchange
on a dunghill, he longs for permanence: "Oh that my words were now
written! oh that they were printed in a book! / That they were graven with
an iron pen and lead in the rock for ever!" (Job 19:23, 24). Clarissa also
longs for permanence, and these words of Job's are the very lines with
which she ends her first meditation (15 July; contained in Lovelace's L 364
to Belford of 24 July, 1125). But her own words are not the only ones that
must be recorded. Job longs for the record of the other side as well: "Behold,
my desire is . . . that mine adversary had written a book" (Job 31:35). Now
Clarissa's adversary, unlike Job's, has written, and Belford's work on her
behalf brings Lovelace's letters first into the scope of her understanding
and then into the book of her life. What Clarissa performs in this collabora-
tive bookmaking is neither mere self-justification nor even mere record-
keeping, important as the public record will be. Preparing the "book" is a
laborious business during the course of which she must relive her entire
experience and rectify her response to it—recreate and examine it through
writing—in order to prepare fully the Self she will present to God. By
means of this strenuous and absorbing exercise in meditation, she probes
the wounds of violation, struggles with the necessity of forgiving her abus-
ers, rejoices in and counsels her friends, leaves instructions for those who
will survive her, and thereby wins the battle against the temptation to despair.

In this forensic enterprise truth must be sought first. Though Belford
helps, it is Clarissa who primarily flushes out the facts. Even in her Papers,
where her grief flails in all directions, one of the salient efforts is simply to
interrogate the facts. As wit and purpose return and she struggles to extri-
cate herself from Mrs. Sinclair's house, one of her worst torments is that
she has no independent means of finding out the truth about anything.
Nevertheless, she is increasingly aware of the machinations within machinations that envelop her, so that by the time she wisely refuses to accom-

pany Dorcas to the coach of "Mother H" it is partly from suspicion at the
ease with which a variety of seemingly improvisational connections have
arranged themselves (L273, RL to JB, 21 June, 926–27).

But being able to see the truth about others requires first that she be
able to speak the truth about herself. Ironically, it is Lovelace who, by
setting up the penknife scene, first enables her to say quite baldly what has
happened to her. On 23 June, after his manipulations have provoked
Clarissa's affidavit promising Dorcas a life annuity in exchange for help-
ing her escape, Lovelace attempts a preemptive move. He puts Clarissa on
trial, anticipating the pleasures of highly charged histrionics to be followed
by a second rape:

> Now, Belford, see us all sitting in judgement, resolved to punish the fair
> briberess—I, and the mother, the hitherto *dreaded* mother, the nieces
> Sally, Polly, the traitress Dorcas, and Mabel, a guard as it were over
> [Dorcas] that she might not run away and hide herself: all pre-deter-
> mined. . . . (L281, 23/24 June, 948–49)

But when Clarissa confronts them she immediately takes the trial into her
own hands, in the least expected way, by laying claim to her own ruin:
"And ye, vile women, . . . know that I am not married—ruined as I am by
your helps, I bless God, I am *not* married to this miscreant" (949). That
"truth" move announces disaster for Lovelace, did he but know it. He has
counted on her sense of shame to cover the evidence of his guilt:

> For a rape . . . to us rakes is far from being an undesirable thing. Nothing
> but the law stands in our way . . . ; and the opinion of what a modest
> woman will suffer, rather than become a *viva voce* accuser, lessens much
> an honest fellow's apprehensions on that score. (L 261, 16 June, 896–97)

Clarissa is the most modest woman he has ever met, thus extortion should
work best upon her. But as Clarissa says later to Lady Betty and as Belford
quotes her to Lovelace, "Why should I seek to conceal that disgrace from
others, which I cannot hide from myself?" (L 306, 3 July, 985; L 336, 17
July, 1073). Having thus sloughed off the major pretense that burdened
her, the pretense to marriage, once her residence at the Smiths' gives her
freedom of correspondence she goes after the facts. She sends inquiries to
Lady Betty, to Uncle John's housekeeper, to Mrs. Norton, to Miss Rawlins,
to Anna Howe—Did you write at such and such a time and to such and such

a purpose? Does my uncle know a Captain Tomlinson? Were my family gathered to celebrate my uncle's birthday? Who (for it was not I) was lying flushed and bloated upon the sofa at Hampstead? And the evidence comes in, while Clarissa mourns and marvels over not just the malice but the sheer complication of it all.[13]

Throughout, Clarissa practices stating what has happened to her. To Lady Betty, to Mrs. Norton, to the Howes she conveys with various degrees of detail the information that she is unmarried, raped and without prospects. Of course it takes practice, this stating, as it takes time and testing to be certain of what the facts are and who her friends are. By 21 July she is essentially finished with fact finding, and therefore ready for the scene in which she recounts her history to Belford, Mrs. Lovick, and Mr. and Mrs. Smith (L349, JB to RL, [21 July], 1104–6). She tells it all, all but Lovelace's name: the months of correspondence and flight and delusion with Lovelace, the rape and the escape and the arrest for debt, her name and her family history and her erstwhile prospects, her father's malediction, her blighted hopes. She states openly and repeatedly that she is not married; she makes clear that she will not be married. What is astonishing about this trial scene is Clarissa's lack of embarrassment. We might have imagined her able to say what she does before Belford, who knows it all anyway, or before the motherly women. But to serenely welcome Mr. Smith into their midst is to go public.

Clarissa can do so because she has examined the facts and her conscience and knows both her culpability and her innocence. Her second letter to Lady Betty (L 306, 3 July), the one which refuses to conceal from others what she cannot hide from herself, acknowledges all the key features: her presumption in attempting to reclaim an unreclaimable man, her disobedience to those to whom she owed obedience, and her innocence in her behavior toward Lovelace. Her summary is helped toward a judicious balance and accuracy by being directed at a personally distant audience:

> I will not offer to clear myself entirely of blame: but, as to *him*, I have no fault to accuse myself of. My crime was the corresponding with him at first, when prohibited so to do by those who had a right to my obedience; made still more inexcusable by giving him a clandestine meeting, which put me into the power of his arts. And for this, I am content to be punished: thankful that at last I have escaped from him; and have it in my power to reject so wicked a man for my husband: and glad if I may be a warning, since I cannot be an example: which once (very vain, and very conceited as I was!) I proposed to myself to be! (985)

This sober and unflinching assessment of her own behavior may stand as a clean and neutral summary of the facts.

But though finding and stating the truth is the necessary first step, it still has as its goal the reconciliation which should follow. The Trial is designed to correct and to heal. Clarissa's family and friends know the traditional ways this is done, both of which would force restitution from Lovelace. Mrs. Howe, her opinion conveyed by her daughter, baldly broaches the alternatives—marry or die:

> To this purpose, the custom in the Isle of Man is a very good one—'If a single woman there prosecutes a single man for a rape, . . . if he be convicted, the deemster, or judge, delivers to the woman a rope, a sword, and a ring; and she has it in her choice to have him hanged, beheaded, or to marry him.' (L 317, 10 July, 1017)

Lovelace himself counts on this Manx scenario, as we see in his 18 July note to Anna Howe begging

> that if I may be once more admitted to pay my duty to the most deserving and most injured of her sex, I will be content to do it with a halter about my neck; and attended by a parson on my right hand, and the hangman on my left, to be doomed, at her will, either to the church or the gallows. (L 332.2, 1050)

By this point, when Lovelace is happy to play the marriage card, there is every evidence that the victory which would accrue from bringing him to the altar, eased by the flattering civilities of Lord M's family, would indeed eventually reconcile the Harlowes to their daughter and each other. But victory they must have.

The logic of their position forces the subsequent step. If marriage is not possible, a capital prosecution is the alternative. To the bafflement of all, marriage is out, not because Lovelace will not, but because Clarissa will not. So prosecution becomes the cry. The most cogent case for it, and the one which because of its source Clarissa would be most likely to admit, is Dr. Lewen's. Lewen's argument is twofold: that for the sake of public safety and morals such wickedness should not go unpunished; nor should it for the sake of family harmony, as he fears "mischiefs" between Lovelace and either James or Morden. Since "the reparation of your family dishonour," he says to Clarissa, can go forward only by either marriage or a capital prosecution, and since you refuse to marry, you must prosecute in defense and proof of your modesty and innocence:

> To pretend to pardon, while we are labouring under the pain or dishonour of [indignities of any kind], will be thought by some to be but the vaunted mercy of a pusillanimous heart trembling to resent them. The remedy I propose is a severe one; but what pain can be more severe than the injury? or how will injuries be believed to grieve us, that are never honourably complained of? . . . Little, very little difference, is there, my dear young lady, between a *suppressed* evidence, and *false* one. (L427, 18 Aug., 1252)

In short, Dr. Lewen is saying, the world, especially the world of your family, must be brought to believe that you are innocent and must be allowed to vent its spleen on the offender, or there will be no peace. To prove your resentment and your desire for reconciliation, you must revenge.

In the meantime, Clarissa has been coming to quite another position, based on the recognition that a legal process would neither punish nor reform Lovelace. She understands Dr. Lewen's argument, to be sure. She used it to free herself in the penknife scene where, having rejected the lie that she was married, she was free to threaten "the LAW." But there are laws and laws, witnesses and witnesses, friends and friends. Clarissa comes to understand that Lovelace cannot be gotten at by an earthly judicial process; he would enjoy it too much to profit from it. "Such is the assurance of [this] man, . . . and such his inveteracy to my family . . . , that he would not have been sorry to have an opportunity to confront me and my father, uncles, and brother, at the bar of a court of justice, on such an occasion" (L 428, to Dr. Lewen, 19 Aug., 1254). She wants for him the punishment of self-purifying change: "All the ill I wish him is that he may reform" (L 306, to Lady Betty, 3 July, 985). She wants him to undergo a truly effective process: "He will have his account to make up somewhere else; not to me" (L 336, JB to RL, 17 July, 1071). She refuses Belford's account of the Montague family's "trial" because it is not the significant one: "She cut me short, saying that was a cause before another tribunal" (L 339, 18 July, 1077).

But neither would a legal process reconcile the family with each other or with her. They would be caught up all over again in the struggle with Lovelace, too preoccupied to hear or see the truth. Further, a courtroom trial would not produce the necessary evidence; by its form it would suppress and falsify what most needs to be told. After all, Mr. Brand has confirmed to the family what the whole world already knows and Uncle Antony assures her of: that she lived "several guilty weeks at bed as well as board no doubt" with "one of the vilest fellows that ever drew breath" (L 407, 13 Aug., 1195)—and so why shouldn't they ask whether she is pregnant? And they hope it isn't true what they hear more, that after she ran away from Lovelace she now entertains his equally profligate friend——. A court of law would flourish this kind of "fact." As for Clarissa, she is not surprised that slander can be propagated when even her family have given up on her (1196–97). She understands their shock: "The fall of a regular person no doubt is dreadful and inexcusable. It is like the sin of apostasy. Would to Heaven, however, that I had had the circumstances of mine inquired into!" (1196). If the real problem is how to inquire into the circumstances of her case—how to conduct this particular casuistical investigation in such a fashion that her family will come to know and eventually live in some sort of peace with the full truth—then a trial in a court of law is not the way. A court battle would finally only disguise, distort, and inflame.

In considering Clarissa's conduct of her Trial, we have discussed two plot moves, her search after the facts and her efforts at familial reconciliation. The outcomes of the two efforts are related: although she satisfies herself as to the facts, her family is not receptive to the truth, which means that reconciliation is not yet possible. They cannot yet understand what happened because they cannot yet face a full description of events, which would include their own involvement and responsibility. Hence the third plot move of Clarissa's Trial, her turn from father Harlowe to God the Father as first the ultimate, and then the only, judge of her case. We have already remarked on how difficult this turn is for Richardson to convey in a realistic script, for who is left to play God but God Himself? The conversation with God that Clarissa learns to seek and dies believing she has engaged in must necessarily, for the reader, be carried out inferentially. It is accomplished by implication, by negation, by a subtle recourse to texts whose echoes Richardson expects his readers to recognize even when his characters do not.

In the plot turn from father to Father, the most interesting and subtle text is the one that marks its beginning. Paper II—"(Scratched through and thrown under the table)"—is Clarissa's appeal to her "dear honoured papa" (copied in L 261, RL to JB, 16 June, 890). This is the first text in which the paternal identity is explicitly ambiguous. In it, the cry of the abandoned child to the absent father is designed to conjure not just the relationship between Clarissa and Mr. Harlowe but that between all Christians and their God. The textual allusion behind the fragment is the "Prayer of Humble Access" which in the Anglican Communion Service directly precedes the administration of the Sacrament. That prayer opens with a statement about the relationship between the petitioner and God, a relationship which then makes it possible for the communicant to request access to the Sacrament:

> (The statement of relationship) We do not presume to come to this thy Table, O merciful Lord, trusting in our own righteousness, but in thy manifold and great mercies. We are not worthy so much as to gather up the crumbs under thy Table. But thou art the same Lord, whose property is always to have mercy:
>
> (The request) Grant us therefore (and the text moves to consider the acts and the significance of the Eucharist).[14]

The statement portion of this prayer not only does what Clarissa is attempting to do, but does it in much the same language. The difference lies in the degree of sureness with which the statement is unfolded: Clarissa is forced to try to establish the foundation for each of her points, to assert her filial right to use this language and perform this act, whereas the prayer assumes that right.

What evokes this prayer for the reader of Paper II is, first, situation: the very need for a "prayer of humble access" in which the petitioner reestablishes, by reference to the fundamental nature of the relationship and characters of petitioner and petitioned, the essence of the bond between created and creator. The second evocation lies in two key words, I do not *presume* and I am not *worthy,* by means of the juxtaposition of which Richardson will call up the text he wants. The third means of evocation lies in the contrastive rhetorical movement of the two passages as they invoke the natures of the beings involved: *not* our righteousness *but* thy manifold and great mercies; *not* our worth *but* thy essential property of mercy. The chief difference between the texts is that Clarissa's movement between the two natures, her own and her father's, is not nearly so smooth nor so confident. Further, it takes place in not two backings and fillings but four: Can you? But I am sure you would not; Will nobody? Why, let it be your own act; I don't presume. . . But you are my own papa; I am unworthy, yet I am your child.

The power of this prayer and of Clarissa's petition is the power that Job knows finally to call upon: the power of definition itself. Given the Being that you are, and the being that I am, here is our relationship. To deny me is to deny Yourself. And Clarissa's case is made, though in uncertainty and agony of spirit, for Clarissa's Paper ends up a crumb under the table. Given the mental state evinced by the sum of the Papers, it is safe to say that Clarissa does not know what she is doing here: not consciously. She is only preparing to understand that her comfort will be in God alone. She does not yet know that she will die having achieved the conversation that she comes to crave the most, for such is what her "assurances" mean (see for example L 465, to Mrs. Norton, [5 Sept.], 1338). But in Paper II she takes up a richly familiar language the nuances of which she will eventually understand fully and command completely. Even now though, in the confusion and agony after the rape, she knows where Paper II and the other Papers belong: "Dorcas thinks her lady will ask for them: so wishes to have them to lay again under her table" (889).

There is no sign that Lovelace understands the work Clarissa is beginning with such difficulty to do. The religious texts and practices to which she is turning are a mystery to many of the characters, and we need to read that fact as judiciously as we read the textual echoes themselves. Given his profession, the Reverend Mr. Brand is the most blatantly ignorant, and his misreading of Clarissa's spiritual work during the month of August is intended to be illuminatingly egregious. The usually charitable Mrs. Norton, who "can't say l like him, either in the pulpit or out of it," helps us with a scathing description of his inability to understand and elucidate the gospel he pretends to be teaching (L 381, 31 July, 1167). We are less surprised that Lovelace at Hampstead should use Jeremy Taylor as a masquerade prop, or that Sally Martin, pursuing the phony suit at Rowland the bailiff's, should mockingly admire the way Clarissa's Bible opens itself to the Book of Job and prove herself a scriptural scholar by knowing that Ecclesiasticus is Apocrypha. Even earnest John Belford, describing with increasing moral dismay first this deathbed and then that, hardly understands the full import of the biblical passages he hears and the John Norris he himself cites. But as she regains sanity and purpose, Clarissa herself comes to master those texts and that language.

By 22 August her shift in hierarchical focus is both conscious and complete. Her new business is the subject of the famous letter to Lovelace (copied in L 421, RL to JB, 23 Aug., 1233). I am going home to my father's house, she says, announcing with utmost exactness and economy precisely that shift from father to Father that Richardson's version of the Trial incorporates. After Paper II, what must first strike us about this text is the sureness with which it moves:

> I have good news to tell you. I am setting out with all diligence for my father's house. I am bid to hope that he will receive his poor penitent with a goodness peculiar to himself; for I am overjoyed with the assurance of a thorough reconciliation through the interposition of a dear blessed friend, whom I have always loved and honoured. I am so taken up with my preparation for this joyful and long-wished-for journey, that I cannot spare one moment for any other business, having several matters of the last importance to settle first.

Clarissa's language is always plain and direct; here it is confident as well. It is also doctrinally sound, which is one reason for its confidence. Clarissa sees exactly where she is in her Christian journey and knows what last things remain for her to do. Further, the letter brilliantly extends the analysis of authority functions which is the heart of the Tested Woman Plot. In this letter not only does Clarissa recognize that God the Father must be her ultimate Judge, but she acknowledges that her ultimate Defender is the Christian's "dear blessed friend" Jesus. Thus the divided authority of the Hebraic Heavenly Court from which sprang the testing of Job finds its reconciliation in the unity of the Christian Trinity. Clarissa's deathbed publicly and joyfully confirms her confidence in her reception.

But what about those Clarissa leaves behind? Whither the drive to earthly reconciliation and reintegration with which the Tested Woman Plot traditionally closes? That reconciliation is by no means complete, and it certainly is not conducted in stereotypical fashion. Yet Richardson has his eye unceasingly on the issue. The freedom Clarissa achieves by means of her dying allows her to speak forcefully and, she hopes, persuasively to those she loves and might have loved. Within the context of the Tested Woman Plot, here is in good part the "reason" that Clarissa dies, the plot purpose that her death carries out. Death gives her a whole life to tell, and the freedom to tell it. Peter Brooks, discussing this plot function of the focal character's death, evokes Walter Benjamin in a passage perfectly descriptive of Richardson's novel: "If in Benjamin's thesis . . . 'Death is the sanction of everything that the storyteller can tell,' it is because it is at the moment of death that life becomes *transmissible*."[15] Though her will is the document through which Clarissa transmits specific messages, it is her completed life that transmits her entire intentions and actions.

The shock of Clarissa's death, however, provides a psychological opening from which the living can profit only as their natures allow. The Harlowes, it turns out, cannot rise above themselves. A disarming feature of the last part of the novel is the tension between Clarissa's posthumously expressed desire to assuage the guilt and anger of her family, and Richardson's insistence upon showing them up. Their grief is disabling to the degree that their guilt is profound, and it is the disability that Richardson chiefly brings home. We are hardly surprised that Miss Howe refuses to temper her contempt. But the telling details of sheer ineffectuality provided by Mrs. Norton, Colonel Morden, and the servants, none of them enemies of the family, are what reduce Harlovian pretensions to their sordid actuality. Upon their receipt of Dr. H.'s letter announcing Clarissa's imminent death, the family finally starts to come round. Do hurry up to London, they entreat Mrs. Norton, and tell our Clary all manner of nice things from us. But they make no move to go themselves. Nor does it occur to them to wonder how this aging and impecunious widow is going to get there, so naturally they do not think to offer the family chariot (L 483, Mrs. N to CH, 6 Sept., 1364). Mrs. Norton makes a point of the problem, several times, for Richardson does not want us to miss it. Nor does he want us to miss the reception of Clarissa's death. Belford's news-carrying servant Harry (who gets a name because his report is significant) relays the total breakdown of order and social decency at Harlowe Place to the point where he is neither rested, fed, nor even interviewed, a state of collapse contrasted with his reception at the Howes' (L 494, JB to RL, [9 Sept.], 1379). As for Morden, when he arrives at Clarissa's home with her body he encounters such an orgy of mutual recrimination and ostentatiously impotent grief as embarrasses him to report (L 500, to JB, 10 Sept., 1394; and continuations). The only relief comes from the unexpectedly decorous behavior of the working folk who sort out their precedence in whispers as they crowd forward to carry her casket into the hall (1398). After the meticulous and effectual caring that manifested itself those last days in London, the family's hysteria seems freshly shocking. How ill-prepared the Harlowes always are, we reflect. To point the moral, Morden comments on how accurately Clarissa foresaw the effect her death would have on them (1399). We are hardly surprised to hear in Belford's "Conclusion" that father and mother sink shortly to unhappy deaths, and that brother and sister, still festering with spite, construct miserable marriages precisely modeled on their previous familial habits.

Nor can Lovelace profit from Clarissa's efforts. His incapacity is sufficiently complex and interesting to merit a separate discussion, to which we will turn in chapter 5, but here we must note his inability to admit the truth about others or about himself. Again and again we watch him come face to face with an understanding so painful that he must reject it. His letter of 21 August to Belford, for all its frenetic, self-preening amusement at the glove-play at Smith's and at Sally's aping of Clarissa, can momentarily tell the truth about Clarissa's integrity:

> Oh this sex! this artful sex! There's no minding them. At first, indeed, their grief and their concern may be real: but give way to the hurricane, and it will soon die away in soft murmurs, trilling upon your ears like the notes of a well-tuned viol. And, by Sally, one sees that art will generally so well supply the place of nature, that you shall not easily know the difference. Miss Harlowe, indeed, is the only woman in the world, I believe, that can say, in the words of her favourite Job (for I can quote a text as well as she), *But it is not so with me.*" (L 416, 1217)

Having said this, however, he nevertheless cannot believe in the possibility of her dying. He is tricked by the "father's house" letter of 22 August because he insists upon it. He was on the verge of a sound reading: "And yet Cousin Charlotte, who pretends to have the eye of an eagle, was for finding out some mystery in the style and manner, till I overbore her, and laughed her out of it" (L 439, 28 Aug., 1270). "Till I overbore her" is precisely right. Lovelace must veer away, is psychologically incapable of admitting his incipient knowledge of Clarissa's independence because it would force his total reorganization.

When Clarissa's death proves her "grief" and "concern" Lovelace unravels, but unlike Clarissa he has neither the sound training nor the new agenda which might allow him to reconstruct himself. His "recovery" is mere intermittent imitation of his previous behavior and it is poor stuff, adequate only to temporarily remesmerize Mowbray and Tourville. Miss Howe remarks on the "meanness" with which he heaps blame on Sinclair and his other sidekicks for actions for which he had always insisted upon taking exclusive credit (L 522, to JB, 30 Sept., 1454). We see for ourselves the lie with which he salves his conscience over challenging Morden, for despite his claims to the contrary it is he himself who provokes the duel.

Belford's account to Lord M shows how much the last interviews with his friend consist of damage control. Refusing to be provoked, alternately playing Lovelace's game and evading it, Belford eases into exile the man he still loves but can no longer admire or even find very interesting. The final tavern scenes bear out the degree to which Lovelace has become a pointless nuisance not just to Clarissa but to all his world, and nowhere more than to himself.

What a fitting, and healing, relationship between the plot's authority functions and a character's individual life purpose might look like is modestly exemplified by Belford. Attracted first by guilt and admiration, then by Clarissa's own sense of purpose, Belford not only becomes her active abettor but himself undergoes a transformation triggered by her example and confirmed by the horrific deaths of his cohorts and acquaintances. The cautionary flavor of those experiences is less compelling, for the reader certainly and for Belford himself perhaps, than the exercise of personal power and independence that reformation entails. As he retrains himself step by cautious step and reports with nervous exaltation on his progress, his education in virtue becomes an imitation, wan but waxing, of Clarissa herself. Belford has learned from Clarissa's trial how to shape his own life. It is he who, by marriage with Charlotte Montague, will live a real man's life, "a life of reason" (L 344, to RL, 20 July, 1090). It is their son who will inherit Lovelace's patrimony.

Before the last letters take us to the events on the Continent, in fact, we have an intimate look at a subtle and gratifying social development centered around but by no means restricted to Belford. For the first time in the novel, we see a community being built rather than torn apart by means of the letters we are reading. The common note of these letters is a blend of civility, frankness and common purpose that we have not had occasion to enjoy before. Now that both Lovelace and the Harlowes have eliminated themselves from the social enterprise, the new family that Clarissa had begun to build starts to achieve a solidarity among its members. This is no mere matter of common sentimental attachment to Clarissa's memory. It is a matter of independent truth-telling and contract-making. Belford can be frank with Lord M about Lovelace's behavior and prospects. Morden trusts Belford enough to describe the quandary Lovelace's behavior has put him in as a man of honor, spirit, and familial piety. Anna Howe can admit to Belford her admiration for Hickman and her resolve to marry. Hickman himself serves as a curious bellwether figure. Even more of an epistolary cipher than Mr. Harlowe, Hickman comes by the end of the novel to enjoy considerable moral and social stature and presence. Eventually successful suitor, husband and father—and one of the few men in the novel to hold his own against Lovelace—while we were looking elsewhere he has been gaining stature. He helps unite the women's world with which we had associated him with the men's world from which he had seemed excluded, for Morden, asking Belford to be his executor, reveals that he has requested the same service of Hickman. Belford agrees upon the condition that Morden will serve in the same capacity for him. By the end of the novel we realize that Charlotte Montague, Anna Howe, Morden, Hickman, Belford, and to a lesser degree Lord M have become joined in a variety of formally contracted intimacies based on mutual esteem.[16]

For the world of the novel, this is a remarkable social network because it is formed by free contract rather than the enforcement of either Lovelace's predation or James's prerogative. It is remarkable also for the full integration of its women. Anna Howe's "marriage letter" to Belford (L 523, 2 Oct., 1455) is amusingly characteristic of her high spirits, which we are delighted to see her recovering, but it also asks a key question. To put it baldly, as does Miss Howe, why would anyone of spirit and good sense contract herself to either a Harlovian or a Lovelacean world? The question, so put, answers itself. It reminds us that Clarissa's two great refusals rejected both kinds of enforcement. And that it is thanks to her strenuous work that the friends who have also refused those worlds, though at far less cost to themselves, will prosper together in respect and love.

5

The Don Juan Plot

In *Clarissa*, Richardson's conscious adherence to the Tested Woman Plot is unmistakable. But while this plot accounts for much that is both distinctive and unexpected in the novel, it cannot adequately account for Lovelace. It does not explain his relationship with Morden or the manner of his death. Nor does it explain why, when his plot purpose is lost, he can neither change his function nor quit the story. The problem is not merely that in Lovelace Richardson has conceived a most compelling Tempter. It is that the plot in which Clarissa finds herself seems not to be precisely the plot of which Lovelace believes himself a part.

I think that in a sense this explanation is accurate. In addition to the Tested Woman Plot, Clarissa exhibits the pull of another entire structure, the Don Juan Plot. The Don Juan Plot is no mere rake's progress, any more than the Tested Woman Plot is simply the story of a woman abused. As a genuine plot, it exhibits a strong coherence of both events and character types. And the feature that most accounts for Lovelace's treatment is that its Tempter protagonist maintains his singularity to the point of, even in despite of, death. But Richardson seems to handle the Don Juan Plot less masterfully than the older structure, perhaps because it is comparatively simplistic and lacks the rich variety of the testing plot, perhaps because it is innately less well suited to his positive didactic purposes. Some of the difficulties of *Clarissa* stem from the cross-purposes set up by his attempt to graft the Tested Woman Plot with a plot which is its structural antitype.

Unlike the truly venerable Tested Woman Plot, the Don Juan Plot is essentially an Enlightenment artifact. The first literary version, Tirso de Molina's play *El Burlador de Sevilla,* was published in 1630. The story was immediately popular, especially among dramatists, and renditions, the more hackneyed the more typical, were legion. According to Leo Weinstein's study *The Metamorphoses of Don Juan,* in the slightly more than 100 years before *Clarissa* there were thirty-one literary treatments, virtually all of them continental. To modern readers the best known of the pre-Richardson versions is surely Molière's *Dom Juan, ou Le Festin de pierre* (1665). The greatest rendering of the Don Juan Plot, however, is unquestionably the Mozart/Da Ponte *Don Giovanni*. Written and performed in 1787, the opera naturally had no influence on Richardson. But partly because of the structural starkness of opera, partly because it was the last great version uncontaminated by the Romantic glorification of self-aggrandizement, *Don Giovanni* tells us much about the plot's essential structure and, as we will see later, is therefore helpful to our understanding of *Clarissa*.

The one significant English version of the Don Juan Plot before Richardson is Thomas Shadwell's *Libertine,* published in 1676. Its chief virtues are energy and a strict adherence to the already stereotyped plot. Shadwell, who took positive pride in being a hack, vaunts himself in the play's preface on having spent no more than five days writing any of the acts, and from the reading I do not doubt him. *The Libertine* remained part of the standard London stage repertory for decades, enjoyed the additional fame of incidental music written by Henry Purcell for a revival in 1692, and was performed at Drury Lane until as late as 1740. It probably even served as the source for the Don Juan pantomime produced by David Garrick some time before his death in 1779.[1] Richardson is unlikely to have read Tirso, Molière, or other continental Don Juan plays, though he could have heard of them. But he probably read or attended Shadwell's play: Jocelyn Harris ("Richardson," 198–200) catalogues not just the similarities of character and event which we would expect whatever Richardson's source, but verbal echoes of Shadwell which in a few instances go beyond the stage-ravisher commonplaces. By the time of *Clarissa's* composition, at any rate, the Don Juan Plot was part of English theatrical lore.

One of the striking features of the Don Juan story, at least in its seventeenth- and eighteenth-century renditions, is its schematic rigidity—hence Shadwell's quickie. The plot always contains three agonistic groups of characters. *Don Juan himself,* the constant focus of the plot, is often abetted by a cluster of fellow rakes and usually accompanied by a servant whom he bullies and patronizes. He preys upon *a succession of woman victims,* both high-born and low-born, against one or two of whom he has especially offended either by promising marriage or by killing the father, the husband, or the betrothed. At the end he faces *the figure of Death,* usually a stone statue representing the slain relative.

These characters are involved in a characteristic, virtually an inevitable, event sequence. Early in the play Juan or his cronies engage in *a defense of libertinage,* which is associated with *a cataloguing of Juan's female victims.* Throughout the first part of the plot, we are entertained with *the alternating seductions of highborn and lowborn women,* and, at some point, *Juan's killing of the male relative of one of the women.* Midway through the story Juan issues *an impious invitation to the statue of the slain man* and the statue comes to life to issue *a counter-invitation.* Juan arrives *at the tomb or crypt* to which he has been invited, where the statue welcomes him in funereal surroundings, often to a stone feast. There, in a swift winding down of the plot, Juan *refuses the statue's demand that he repent,* boldly accepts the *statue's handshake of Death,* and *descends into Hell.*[2]

Because this plot, unlike the Tested Woman Plot, is singlemindedly focused on the protagonist, it is not surprising to find in him the same kind of stereotypicality we find in the plot structure. Two psychological traits are consistently associated with the Don Juan character. One is that Juan is less the lover than the trickster, the "burlador" of Tirso's title. He is conspicuous for his strongly histrionic flair, frequently involving role-playing and costume changes, and for his delight in improvisation. He is typically far more interested in the pleasurable challenges of his devious and often cruelly exploitive pursuits than he is in the sexual pleasure that is his putative goal. Even more famously, Don Juan is marked by his impiety or disregard for Providence, his "libertinage." This trait may take the form, as it does in Tirso's play, of his bold refusal to fear the Divine power in which he professes belief. Or it may appear as the frank unbelief of late Renaissance and Enlightenment freethinking or "atheism": the "Nature, thou art my God" strain of Shadwell's John. In either case, Juan's impiety is related to his abuse of promises, especially the promise of marriage, as a means to seduce. And it accounts for his provocation of Death, for the invitation to the statue, always an impious invitation, comes first from him.

Such in fact is what "libertine" means, to Juan, to Shadwell, and to the Enlightenment. Though in the letters of a real-life Rochester or the dialogue of a stage Horner the sensational (and, I might add, the politically safe) emphasis is on *sexual* libertinism, which is characterized by James Grantham Turner as a "*mélange* of Ovidian seduction-theory and Epicurean philosophy" ("Lovelace," 71), *libertine* is by no means a restrictedly sexual description. More broadly, it names Juan's refusal to be bound by Christian doctrine and moral causality. This trait is reflected at the end of the story in his unflinching willingness to accept the Statue's handshake despite the threat of hellfire. In terms of the event sequence as a whole, his libertinage is reflected in the importance of the issue of promises. Don Juan seduces by promising fidelity, usually marriage. But he never returns. The heart of the matter, one of the features that makes the Don Juan Plot the antitype of the Tested Woman Plot, is thus the attitude of its protagonist toward contract. The Tested Woman Plot contains a team of male characters who, in a highly synchronized though vigorously agonistic dance, cooperatively act out the common contractual assumptions of a patriarchal society. The Don Juan Plot, by contrast, focuses on a single individual who violates those assumptions. But he violates them by negation, by not holding them. It is not that Don Juan breaks real contracts, it is that he makes specious or phony ones, casually, nonchalantly, as the nonbeliever can blaspheme with nonchalance, there being for him no such thing as blasphemy. It is in this regard especially that Don Juan is the trickster. He is a confidence man, a speculator in phony promises and phony contracts, a professional hypocrite.[3] To the patriarchalist by right of nature (the father) and the patriarchalist by right of contract (the husband) has been added their antitype, the patriarchalist by right of fraud. Thus Juan the libertine is the antitype of Lothario the seducer, who never promised more than pleasure, and who longs to pay what he promised.

Don Juan's attitude toward contract may be understood as an expression of his attitude toward time. Jean Rousset, to whose tight and suggestive structural analysis of the Don Juan myth I am much indebted, calls Don Juan a "paladin of the present moment" (*Le Mythe de Don Juan,* 101) and links his inability to maintain contract with his lack of a sense of continuity:

> A man living only in the present cannot know either past or future, so how can he deliver on what he has promised? At the moment he commits himself, he simply cannot conceive that later he might be called to account. He cannot conjugate the future, it escapes him, because it lies outside the framework of his desire. . . . And when the future does intrude upon the present, the moment of contract has already been swallowed up in a forgotten past. For Don Juan lacks memory as well as foresight. (100; my translation)[4]

Don Juan's failure to acknowledge the past and future in the present is most marked in his relations with women. But it is manifested everywhere in his human relations. Such at least is the implication of the blackly comic ending of Molière's *Dom Juan*, in which the servant Sganarelle howls his anguish as his master descends into hell: "Mes gages! mes gages!" My wages, my wages: the play ends on the theme of the broken contract. For Don Juan, only the promise to Death is unimpeachable.

Readers have always seen that *Clarissa* shares themes and motifs with the Don Juan story. The most striking involve the characterization of Lovelace himself, some of whose Juanesque features are even exaggerated by the novel's extension. Lovelace's histrionic flair is pronounced: he adopts roles, dons disguises, delights in the improvisation of seductive ploys. Bullying and exploiting his gap-toothed manservant Will, surrounded by his admiring, imitative gang of fellow rakes with whom he exchanges paeons to the life of libertinage, he catalogues and takes a craftsman's credit for the dizzying succession of gentlewomen, shop girls, and innkeepers' daughters who have challenged his attention and his skill. When they are not at hand, he fantasizes: Imagine the triumphant serial seductions of Anna Howe (interfering creature) *and* her mother *and* the maid![5] Or he literally dreams, as when in the Mother H. sequence his concubine Clarissa continues on the warmest of terms with his concubine Anna, and his children by the two women marry "(for neither have dreams regard to *consanguinity*)" in order "to consolidate their mamas' friendships" (L271, [20 June], 922). Such self-congratulatory *sprezzatura* is pure Don Juan, and it is one of the triumphs of Richardson's art. He is not finally writing a Don Juan novel, but in this regard he has created the most typical and unquestionably the most attractive Juan in literature.

One thing Lovelace is not, however, is an atheist, an unbeliever. As Leo Weinstein reminds us (*The Metamorphoses of Don Juan,* 18–19), Tirso's type specimen is no atheist either; believing in the risk, nay the certainty, of eternal damnation, he runs it with bold aplomb. But by the mid-eighteenth century the issue of religious libertinage was so closely associated with the Don Juan figure that Richardson went out of his way to protect himself from its charges and to deny Lovelace its taint. Richardson protests as much in the postscript to the third edition: "But the reader must have observed that, great, and, it is hoped, good use, has been made throughout the work, by drawing Lovelace an infidel, only in practice, ..." And Richardson goes on to remind the reader of Clarissa's consolation to herself that "'he is not an infidel, an unbeliever,'" which means that she can continue to remain hopeful on his behalf. Richardson knows, as does Clarissa, that if Lovelace were a religious libertine he could not keep it to himself: "It must be observed that scoffers are too witty in their own opinion (in other words, value themselves too much upon their profligacy), to aim at concealing it."[6]

Nevertheless Richardson protests too much, is obliged to do so because the theme of the abuse of contract figures so strongly in his portrayal. The Lovelace Richardson has created is a man who does not comprehend moral causality. He can abuse the promise of marriage by the subtleties of pretense, implication, and plausible denial because like Don Juan he is incapable of genuine contract with a woman. He acknowledges as much to Belford: "It would be strange if I kept my word—In love-cases, I mean; for as to the rest, I am an honest moral man, as all who know me can testify" (L 439, 26 Aug., 1270). We are entitled to our doubts about Lovelace's honesty with regard to "the rest." Concerning "love-cases" we can have no doubts; we know that the succession of seductions which preeminently characterizes the Don Juan stalls with Clarissa only because she is unattainable on the only terms Lovelace knows with women. No matter what he had promised, were she snivelingly acquiescent or even adoringly compliant she would be a mere number in the ledger; he would instantly move on. This is one of the underlying psychological reasons why *Clarissa* is not a courtship story. To the degree that he partakes of the Don Juan type, Lovelace does not hold the same psychological ground toward contract as those around him. Lovelace does not truly court Clarissa, unlike Solmes, who truly does court her (that is the horror), or Hickman, who truly courts Miss Howe. Lovelace perverts the gestures and language of courtship with their implications of contract, and he perverts even formal contract itself. When after the rape Clarissa holds up the marriage license to him (L 260, RL to JB, [15 June], 887), she is not attempting to hold him to a promise. She is not begging for marriage, as she makes unequivocally plain the moment her wits are hers to command (L 263, RL to JB, 18 June], 901): *"The man who has been the villain to me you have been, shall never make me his wife."* Instead she is signaling her belated understanding of the total fraudulence of his language of commitment.

Actually Richardson wants to have it both ways. By maintaining that Lovelace is a practicing rather than a professing atheist, Richardson is arguing that his unbelief is psychological rather than theological. This is precisely Richardson's point about him throughout—and Clarissa's and eventually Belford's point. Lovelace has no emotional, no psychological, teleology, no sense that a person's mental and emotional habits build upon themselves to construct the creature he becomes. Especially is this true regarding death, whether his own or that of others. Because people prepare their ends by the way they have lived, worthy preparation requires consciousness of an ending. Belford contrasts the deathbed terrors of Belton and Mother Sinclair with his own moral reformation and Clarissa's beatific passing in order to lift his friend beyond the solipsistically compelling moment and educate him into a sense of spiritual causality. It is not a point that takes with Lovelace. Commenting on Belton's guilt over causing the death of the brother of a woman he seduced, Lovelace excoriates the messenger: "Why didst thou not comfort the poor man about the rencounter between him and that poltroon Metcalfe? He acted in that affair like a man of true honour, and as I should have acted in the same circumstances. Tell him I say so, and what happened he could neither help nor foresee" (L 422, 23 Aug.). As for foreseeing his own responsibility, though he accepts first grudgingly, then hysterically, that Clarissa's death is somehow his doing, he hopes that his own unlooked-for death will balance and thereby expiate it. That hope reads very much like the last of his improvisational quick-change schemes.

The portrayal of Lovelace's moral psychology represents Richardson at work upon some of the most promising material of the Don Juan character. Every Richardsonian innovation deepens and complicates Juan's nature. For instance, Lovelace differs conspicuously from the type specimen in the staying power he brings to his intrigue with Clarissa. The typical Don Juan seduction—the sighting, the subterfuges, the pitch, the conquest—is over in a mere moment; from night to night, we are to believe, Juan moves from woman to woman, not merely because his inevitable success allows him to do so, but because he is too impatient, too mercurial, to do otherwise. As Lovelace says it, "Variety has irresistible charms. I cannot live without variety" (L 261,16 June, 897).[7] This character trait is influenced in part by genre. It is all very well for critics to speak Juan's philosophical entrapment in the present, but such an emphasis on the momentary and the instantaneous is also an economical literary means for making the dramatic point about his prowess. The two-hour play, especially if contaminated by the specious demands of the dramatic unities, will often attempt to get its drive from frenetic repetition of the act itself. It is a quick and dirty way to write the commercial dramatic property, and we see Shadwell embracing it with gusto. Richardson, however, reveling in the leisure and extension of his enormous novel, brings us a Juan uncharacteristically patient in design, with uncharacteristic wind and bottom for the chase, a Juan who seems to enjoy delaying as much as pressing his suit. Telling Belford how much he craves variety, Lovelace can go on to assuage that craving by reveling in a new scheme to redeploy the Widow Bevis and the rest of the Hampstead crew. If we are examining the capacity to understand and control human behavior, Lovelace is a character for whom the causality of intrigue and enforcement has the most constant fascination.

Which is why his moral emptiness is so strange, and for Clarissa so deceiving. For months and months, she simply cannot comprehend that a man of such wit, such imaginative élan, such an ability to imitate the various passions and behaviors of others, such control and patience and staying power, can remain so unchanged by what he does. It is as though he has no life other than the life of his various roles and intrigues and seduction ploys. And there we have an explanation of Richardson's technique. Within Lovelace's theatrical life, so to speak—within his life in the Don Juan role—there is past and future aplenty. But there is nothing beyond that role, with the result that nothing he performs really matters to him morally or spiritually. Lovelace is an infidel only in practice because the practice, the stage role, is all there is. Richardson has gained his literary effect by lifting the most histrionic of characters from drama into the novel, elaborating him in all the ways novelistic extension allows, yet never releasing him from his theatrical bondage to the eternal present. It is this bondage that is finally the source of his existential despair.[8]

James Grantham Turner makes clear that Lovelace's bondage is typical of the double bind of the Enlightenment libertine in general. The libertine sexual code was a double program of indulgence in the life of the senses and of tactically intricate and method-driven mastery of women. Supposedly spontaneous behavior was coupled with set procedures designed to prove fixed maxims: that women like "an uncontrollable passion," that they want to be seduced and even raped by men of "violent spirit," that the greatest prudes are the greatest lechers, that "every woman is at heart a rake." The paradox, says Turner, is that this "experimental and tendentious approach to seduction . . . undermines the libertine's claim to originality. The intense assertion of individual rebellion and individual libido turns out to be quite conformist, since it aims to prove an existing theory, an established (if scandalous) ideology of female submission and female arousal. It confirms a script already written" ("Lovelace," 72). The libertine's entrapment in the already written script extends far beyond his sexual behavior. Turner cites Claude Reichler's suggestion that "the central problem of libertinism, once it had rejected traditional religious beliefs, was to maintain an authentic self in a world increasingly constituted by 'representations'. Reichler traces the oscillation of the libertine character between two extreme positions—a fierce individualism that underestimated the power of social forces, and a compliance to social conventions which, though intended to be ironic and self-liberating, eventually traps the self within the mask."[9] In Lovelace Richardson has vividly dramatized this self-defeating libertine code.

In this discussion of Richardson's use of the Don Juan Plot, I have thus far commented on striking aspects of theme and characterization. A plot structure is more than a collection of themes and character traits, however, or even of discrete events. A plot has an inevitable direction. With the same compulsion by which the Tested Woman Plot seeks judgment of the woman, the Don Juan Plot seeks not just the challenge of women but the challenge to Death. The type story—and the plot logic—drives toward a confrontation with the supernatural that annihilates the protagonist. This plot feature seems strongly linked with the phenomenon of Juan's histrionic entrapment. H. G. Tan (*La Matière de Don Juan,* 113–17) points out that the essence of the Don Juan story is the act itself—even the act repeated—rather than language about or contemplation of the act. This is why the Don Juan story is uniquely at home in drama rather than fiction, in fact at home in drama of a very particular style and pacing. The act in question is the act of seduction, during which for the fleetest of moments Juan escapes from himself by his participation in the desire of another. But since her seduction transforms the woman into his mere adjunct, his creature, it is an act that can only be repeated with someone new. Hence the typical sequentially introduced cast of female characters in the typical Don Juan play. The typical way to put an end to this progression is by means of death, for the exquisitely simple reason that there is no other way off the existential treadmill. In fact Juan typically goes to his death by literally falling off the stage through the trap door. Another way to stop the treadmill would be to have Don Juan fall genuinely in love. But although such a plot move is the frequent recourse of the nineteenth century, it bears no relation to what the original Don Juan story is about. If Juan were able to repose his confidence in an other, if he could have faith in her otherness instead of seeking to possess and destroy it, he would not be the mechanical man he is. In his momentary accesses of conscience, Lovelace knows this: "To be *excelled by a WIFE . . . . To take lessons, to take instructions,* from a WIFE!—. . . .

I am so goaded on—Yet 'tis poor too, to think myself a machine—I am *no machine*—Lovelace, thou art base to thyself, but to *suppose* thyself a machine" (L 202, 23 May, 658). But Juan the libertine, the infidel, the everlastingly self-creating man of the original plot, cannot have faith. "So now, Belford, as thou hast said, I am a machine at last, and no free agent" (L 246, 10 June, 848). He challenges Death because it is the only way to bring about his own release.

Now Jean Rousset denies that Lovelace is a Don Juan figure because he has not fought with Death—"il [se] manque d'avoir combattu contre le Mort" (*Le Mythe de Don Juan,* 17). Rousset is correct to see the challenge to Death as the signature event of the Don Juan Plot. He is wrong, however, to deny its presence in *Clarissa*. Richardson has a realistic novel to conduct, one that hardly lends itself to talking statues or stage traps opening over Hell Mouth. But the key elements of the Don Juan Plot's conclusion do appear, some of them intriguingly displaced for the sake of realistic psychological demonstration.

In the Don Juan Plot, with its economy of male roles and plot moves, the lethal fight with the protecting male relative directly sets up the encounter with Death because it makes possible the dead man's metamorphosis into the stone statue. In *Clarissa*, the fight with the relative actually precedes the novel's opening, since Lovelace has had his duel with Brother James before Miss Howe's first letter. Only James's self-esteem is slain in the encounter, though that death is enough to ruin the peace of the Harlowe family forever. James is too contemptible to stand as the figure of Death, however, and besides, the Tested Woman Plot has used him up elsewhere. This then is where the seemingly incompletely used Morden comes in. His name, like those of Lovelace and Clarissa, announces his symbolic meaning. He is the representation of Death, the character whom Lovelace will be compelled by his despair to encounter. Lovelace's psyche knows this with a certainty terrible in its prescience. The dream he recounts to Belford in his letter of 22 August (L 417, 1218–9) plays out the funereal final sequence of the Don Juan Plot. In the dream we have the assembled family members dressed in mourning, the supernatural appearance of Morden, his demand for Lovelace's repentance, Lovelace's refusal, the opening of the floor and Lovelace's descent into Eldon. As in the Don Juan story, so in the dream Morden does not kill, for the fight that Lovelace attempts as one man with another is prevented. Morden is catalyst only, the sign of the presence of Death which is the occasion by which Lovelace passes to judgment.

In the novel's realistic denouement, however, Morden does kill. It is a puzzling ending to the Tested Woman Plot, since it is an ending specifically forbidden by Clarissa herself, the terms of whose death and will have become a sacred trust to Morden as well as Belford. The Tested Woman Plot, after all, seeks judgment of the woman and reconciliation among the family; nothing done to Lovelace will aid in either. But grafting Don Juanesque elements onto the story has given Lovelace a plot of his own to which he may respond beyond or even despite the exigencies of Clarissa's story. So it is with his death. Not that Morden pursues him. Morden simply makes himself available, on the Continent where a duel may be more easily arranged than in England and where national borders offer escape, and Lovelace finally cannot but seek him out. The initial approach comes from Lovelace, as it must: "I have heard, with a great deal of surprise, that you have thought fit to throw out some menacing expressions against me" (L. 534.1, 10–21 Nov., 1479). The subsequent exchanges lead with stately scrupulosity to the dueling ground. As in Don Juan's encounter with the Statue, impetuous improvisation has no place here; no pickup match just because the principals happen to find themselves surveying the field. And no broken faith either. The challenge to Death has for Lovelace, as for Don Juan, an unimpeachable seriousness unavailable to him in his relations with women. Not that Lovelace expected to die, the French valet assures Belford. We however know differently, we and Lovelace's psyche. We know that the Tested Woman Plot has no more use for him, and the Don Juan Plot only this one end.

The Don Juan Plot focuses almost claustrophobically on its protagonist, which means that it teaches us most about Lovelace. But it also teaches us about Clarissa because it corroborates our understanding of the way the Tested Woman Plot responds to his plot. Which means, of course, how he chooses to seduce and she to refuse. To examine the relationship of seduction and refusal in the light of the Don Juan Plot, I wish to invoke the evidence of Mozart's opera. The fact that opera as a genre has little space for anything but music means that plot and characters are trimmed to their essentials. What the Da Ponte libretto chooses to regard as essential especially illuminates the plot's female characters, and thus the plot possibilities open to a Clarissa. Don Juan is the seducer of hundreds of women. Most versions of the plot, as for instance Molière's, characterize at least four, giving thereby the illusion of infinite numbers. *Don Giovanni,* however, has only three characterized women, giving thereby the impression of the closed set.

Operatically, the reason has to do with manipulating the limited number of naturally available vocal slots and creating optimal musical configurations and partnerships. But a deeper dramatic economy seems to be operating. The three women of *Don Giovanni* embody three forms of female obsession, counterparts to the three styles wherewith Don Juan brings women to the point of submission. Clarissa is pressed by Lovelace to succumb to the temptations of all three of these forms. It is these women's obsessions—the "idols of the Don Juan Plot"—that she comes specifically to understand and to refuse.

The first is the temptation of the flattery of power. This is Don Giovanni's way with the peasant Zerlina—the generic lower-class woman. It is Don Juan's only way with lower-class women; hence the psychological redundancy of Molière's second peasant. Flattery is always a power move, which is why it rarely occurs between equals. Flattery practiced by a superior on an inferior, further, always combines a promise and a threat: that such a man as Il Cavaliere desires such a woman as Zerlina promises to enhance her, does enhance her, but the power to enhance carries with it a reminder of the power to ruin. Such flattery is one of Lovelace's styles as well. The possibility of marriage need not be part of the enhancing and threatening attention he bestows—no one pretends in the Rosebud episode that it is— but with Clarissa the prospect of marriage is part of the campaign. Clarissa is expected to be flattered by Lovelace's attention. Arabella and the rest of the Harlowes are. They are also fearful of Lovelace's social power, since his capacity to flatter reflects hierarchical position: it arises from perceived inequality. The fact that marriage is socially acceptable between the socially unequal Clarissa and Lovelace represents one of the most brilliant moves on Richardson's part, for that possibility makes the seeming obligation of Clarissa to marry her violator all the stronger—as Lovelace knows. The world would regard marriage as a social as well as moral victory for Clarissa. How could anyone lose—so long as the will to marriage proceeds from the one in power?

The second temptation for the women in Mozart's opera is the temptation of passion, Don Giovanni's way with Donna Elvira. Elvira's bitterness is palpable—she cannot reconcile herself to having been wooed, won, and abandoned—but her consuming passion is not the desire for vengeance but a cruelly masochistic love. When she experiences renewed hope that Giovanni loves her, it is because Leporello, in the costume of his master, has been assigned to court her as a diversionary measure. She pours out her soul to a servant and a mask, and is again both caught and cheated. But Don Giovanni does not want Elvira; he has had her. For him, the awakening of her capacity for passion is merely one style of seduction. This style is part of Lovelace's enterprise as well. Though he commences his courtship of Clarissa intent primarily upon flattery and compulsively attentive to the slights her family has visited upon him, as he begins to understand her complexity and self-containment he turns to the awakening of passion as his putative central goal. That she is cold and he will thaw her, that she is reluctant and he will make her willing and then eager and finally utterly dependent, becomes increasingly his fantasy. The rape belongs in part to this second style of seduction and obsession because Lovelace designs it as a form of sexual tutelage and when it does not take even proposes to perform it again on a fully conscious victim.

The third temptation of the opera, represented by Donna Ana, is the temptation of vengeance for the rape attempt and her father's death. We know next to nothing about the rape attempt except what we learn subsequently about Ana's family and situation: she had a father; she has a fiancé who loved and honored her father; she did not know Don Giovanni; she was broken in upon by him; she fought off his attack and her screams sent him running; her father met him, and death, in the courtyard; she and Ottavio vow vengeance. Ana is the woman indifferent alike to the temptations of position and passion. The rape was designed to break through her indifference, but it failed. Yet Giovanni takes her too—in fact, her bondage is more long-lived than that of either of the other women, for as the opera ends she requires of Ottavio a year of wan abstinence while she completes her psychological recuperation. How has Don Giovanni managed her seduction? He killed her father as recompense for the failure of the rape, it is true, but that death gave Giovanni himself no satisfaction. And while it punishes Ana, it does not control her—unless she allows it to. But allows it she does. Vengeance becomes her fixation. Lovelace's motive for rape is likewise in part the motive of Clarissa's perceived indifference: this she cannot ignore! Though from his viewpoint rape has its uses in furthering the style of flattery (now she must admit my generous offer of marriage) and in furthering the style of the awakening of passion (now she knows what sex is and will want more), Clarissa herself comes during the last few weeks of her life to perceive the danger of the rape primarily in terms of this third category of obsession. If she allows herself to become obsessed by the desire for vengeance, the rape will be a recurrent event and Lovelace will possess her indeed.

Again and again we have seen how Lovelace's real agenda, to force Clarissa's hand, her body, her will, underlies his pretense to persuasion. "What does it mean to persuade?" asks Paul Ricoeur. "What distinguishes persuasion from flattery, from seduction, from threat—that is to say, from the subtlest forms of violence?" (*The Rule of Metaphor,* 11). That distinction is what Clarissa must learn to make. Those "subtlest forms of violence" are exactly what Don Juan practices, which is why understanding his plot helps us understand hers.

At the beginning of this chapter I described the Don Juan Plot as the structural antitype of the Tested Woman Plot. We are now in a position to see how this antithesis works psychologically, and how Richardson attempts to take advantage of it. In the bald plot terms of character function and event sequence, the Tested Woman Plot is antithetical first because of its focus on one woman. Thus *Clarissa* lacks the unending sequentiality of Don Juan's women. These women people Lovelace's past, to be sure, but his present becomes compulsively focused on Clarissa. Here we have Richardson's technical method for crossing the two plots, a method which ends the unending sequentiality of female characters while continuing the endless attempts at seduction. For, says Richardson's novel, suppose Don Juan were to meet an unattainable woman? The result would not be love, exactly; it would be a frustrating of the capacity to move on. By definition Don Juan the seducer never loses and never gives up. But suppose that, without losing, he could nevertheless not win? Suppose he were forced, not to move on to the next woman, but to move always back to the same woman, so that the infinite variety of technique—which he and we enjoy the most but cannot see to its full effect because the shift in prey obscures it—were to become the heart of the presentation of his character? Were this to occur, we would have a perfect meeting of plots, for just as Don Juan returns again and again to the attempt, the Tested Woman is again and again attemptable. The most mesmerizing feature of *Clarissa* lies here, in the variety with which Lovelace acts out his single compulsion.

But no dramatic action can remain so poised forever and Richardson unbalances it by showing us the terror of psychic entropy. Even success, Lovelace intuits, would turn pale: "The worst respecting myself in the case before me, is that my triumph, when completed, will be so glorious a one, that I shall never be able to keep up to it. All my future attempts must be poor to this" (L 171, [3 May], 559). But the actual worst turns out to be the absence of that completed triumph. Suppose that Don Juan began to lose his capacity to recreate himself because he began to sense that while he cannot win at what is his game, he cannot stand to move on without winning? And cannot change the game, because to do so would be to change his nature? "If I give up my contrivances, my joy in stratagem, and plot, and invention, I shall be but a common man" (L 264, 19 June, 907). Yet suppose he cannot tolerate any longer the situation he is in, because it has come to resemble stasis, and stasis is against his nature? For the actor must act, or he ceases to exist. What then?

Then he can rape. To Don Juan, rape is intended as a form of seduction. It is seduction by means of the language of the body and it is predicated on the assumption of his irresistibility. He does not see, or he pretends not to see, that it is violation. He believes, or pretends to believe, that it is merely the most forceful and passionate expression of the source of his essential attraction, his desire. If he can only bring that essence home to the woman, she will despite her misery consider herself blessed—for to be the object of desire is to be blessed. Then he can at last move on, unless stopped by that force external to the woman which is death. In play after play, this is the way the Don Juan Plot goes. But that plot shape is possible only if a certain notion of integrity, from which stems the notion of violation, has lost its centrality.

Imagine however that at a certain moment in the eighteenth century this new plot finds itself coupled to the Tested Woman Plot, in which the ideas of integrity and violation remain central, so that the woman whom Juan attempts is precisely the prototypal tested woman. And imagine that when Juan employs his ultimate tool of seduction—rape—he discovers that although stasis has been broken, it has not been in the direction of seduction at all, which would make him all-important to the woman, but in the direction of its opposite, the removal of the woman from his sphere of influence. We know that though the Tested Woman Plot requires the figure of the Tempter, for the woman cannot be tested unless he is present and active, it requires him only during the testing action itself. The Test completed, he loses his function. Once her plot moves into the Trial action, the Tempter has only historic interest. The rape, in short, signals "end of Test" but it also signals "end of Tempter." It is not that the Tempter has lost the woman, for he may never have had her. It is that he has lost the action to another action that has no room for him. The Tested Woman Plot has moved into its second phase, which Don Juan never recognized as the purpose of the first action, and he made it happen. The drama will continue but it will not be his drama; he can get back into it only by changing his function.

To the typical Renaissance Tempter of the Tested Woman Plot, the function change we are describing is not felt as existential trauma because the "character" and the "function" are different matters. Sometimes, the play needing a certain function, it creates for the purpose a character who is dropped when the function is dropped. At other times, in the interests of dramatic economy, one of the characters already in the plot gets to perform a certain function. Such a character does not define himself by his function, he takes on that function. It is not that he is Tempter, but that he plays the Tempter and so long as he does so behaves in certain ways. But in the Don Juan Plot the protagonist *is* the Tempter. His plot is supposed to honor his centrality and to remain his until his death. It is a plot both about how he does not change because he cannot change, and about how he does not have to change because his essential nature is what controls his plot and carries it to its necessary conclusion.

Take Don Juan's plot away from him and what happens? He can do what Lovelace does: flail about in an attempt to find a place for himself. Lovelace tries out a dizzying variety of plot continuations, none of which really carries conviction. Intermittently and halfheartedly he proposes to resume his Juanesque game by pretending that because he has raped Clarissa he has seduced her and is now free to go on to other women. But this move is stymied by her refusal to be seduced, even seduced by the compulsion to seek revenge.[10] More determinedly, Lovelace tries to pretend that Clarissa is still psychologically susceptible to him so that he can plan concubinage or marriage as the next state to which she is to be reduced. But this does not work because she is no longer psychologically available. Or he can attempt to take on one of the functions available in the Trial action of the Tested Woman Plot, acting as Defender against those who would maintain her fault or make her miserable because of it. Lovelace repeatedly attempts a specious version of this move, ranging from the mad demand for Clarissa's heart and bowels to charges against her family, recriminations against Belford, and protestations of the power of his remorse. But because the Defender must seek and speak truth, whereas Lovelace cannot see the truth either about himself or about Clarissa, this move does not work either. His remaining option is to carry out the conclusion of the Don Juan Plot, the point of which is existential annihilation. This is what Lovelace does, inviting the encounter with Morden who leads him to Death.

In so describing Lovelace we are describing failure. This failure is surprising, almost tantalizing, because it seems not just a moral failure but a failure of the artistic imagination in a character who seems in some ways the consummately imaginative artist. Despite his increasing at-least-purported willingness to encounter Clarissa on her own terms, Lovelace cannot bring her or his relationship to her into any kind of accurate focus. He never manages to see and describe, for more than a few sentences at a time, what is actually there. Iris Murdoch might be thinking of him when she sees the moral problem and the imaginative problem as essentially the same: "The chief enemy of excellence in morality (and also in art) is personal fantasy: the tissue of self-aggrandizing and consoling wishes and dreams which prevents one from seeing what is there outside one" ("On 'God' and 'Good'," 78). Such is the case with Lovelace, whose personal fantasy cripples and finally destroys not just his morals but his art.

6

Prudence: The Plot of
the Purposeful Life

Yet there is one more story to be told, one more plot to describe. Why is it that, unlike most Tested Women, Clarissa does not move to the periphery of our attention once her choice has been made? We have partially explained this phenomenon by noting that in the absence of a reliable earthly judge Clarissa must undertake the conduct of her own trial, assembling and interpreting the evidence about what has happened to her. But the fact is that such an obligation, like the other obligations of the Tested Woman Plot, still puts the woman in an essentially reactive role. It makes her the patient or sufferer rather than the agent of her story—as Job is the patient of his. Yet our experience of Clarissa contradicts the impression of mere reactiveness, even passivity, that the Tested Woman Plot structure seems to require. We know her as active, not merely reactive; unlike the terminally frustrated Lovelace, she seems to us in some way both purposeful and fulfilled.

To examine Clarissa's purposes, let us begin with her two great acts of refusal, where the impression of mere reactiveness ought to be strongest. These acts are very similar: they are the refusal to marry Solmes and the refusal to marry Lovelace. There are myriad lesser refusals as well: Clarissa will not be provoked by the servant Betty's officiousness, nor cease to defend her family to Miss Howe, nor be sent to her Uncle Antony's house, nor cease her letter-writing, nor be seduced by Lovelace, nor remain at Mother Sinclair's, nor allow a repentant Lovelace to visit her, nor allow Morden to revenge her, nor allow Miss Howe or Mrs. Norton to come to her deathbed . . . So put, her life would seem an exercise in preferring not to. Yet where Melville's Bartleby is death incarnate, Clarissa pulses with life, even in her dying. So what is she doing? We have described the refusals of marriage in the negative terms that the very notion of *refusal* encourages. In each case, Clarissa's action involves a refusal to enter into a relationship of mutual obligation with a man she cannot honor and respect and therefore cannot love. She will not marry either Lovelace or Solmes because in either case the act would violate her life project. Yet these refusals are made relatively early in the novel. How can she continue to have a life project when she knows that she is not waiting for some other marital possibility? When she knows, all too soon, that she is dying? Still she continues to behave as though she is doing something systematic and purposeful. And she is. She is creating her Self. This project constitutes Richardson's third plot, the plot of which he is most fully conscious and most strongly in control. It is this plot, and this alone, of which Clarissa is the fully active agent.

The notion of the creation of a Self may seem an inappropriately modern idea to foist upon Richardson, and the charge of anachronism might be justified if we were thinking in terms of modern psychology. But if we think of Richardson's own psychology, based on classical virtue ethics expressed in the democratized and Christianized language of Anglican homiletics, we have the terms in which Clarissa does her work. Note that I am drawing our attention to a theory of moral psychology, for Richardson has no other kind. However splendidly broad and detailed his understanding of the workings of the human heart, his inherited formal psychological system and the language in which it works is based on a specifically moral philosophy: it focuses upon theories, descriptions and prescriptions about the way virtue and vice operate in men and women.

One way to get at this system is to turn our attention from Clarissa's specific, discrete, seemingly reactive actions to the ethical patterns and epithets designed to generalize or encode her nature and personality for us. Material for investigation can be found from the opening letter in which the theme of Prudence is announced. We know that the virtue of prudence is Clarissa's salient virtue. It represents both her moral goal and, as far as her doting circle are initially concerned, her daily achievement. As we saw in chapter 3, prudence or practical wisdom is the executive virtue of both Old Testament and classical traditions. Because it is preeminently the skill of acting wisely in the light of events past, present, and to come, it supervises or manages the whole moral performance of the individual. But whereas in chapter 3 we were concerned primarily with how Clarissa chooses and judges under the pressure of particular events, in this chapter we are concerned primarily with what she is—how she conceives of self and life as whole structures. Much of the evidence is to be found in the retrospectives during and after her dying. Miss Howe's "character" of Clarissa in the letter to Belford of 12 October (L 529, 1465ff.) is its most concentrated expression, other self-consciously epitomizing descriptions being Morden's letter to Belford of 23 September (L 519, 1445ff.) and Belford's to Lovelace describing Clarissa's death (L 481, [7 Sept.], 1363). Though most of this material comes from onlookers, Miss Howe's letter contains swatches of Clarissa's own version of her moral program, in part in Clarissa's own words. How, in these various chunks of material, is Clarissa portrayed?

Three features are particularly notable: her innate gifts, her education, and the pleasure she takes in her life. Underlying all is the unceasing emphasis on Clarissa's natural excellences of body and mind. Miss Howe praises her excellence "from her infancy"; her perfection of shape, proportion, features, and complexion; her natural facility in learning languages; her *native* dignity," her "natural ease and dignity" (1466–68). Belford and Lovelace likewise value this native excellence. It has been a strain in Lovelace's admiration throughout, and Belford reminds him of it in the death letter: "Well dost thou know how much she excelled in the graces, both of mind and person, natural and acquired, all that is woman" (1363). Certainly Lovelace has never wearied of reminding us that Clarissa far excels all that is Harlowe, and the entire novel joins him in presenting its heroine as one of nature's nobility. That Clarissa knows both her own native excellence and its dangers is suggested by one of her 'sentences': "Persons of accidental or shadowy merit may be proud: but inborn worth must be always as much above conceit as arrogance" (1466).

But the unhappy example of Lovelace himself is sufficient to warn us that natural excellence is dangerously insufficient without the right training. Hence the novel's extended attention to Clarissa's education. It is characteristic of the tradition in which Clarissa is steeped that this education has followed a specific sequence: careful early training, followed by vigorous self-discipline, until her virtues acquire the status of habit. Responding to Belford's question about how such a young woman managed to become so accomplished, Miss Howe tells us about Clarissa's disciplined use of time:

> I will premise that she was from infancy inured to rise early in a morning, by an excellent and, as I may say, a learned woman, Mrs Norton, to whose care, wisdom, and example, she was beholden for the groundwork of her taste and acquirements, which meeting with such a genius, made it the less wonder that she surpassed most of her age and sex. (1469)

Clarissa's detailed attention to the debits and credits of each day demonstrates, says Miss Howe, that "had she calculated according to the practice of *too many*, she had actually lived more years at *sixteen*, than *they* had at *twenty-six*" (1470). This picture of disciplined female vigor is already refreshing in an age in which one of the chief literary complaints about upper-class women was that they lay in bed until noon. But Clarissa's exploitation of the potential of each day must also be seen as her only means of forwarding her education; she will never get to James's university. Arabella would like us to think this regimen the result of a fanatical punctiliousness (L 42, CH to AH, 21 March, 192). But Arabella is envious and Clarissa knows it; her retort about her sister's use of *her* time completes one of the most satisfactorily catty exchanges of the novel. In fact, Clarissa's regimen serves her enormous appetite for life, an appetite which Clarissa has and Arabella does not.

And lastly, Clarissa takes active pleasure in her life. Miss Howe's description of her openness ("above reserve or disguise"—1468), her affability and graciousness (1466), her ease, satisfaction and cheerfulness in company (1471), all contribute to this portrait, as do Clarissa's descriptions of how "pleasant" she finds keeping her time-accounts (1472) and the "delight" she takes in her writing. Her life has been lived at the "highest pitch of felicity," Belford reminds us (1363), and she herself tells Miss Howe that eighteen out of her nineteen years were "very pleasant." The crowning feature of her felicity is the regard in which she is held. She is admired for her excellence and she deserves to be admired.

Clarissa's character is exemplary in the terms of classical virtue ethics, of Aristotle's *Nicomachean Ethics* or Cicero's *De officiis:* natural and acquired excellences of both body and mind; virtuous habits; felicity both enjoyed by oneself and acknowledged admiringly by others. Miss Howe's character of her friend catalogues the classical excellences of the mean: true generosity is "the happy medium between parsimony and profusion" and benevolence lies in "prudent distribution"; the virtuous person is severe to vileness but charitable to human weakness; she always joins action to precept; she seeks always a decorum of behavior: *"Propriety,* another word for *nature*, was her law, as it is the foundation of all true judgement" (1468). Belford's brief eulogy, addressed to a Lovelace who is expected to recognize and value its provenance, continues the list of classical virtues: "extensive knowledge," "watchful prudence," "discreet generosity," "noble presence of mind," "true magnanimity" (1363). Magnanimity? Greatness of soul? A superb disdain for the petty and an ambition for the *greatly* good? Indeed. Mrs. Norton, no less, commends Clarissa to the support of her "resumed and accustomed magnanimity" (1328). Lest we think of this as some form of capitulation, let us remember with Lovelace Clarissa's most accurate and most cutting judgment of the difference between them: "My soul is above thee."

Much of the novel's ethical elaboration is carried out in such comparative terms. The various characters who people it do so in part to exemplify varieties of vice, or of less-than-virtue. Often the comparisons are both explicit and insistent. Solmes fails egregiously in the category of generosity, his stinginess an expression of the meanness of his soul. James is the victim of constant irascibility to which both Lovelace's coolness and Clarissa's mildness stand in reproof. Arabella lacks both true wit and true friendliness or sociability. Mrs. Harlowe lacks fortitude, the courage of her convictions. Mr. Harlowe fails in the virtue of justice, the virtue which as patriarch he needs most. Lovelace lacks largeness of soul, true honor. All such failures are accompanied by their simulacra: Arabella's snide quickness; Mrs. Harlowe's pursuit of a destructively specious "harmony"; Lovelace's aristocratic *sprezzatura;* Solmes's pretense to being, in Uncle Antony's words, "a saving man." Yet Uncle Antony is making a good Aristotelian distinction when he points out to Clarissa the role of our choice of moral epithets in our assessment of character: "What names will perverseness call things by—" (L 32.4, 14 March, 154). The capacity to name virtue and vice accurately, to assess truly the mean relative to the person and the situation (Aristotle, *Nicomachean Ethics,* II.vi.1106b), is itself one of the principal and most difficult tasks of virtue. It is in part by comparing herself with others that Clarissa learns how to judge and to train herself. It is in part by comparing her to those others that we learn to judge and to value her.

The most subtle and useful comparisons match Clarissa against persons with excellences of their own, those who are or who could have been her friends: Anna Howe and Lovelace himself. Again the reason is very classical.[1] Aristotle sees complete friendship, the friendship which exists for more than utility or pleasure, as possible only between excellent people (the *phronemoi* or friends-in-practical-wisdom). This means that its existence between Clarissa and Miss Howe and its failure to develop between Clarissa and Lovelace reflect the human natures involved. The friendship of the two women is the most complete relationship in the novel. Though Morden is certain that "friendship, generally speaking, is too fervent a flame

for female minds to manage," he also admits to exceptions, telling us what,
as usual, the novel itself has already said:

> This I mention as a *general observation:* but the friendship that subsisted
> between these two ladies affords a remarkable exception to it: which I
> account for from those qualities and attainments in *both*, which, were
> they more common, would furnish more exceptions still in favour of the
> sex. Both had an *enlarged*, and even a *liberal* education: both had minds
> thirsting after virtuous knowledge. Great readers both: great writers—
> . . . Both generous. High in fortune; therefore above that dependence each
> on the other that frequently destroys the familiarity which is the cement
> of friendship. Both excelling in *different ways*, in which neither sought to
> emulate the other. Both blessed with clear and distinguishing faculties;
> with solid sense; and from their first intimacy . . . each seeing something
> in the other to *fear*, as well as *love;* yet making it an indispensable condi-
> tion of their friendship each to tell the other of her failings; and to be
> thankful for the freedom taken. One by nature *gentle;* the other *made so*
> by her *love* and *admiration* of her exalted friend—impossible that there
> could be a friendship better calculated for duration. (To Belford, 26 Sept.,
> 1449–50)

Morden's commentary on this friendship summarizes all over again the
classical description of the nature and genealogy of virtue. Friendship both
reflects and shapes the whole self. Clarissa is in part Anna Howe's creation, just as Miss Howe has been shaped and molded by Clarissa, and
continues to be so from beyond the grave.

When Clarissa feels the first stirrings in Lovelace's favor, she examines his character for the potential of friendship in this sense. This is what
she will have in marriage, this or nothing. From the first she has her doubts.
As their contact grows, she is made increasingly uneasy by his lack of
frankness and his inability to respond to her influence as she would expect
to be shaped by his if he were indeed "THE man." Yet much of the native
material is there; his various natural excellences are potentially compatible
with Clarissa's own intelligence, vividness and joy of life. It is in this crucial matter of the role of friendship in shaping the self that Clarissa makes
her biggest generic mistake, says Richardson, falling temporarily into the
trap of thinking that the rake can be reformed. Yet there is more to it than
that, for Belford is reformed by her example. But Lovelace cannot do what
Belford can do, he cannot change—what? His habits. Given the role of
habit and self-discipline in the classical ethical program, Lovelace's failure

must not be seen as a petty matter: it is of the essence.[2] He cannot discipline and enlarge his deepest habits of mind and soul. He himself acknowledges the lack of proper training in his youth, but this very acknowledgment is an excuse to avoid facing his own responsibility for creating himself.

The descriptions supplied by Belford, Morden, and Anna Howe show Clarissa to be a conscious practitioner of the aretic, or virtue-based, moral program of the classical tradition. It is a tradition most systematically presented in Aristotle's *Nicomachean Ethics*, in Cicero's *De officiis*, and in the Christian synthesis and exegesis of Aristotle provided by Aquinas.[3] The following overview of its salient features gives us a thematic epitome of Clarissa's endeavor. The goal of human life is happiness, says Aristotle, and happiness comes from the pleasure we take in the fullest and best use of our faculties; this fullest and best activity is precisely what is meant by virtue (*Nicomachean Ethics*, 1099a). To achieve such virtuous activity, we hope to be endowed with natural excellences of body and mind, to which, by the early training and subsequent self-disciplining of our habits, we seek to combine excellence of character. We seek to cultivate both the chief virtues of temperance, courage, justice, and practical wisdom (*phronesis, prudentia*), and such lesser virtues as generosity, magnanimity, mildness, truthfulness, and wit. The relative importance of these various virtues depends upon our circumstances and is likely to change with age, obligations or changes of fortune, but *phronesis* or practical wisdom, the virtue in charge of our actions, is always the virtue we need most. We are aided in the pursuit of excellence by the use of exemplars (for "the excellent person is the standard"—1113b) and especially by deep friendships with excellent people. But there are no mechanical or absolute or abstract measures of the virtues. Excellence, which can only exist in application, must function with propriety or decorum, for to be temperate or courageous or just or prudent can only mean to exercise these virtues in the right place, at the right time, in the right amount, and in regard to the right people. Consequently, we are always engaged in decision-making, and therefore always deliberating within ourselves and with our friends, for we seek by constant attention to achieve the right balance in our lives—not some abstract or arbitrary goal but "the mean relative to us" (1106b).

This account of the classical virtues cannot be the whole story about Clarissa, however. For one thing, we know that in its telling by Belford, Morden and Miss Howe it has been incompletely told. Anna Howe's "character" of Clarissa is an inside story and a true story, but it is the story of the life before 10 April. Miss Howe cannot really continue the story beyond that date, and certainly not beyond 13 June, the moment from which their "views," their perspectives, "must *now* be different—." The men's descriptions reveal even less of Clarissa's interior development: though her defenders, they have never been her *phronemoi*, her friends in that mutually shaping Aristotelian sense. Their descriptions, although written from a post-rape perspective, cannot provide a true, full and interior account of post-rape events. What is missing from all three epitomes is any real sense of the spiritual journey of Clarissa's nineteenth year. That journey is explicitly Christian, and it is part of the plot of the creation of the Self that I am describing.[4] Moreover, the failure of the three epitomes to do it justice is a deliberate device on Richardson's part, a device that emphasizes the incomplete experiences of those who write them and the relatively far richer experience that Clarissa has undergone. Miss Howe has not really suffered in her own projects but has only sympathized with suffering. Morden is engaged in a sincere and strenuous but primarily social performance. Belford, by now versed in the emotional flavor of the struggle for the virtuous Self, nevertheless lacks Clarissa's theological matrix. Describing her death moment, he can recount accurately but not with richness of comprehension:

> She was silent for a few moments, lifting up her eyes and the hand her cousin held not between his. Then, *Oh death!* said she, *where is thy sting?* (The words I remember to have heard in the Burial Service read over my uncle and poor Belton.) And after a pause—*It is good for me that I was afflicted!*—Words of Scripture, I suppose. (L 481, to RL, [17 Sept.], 1361–62)

Here Richardson is slyly delineating a Belford who knows which story her words are from without truly knowing the story.

Who should know the Christian story? Why, none better than the Reverend Mr. Brand. The black humor of his performance (L 444, to John Harlowe, 9 Aug., 1292) explodes upon us with the force it does precisely because of this expectation. Whatever his assessment of Clarissa's specific courses of action, we think, he of all people should recognize the Christian terrain over which she travels. Yet Brand recognizes neither the Christian nor the classical story. A clergyman despatched by John Harlowe to conduct a moral inquiry, he not only has no Christian terms in which to conduct it, he has no moral terms at all. The Latin tags with which he fills his malicious gossip are open to mockery not because they are Latin but because they are not the right Latin. They do not tell even the part of Clarissa's moral history that the classically sensitive Belford, Morden and Lovelace understand and can tell. This is impertinence indeed.

But it is not just Mr. Brand's impertinence. The decline of the virtue tradition had become an eighteenth-century philosophical problem, precisely the problem to which Hume and Kant would respond in their opposite ways.[5] In the *Nicomachean Ethics*, Aristotle had given the first great expression to an ethics which by the early eighteenth century was so mechanically ingrained in the school curriculum and in Christian homiletics that skeptics could scoff at it as old-fashioned and the ignorant could avoid noticing it altogether. In his preface to *A Treatise Concerning Christian Prudence* (1710), John Norris laments the very few modern works explicitly devoted to the tradition as he begins to rectify the omission:

> I have sometimes thought with myself, that if the whole system of *Christian vertues* were distinctly treated of, it would be a very great, useful, and noble work. The first link of this golden chain I have attempted to finish in my Treatise of *Humility*, and I could wish that some other more able hand would go on with the rest, it being for one of my little health, and less abilities, too great an undertaking. But however, though it bee too much for me, to treat of all the Christian vertues singly, yet I have now done that which may in some measure answer the design of such an undertaking in the general, by treating of that vertue which fits at the helm, and governs all the rest, conducts the whole movement of life, and is as it were a kind of *universal* vertue. So that in treating of this, one treats of all, and gives as it were a system of Christian morality, which is what I design in this work. (A3)

John Norris, and his ethics, is important to the intellectual background of *Clarissa*. Rector of Bemerton at his death in 1711, he had a distinguished career as a homileticist and philosopher. He was the last significant follower of the Cambridge Platonists and was best known among contemporary intellectuals for his pamphlet responding to Locke's *Essay Concerning Human Understanding*.[6] As we know from chapter 1, he was also one of the respondents to queries in the *Athenian Mercury*. In *Clarissa*, Norris figures by name as author of the *Miscellanies*, a collection of his essays, poems and letters, first published in 1687, that went through many editions in his lifetime and was frequently reprinted after his death. The *Miscellanies* appears most insistently as the result of a double misunderstanding, for it is between the pages of her copy that Anna Howe sends fifty guineas to Clarissa marooned at St. Albans. Clarissa shortsightedly refuses the money, Miss Howe regrets the refusal, and when Lovelace steals their correspondence he is thrown into a comic froth at the thought of being out-Norrised, though how he is not certain, by a pair of novices.[7] Further on, lines from one of the poems in the *Miscellanies* figure in Belford's correspondence about the death of Belton (L 419, 22 Aug., 1229–30). But though the *Miscellanies* reflects traditional Christian virtue theory, it is Norris's specifically philosophical works which explain that theory. *A Treatise Concerning Christian Prudence* is an extended exegesis of the tradition as represented by Aristotle and Aquinas. In it, Norris is doing philosophy, not homiletics. This is no casebook, no *Athenian Mercury*, but a carefully reasoned 400-page disquisition argued abstractly in the fashion of the Cambridge Platonists. Norris is concerned to make accessible to eighteenth-century readers the logical and psychological case for the primacy of Prudence in the Christian virtue tradition.[8]

In turning to the tradition of virtue ethics, we find ourselves in another moral world from the world of duty described in previous chapters. The vocabulary of "obligation," "obedience," and "ought," with its threat of retribution, has given way to a different vocabulary altogether. Here striving is an artistic enterprise, the balanced excellences necessary for human happiness constitute the goal, and the threat is of inadequacy, mediocrity and disease. In this world, Clarissa seems more agent than victim, more athlete than martyr. The shift is deliberate; a literary plot represents an entire gestalt and we are trying to perceive the several gestalts of which this novel is constituted. We have seen that the Tested Woman Plot operates within the morality of law, in which *specific human actions* regarding duties, obligations, promises, contracts and requirements are measured and judged. In order to make those judgments, it devises tests. By contrast, the plot of the purposeful shaping of the Self operates within the morality of the virtues, in which the *general character of human agents* is scrutinized. In order to conduct that scrutiny, it constructs exemplars. The first could be said to be the morality of the Torah, the second the morality of Attic Greece, and Richardson's Christian world is the inheritor of both.

Behind these different moral attitudes, we see a fundamental contrast in regard to time. The Tested Woman Plot essentially belongs to a cyclical time scheme, while the time scheme of the Prudence Plot is far more linear and progressive. Because the Tested Woman Plot is a forensic or justice plot, that is, it is essentially recursive and backward-looking. It commences in a social and moral balance which is first disrupted by a dilemma forcing moral choice, then rewoven by an ultimately healing judgment about that choice. When the trajectory is tragic, healing is achieved by purgation: the culpable are excluded from the rewoven fabric by the banning actions of shame and death. When the trajectory is comedic, healing is achieved by reconstituting the shattered family. If moral growth occurs, it takes place in the hierarchically powerful men of the plot, who are aided by the passage of time to a recognition of what they should have known all along. Thus, the happiest endings are those which most nearly resemble the beginnings. For the tested woman herself, however, time is primarily something to be endured; the prototypal versions of the plot sequester or incarcerate her, put her to sleep, set her adrift, do her to death, in some fashion suspend her upon a monument for so long as it takes Time to bring forth Truth. The Tested Woman Plot is thus not only tradition-controlled and conservative; in psychological terms it tends to be static. It displays rather than develops moral character, which is why its starkest literary versions contain episodes of seemingly motiveless behavior. For all her prudential character and her prudential concerns, Pamela's *plot* is of this kind. She is what she is: her two volumes are devoted to the display of her qualities and their recognition by others. Like Job, she ends as she began.

But given the nature of the virtue theory we have been describing, a Prudence Plot ought to look quite different. It ought to be generative. It should dramatize the growth of something not there before, and its characters should be agents rather than patients. The Prudence Plot should be explicitly concerned with the relation between intention and act: not what a character has done so much as what she is trying to make of herself. In this plot the happiest endings will not much resemble the beginnings. In this plot time will not be a suspension to be endured but material to be used. Time will preeminently represent opportunity: it will be the medium in which character traits interact with occasions for action to build the ever more adult, more excellent, more virtuous person. A person living the Prudence Plot will be attempting to increase in wisdom and in favor with God and man. That is how the young Jesus' growth is described (Luke 2:52), it is what the imitation of Christ is about, and it is what Clarissa means when in her posthumous letter to Lovelace she says that she is "indebted" to him for his *"real service"* (L 510.4, 1426). Despite his intentions, he has been the source of her most extraordinary opportunities.

This conception of time as the medium for the practice of virtue imbues one of the great handbooks of virtue ethics, Jeremy Taylor's *Holy Living and Holy Dying*. Clarissa knows this book well. She knows that when Lovelace thumbed it at Hampstead it was merely a prop in his false-Lady-Betty charade. "The great deluder was at the farther end of the room another way . . . looking into a book which, had there not been a preconcert, would not have taken his attention for one moment. It was *Taylor's Holy Living and Dying*" (L313, 6 July, 1001). Taylor commences both volumes of his guide in the same way: chapter 1 of *Holy Living* opens with the section entitled "Care of our Time"; chapter 1 of *Holy Dying* begins with "reflections" and "practices" regarding "the Vanity and Shortness of Man's Life" from which it moves to "Rules and Spiritual Arts for Lengthening our Days, and taking off the Objection to a Short Life." As the artist attends to his medium and the athlete to his equipment, so the practitioner of the arts of virtue looks first to time, the stuff he has to work with. Unfortunately, however, the brevity of life is further shortened by nonage and dotage. We can hardly reckon the aged person as fully alive "when his body is possessed by so many degrees of death" (*Holy Dying*, 33), and the life of the unborn or the infant is not a full human life either. "Neither must we think that the life of a man begins when he can feed himself, or walk alone, when he can fight, or beget his like; for so he is contemporary with a camel or a cow" (32). Full human life, involving a "certain, steady use of reason, according to his proportion," comes upon a person "slowly and insensibly" (32–33) and the period available for its exercise is all too brief. Worse, since youth is the least likely period of life in which to develop virtuous habits, young people are prone to behavior which extends their intellectual and spiritual nonage even further. The result is that all too many people are seized by old age while they yet retain the minds and behavior of children and have somehow never found the time for practicing a fully human life, though "when death comes they must be at leisure for that" (34). Continues Taylor, "Such men are like sailors loosing from a port, and tossed immediately in a perpetual tempest lasting till their cordage crack, and either they sink or return back again to the same place: they did not make a voyage, though they were long at sea" (34).

It is Lovelace's particularly ignorant mistake to regard *Holy Living and Holy Dying* as a pious flight from flesh and the world, from the possibilities of a richly human life. Approaching Clarissa with Taylor in his hand—"A smart book, this, my dear!—This old divine affects, I see, a mighty flowery style upon a very solemn subject. But it puts me in mind of an ordinary country funeral, where the young women, in honour of a defunct companion, especially if she were a virgin, or *passed for such*, make a flower-bed of her coffin" (1002). On the contrary, Taylor has no brief for flowered coffins; he is interested in voyages, strenuous voyages that crack cordage in the course of great expeditions. He is particularly urgent that we waste neither our youth nor our dying, that we "make the 'outgoings of the morning and evening,' that is, our infancy and old age, to be taken into the computations of a man"; if we do this, "God gives us time sufficient" (36). In the tradition for which Taylor speaks, Clarissa's cultivation of her youth and the energy she devotes to the conduct of her dying are essential to the economy of happiness.

For Taylor's metaphor of the voyage tells us that in virtue ethics there is a destination, the same destination for the seventeenth-century Christian as for the Greek philosopher: the goal of happiness. This is Clarissa's dying wish for every one of her family and friends, as for Miss Howe: "adieu, and be happy!" (L 473.2, [6 Sept.], 1349). Virtue itself is never the ultimate goal, always only the means. Thus John Norris begins his treatise on Prudence exactly where Aristotle commences the *Nicomachean Ethics:* by placing virtue in a second or mediate position in relation to happiness (*Christian Prudence,* 2–4). Aquinas summarizes the idea by reminding us that "prudence is concerned with the things that *lead to* the final purpose of the whole of life" (*Summa Theologiae,* Q. 55, p. 147; my emphasis). The question then becomes what constitutes "the final purpose of the whole of life," what we mean by "happiness." Here the answer will necessarily be somewhat different for the Christian than for the pagan because of the way the teleological landscape is mapped. If as in the Christian view eternity is a continuation of earthly existence, then "the whole of life" stretches everlastingly. In this case the most important capacity of prudence is to take all the landscape into account, not to be fooled by secondary ends or false summits. For the terrain is immense, and therefore baffling and misleading on a human scale. "Here let me beg my reader to make a short pause," says Norris,

and consider what a vain empty thing the greatness of this present world is, and how vain and little it will appear when beheld in a true *point of view*, and with the lessening end of the prospective, not that which makes it less than it is, but which represents it in its *true littleness*. (47)

Seizing the actual proportions in this vast landscape is the supremely serious
and absorbing task of prudence.

> 'Tis the concern therefore of every Christian, and one great part of his
> prudence and wisdom, after he has fixed this his right end, to endeavour
> by much consideration to possess his mind with a due sense of its moment
> and importance, and of what consequence it is that he should take care to
> succeed in this one affair, whatever he fails or miscarries in besides. (162)

"She should take care to succeed in this one affair, whatever she fails
or miscarries in besides." After her catastrophe this tradition reminds Clarissa
of the entire reach and purpose of her life, *whatever* her failures. For the
Christian even more than for the pagan, Aristotle's ironic point is well
taken: by the pursuit of happiness, we are engaged in something a great
deal tougher than amusing ourselves (1177a). We are engaged in making a
life project. Clarissa is navigating toward that moment when, dying in full
fear and hope of God, she can issue the desiring, confident invitation:
"Come—Oh come—blessed Lord—JESUS" (L 481, JB to RL, 7 Sept.,
1362). It is no accident that these are the final words recommended to the
dying Christian in *The Whole Duty of Man,* that other great seventeenth-
century guide to the whole project of a Christian life.[9] Exactly how deliberate is Richardson's design is made clear in his letter to Aaron Hill just
after the appearance of the third and fourth volumes when he was resisting
the nagging of a public fearful of the catastrophe to come and desirous of a
"happy ending":

> I intend another sort of happiness (founded on the Xn [Christian] system)
> for my heroine, than that which was to depend upon the will and pleasure,
> and uncertain reformation and good behaviour of a vile libertine, whom I
> could not think of giving a person of excellence to . . . . And to rescue her
> from a rake, and give a triumph to her, over not only him but over all her
> oppressors, and the world beside, in a triumphant death (as death must
> have been her lot, had she been ever so prosperous) I thought as noble a
> view, as it was new. (10 May 1748; Carroll, 86–88)

Here his stress is on two features of his plot—Clarissa's pursuit of the goal
of specifically *Christian* prudence, the happiness of eternal life; and his
understanding of the necessity to complete her life story by death—"as
death must have been her lot, had she been ever so prosperous." She does

not die because she has been raped; she dies because she is a human being, and death is what happens to us all. What she does with the rape is what allows her to die triumphantly.

Such a rendition of the prudence tradition cannot but impress by its demand for courage and by its intellectual rigor. That rigor helps explain why "practical wisdom" or "wisdom in action" is probably modernly[10] the translation of choice for the Greek concept of *phronesis* or its Latin version *prudentia*. Aristotle's translator Terence Irwin finally opts simply for *intelligence*, which, while it sacrifices much of the richness of the term, at least retains the rigor. Aquinas's translator Thomas Gilbey remarks that if we feel the term "prudence" to have a grudging ring, we should think of this virtue as "holy discernment, wit, and decisiveness" (*Summa Theologiae,* xiv) and we will be translating it accurately. This is why both patristic and scriptural sources often admonish us, not to be good rather than bad, but to be wise rather than foolish (Norris, *Christian Prudence,* 52–56). Getting it right is an intellectual act.

John Norris helps us see why the practice of prudence is so strenuous—because it is not just a matter of rightly conceived goals but of the right response to specific circumstances. As he cannot cease reiterating, prudence deals with *now,* the immediate occasion—this time, this place and this decision. Our theoretical understanding of morality (or, as Norris terms it, our *notional* or *habitual* understanding) in no way guarantees wise behavior; it is our *actual* understanding, our grasp of the situation at the moment of action, that counts. Thus Norris objects to St. Augustine's definition of prudence—"the knowledge of things to be desired, and to be avoided"—as failing to insist upon the key point: "'tis also a knowledge actually directive of our practice" (68–69). To help us seize the difference, Norris uses a comparison which he must have known well in his role as a respondent for the *Athenian Mercury.* Supposing, he says, you are dealing with a case involving competition between what in theory looks like a "sensible good" on the one hand and a "moral evil" on the other:

> If a man were to answer this question for *another* he would soon do it, and do it right; but neither so soon, nor so well, for *himself.* However he might do it for himself too, if he were to give sentence when he is cool and sedate and unmoved, as a man is when he writes cases of conscience in his study. He would then think this so clear a one, that he would hardly think it worth resolving. But speculation is one thing, and practice is another. In the former our *habitual* knowledge speaks, but our actual in

the latter, and 'tis our *actual* knowledge upon which our practice depends. For we always act by our present light, which at that time generally shines but dimly. So that 'tis one thing to pass a general sentence, . . . and another thing to *act*. (18–19)

Whence the intellectual and emotional demands. Prudence requires that we see the farthest, with the greatest scope and balance, at precisely the same moment that we act with attention to the immediate and the minute. The prudent action, an action of the moment, must nevertheless be performed in the light of everything we know of all things past, present, and to come. Norris insists throughout that there is no willing evil as evil; always when we act we are seeking something, however transitory or misguided, that seems to us good. The task of prudence, then, is to bring our expanded sense of the range of human possibility to bear at the very moment of the individual action. Prudence knows that if we can see that whole range truly, we will choose and act wisely.

There is the ideal. But we run risks even in its most conscientious pursuit. Like all the virtues, prudence has its associated dangers and vices. In chapter 3 we noticed the iconographic representation of its unified intellect by the Janus-faced figure which sees both past and future in the instant. The importance to Prudence of the unified mind that combines memory, understanding and foresight is apparent when we compare Ripa's representation of its simulacrum, the figure of Fraud (see pp. 49–50). Fraud also has two faces, which look in opposing directions. But unlike the faces of Prudence, the faces of Fraud are on separate heads. Fraud's intellect is split; true understanding is not possible because the face of memory, which views the past, is not carried in the same organ as the face of foresight, which views the future. Fraud is unified only below the neck, by the merely corporeal and sensual. This figure, of course, is Lovelace, the "politick cunning man" who is "a sophister in prudence" (Norris, *Christian Prudence*, 95) because he uses intelligent means in pursuit of unworthy ends. For Clarissa, the major external threat is unquestionably the threat of Lovelace's fraudulence, which seeks to fragment her as he himself is fragmented. But there are also the internal vices of excess and deficiency for the prudent person to combat. Because Lovelace-as-Fraud is the simulacrum of Prudence, he knows all about that tradition too: "There is a *too much*, as well as a *too little*, even in righteousness. Perhaps she does not think of that—" (L 453, 1 Sept.,

1309). Given the date, however, we know that she has had ample practice in thinking of both.

First the vice of deficiency. Because prudence is intellectually so strenuous, the prudent person runs the danger of either cognitive dissonance or cognitive overload. Trying to see the future clearly in the light of an accurate assessment of the past may lead to intellectual chaos—"I just don't know; I just can't tell"—which translates into the inability to act at all. Such stasis is what Miss Howe fears when in late April and early May she urges Clarissa to move, to get married now on whatever terms lest she lose the possibility for action altogether. Miss Howe is wrong about the wisdom of marriage to this man, but she is right to fear the stasis brought on by indecision. Such a deficiency becomes, at its worst, a deep-reaching despair, and when Clarissa is faced with the collapse of her entire life project, despair overwhelms her. Because prudence is an intellectual virtue, its deficiency is felt most deeply in the intellect, as Lovelace notices about Clarissa's condition in the two weeks after the rape. The fact that her life is conducted in writing means that we see the intellectual collapse textually reflected through the prudential medium of time. Clarissa becomes temporarily unable to make forward-moving, coherent, and purposeful texts from the language materials of her past life.

Prudence is also vulnerable to the vice of overconfidence, and Clarissa's despair is great to the degree that her confidence in her own prudence has been strong. As usual, she comes to understand the problem better than anyone else. She puts her finger on it when she accuses herself of pride. This is not the personal and social vanity of an Arabella or James Harlowe, or even a Lovelace. Clarissa's pride is much more subtle, well founded, desirable and dangerous: it is a confidence in precisely that practical wisdom which has made her excellent. Lovelace is just the adversary to bring out this pride in her.[11] His reputation puts her on her guard before she lays eyes on him, and the intricacy of the family upheaval he engenders calls upon all her resources of intellect. In response, she can feel herself exercising her prudential care to the utmost. What she cannot count into the equation is the extent and nature of his deceit, which is too persistent and intricate to be either detectable or predictable. Not only does she not know his intentions; she does not know the full measure of his artifice. Her practical wisdom cannot operate fully because it cannot use its deliberative tools: memory is contaminated by the inaccuracy of Lovelace's rendition of the past, and, given his insincerity, foresight is denied its capacity to predict. Her understanding has no firm ground on which to choose and act.

It takes months for Clarissa to fully appreciate her incapacity, though she has no sooner fled with Lovelace than close association gives her information with which to start reevaluating the past. She immediately begins to doubt the wisdom of various of her choices, such as the clandestine correspondence ("fool that I was!"—L 112, 13 April, 434), and to fear her capacity to manage the future. No practical wisdom can operate securely against his deliberate fraud: "Oh Lovelace, you are Satan himself; or he helps you out in everything; and that's as bad!" (L 261.1, 16 June, 894). Long before she knows the full details of his perfidy, she rejects the notion that she simply needed to behave with more deliberation: "But I might have written to you for advice, in my precarious situation, perhaps you will think. But, indeed, my dear Mrs Norton, I was not lost for want of advice" (L 307, 2 July, 988). And she continues, summing up her sense of the seeming bankruptcy of the prudential enterprise in the face of the phenomenon that is Lovelace:

> When I reflect upon all that has happened to me, it is apparent that this generally supposed *thoughtless* seducer has acted by me upon a regular and preconcerted plan of villainy.
>
> In order to set all his vile plots in motion, nothing was wanting from the first, but to prevail upon me either by force or fraud, to throw myself into his power; and when this was effected, nothing less than the intervention of the paternal authority (which I had not deserved to be exerted in my behalf) could have saved me from the effect of his deep machinations. Opposition from any other quarter would but too probably have precipitated his barbarous and ungrateful violence: and had *you yourself* been with me, I have reason *now* to think, that somehow or other you would have suffered in endeavouring to save me: for never was there, as now I see, a plan of wickedness more steadily and uniformly pursued, than his has been, against an unhappy creature who merited better of *him*. But the Almighty has thought fit, according to the general course of his providence, to make the fault bring on its own punishment: and that, perhaps, in consequence of my father's dreadful imprecation, 'That I might be punished *here*' (O my mamma Norton, pray with me that *here* it stop!) 'by the very wretch in whom I had placed my wicked confidence!' (989)

So the issue has been joined, and where it should be—on the problem of providence. The classical project of the cultivation of the virtuous life insistently raised questions about human response to the vagaries of fortune. If the wisest courses of the wisest people are subject to the caprice of fortune, what is the point of a project that seeks the rewards of a life of excellence? All systems of ethics must face this question. The Peripatetic, Stoic and Epicurean systems of Greece and Rome were in business because of it. But Richardson's management of the phenomenon that is Lovelace introduces an expressly Christian complication into the prudential enterprise. For the fact is that Lovelace-as-Fraud seems designed to cooperate with Clarissa's virtues toward her destruction. It is as though he existed to demonstrate the inevitable imperfections of even the most excellent of creatures. Lovelace himself begins by thinking so, and in fact it is true, though not in the way he believes.

Thus far we have been describing Clarissa's life primarily in terms of a classical model of the creation of the Self. More or less thoroughly domesticated to Christian morality from the patristic adoption of Cicero to the eighteenth century, this model cooperates harmoniously with Christianity as far as it goes. It is not sufficient to the project of Christian life, however, because as we saw it lacks the goal-setting concept of an afterlife. Further, it fails to include two other features that profoundly affect Christian moral psychology. For one thing, the pagan account omits the theological virtues of faith, hope, and charity. These are the virtues for which Clarissa must struggle hardest and which in her last months she can take least for granted, for they are in no sense natural excellences. The pagan account also omits the doctrine of original sin, of inevitable human failing, the doctrine that makes the theological virtues both necessary and necessarily hard to attain. From the Christian point of view, Clarissa cannot carry out the project of the creation of the virtuous self by herself alone. She will stumble; she will fall. Because she is human and therefore flawed, she cannot have sufficient practical wisdom to proceed without potentially crippling error in the courses of deliberation and choice that make up her life. Not only will her prudence, however great, not be able to control what fortune puts in her way, but it will not be sufficient to command her response. There are matters in her life, and even in her Self, beyond her control. Lovelace is the artistic creation which dramatizes this inevitability.

But how to project a life that in some sense is doomed to failure? Again the answer lies with the intellect. Aristotle ends the *Nicomachean Ethics* with a discussion of the activity of *theoria* or contemplation. This *theoria*, the "capacity in action" of "seeing with the mind," is the particular provenance of mature wisdom, and in Aristotle's view it is the capstone of the excellent life. Less dependent than the other virtues on the vagaries of worldly fortune, capable unlike the social virtues of being practiced in solitude, contemplation expresses and realizes the supreme element in human nature, the understanding, and is thus the most godlike activity a person can undertake (1178a). Or in Alasdair MacIntyre's paraphrase: "The perfect good is a type of theoretical activity in which the mind contemplates the unchanging and eternal aspects of things, an activity in which the mind, in virtue of that within it which is divine, contemplates in a way that reproduces the activity of God" (*Whose Justice?* 142). "Hence," says Aristotle, "a human being's complete happiness will be this activity, if it receives a complete span of life" (1177b25). The "complete span," that full life which need not necessarily be a long life,[12] is thus in a sense defined by the achievement of contemplation, for which leisure or freedom from distraction is a necessary condition. This tradition is helpful in understanding the way Clarissa conducts her dying. The detachment from emotional upheavals for which she fights so hard and which she guards so jealously in the last two months of her life makes possible the acts of contemplation which develop and exercise her full potential.

For Aristotle, it is clear that contemplation means the practice of beatitude, the practice in this life of the higher happiness which is the earthly reward of the most virtuous people.[13] Such is not entirely true of the Christian, for whom contemplation must mean preparing for beatitude in the life to come. Such preparation is by no means simply a matter of purgation or asceticism for its own sake. It requires an active exercising of the intellect in order to be capable of "reproducing the activity of God" and participating in eternal life in His presence. This view of contemplation is the source of the rich tradition of Christian meditation, and it lies at the heart of Jeremy Taylor's insistence upon the importance of "the practice of the presence of God." Such practice is Taylor's "third instrument of holy living," grouped in chapter 1 of *Holy Living* with "care of our time" and "purity of intention" to form the three "general means serving to a holy life." Given Taylor's unyielding emphasis throughout his career on the insufficiency of deathbed repentance and the necessity of the active life of virtue,[14] it is not surprising that for him this "practice of the presence of God" not only prepares for Heaven but imitates on earth the beatific state: "Indeed the hearts of holy men are Temples in the truth of things, and in type and shadow they are of Heaven it self." Nevertheless, this earthly practice can be but a promise and an apprenticeship, "as infancy is short of manhood"—"The same state of life it is, but not the same age" (37). By definition, Clarissa cannot fully succeed in the prudential courses of this life. She may even fail egregiously, as in fact she does, in part through her own unintended fault. But whatever fails or miscarries besides, she must use this life to exercise for the life to come. And that she manages to do.

By now we can see how the project of the creation of the excellent Self produces a plotted event sequence. The model assumes that the stages of virtuous activity correspond to chronological age and thus to social obligation and opportunity. The classical tradition understands the natural course of a life as a sequence emphasizing the cardinal virtues in turn. Children and the aged, living in a world focused on the senses, especially need the virtue of Temperance; young men, faced with military service, must cultivate Courage; the middle-aged taking up their responsibilities to the *polis* are especially called upon to practice Justice; while the overarching intellectual virtue of Prudence, the virtue connected with deliberation or the making of choices, regulates the application of all the others, increases with experience, and culminates for the wisest in the joys of contemplation. Christianity opens Aristotle's exclusively upper-class male tradition to all people, male and female, of whatever class and nation. It too, however, stresses appropriate stages of training and social activity: when the twelve-year-old Jesus anticipates ("I must be about my Father's business") the tradition reins him in and returns him to his apprenticeship. Nevertheless the application of these stages to the life of a genteel eighteenth-century Englishwoman requires some readjustment: she does not face military service (the need for physical courage comes preeminently with childbearing), and one of the life stages most requiring deliberative capacity comes early, during courtship. Still the concept of the progression of life stages and their attendant virtues is strongly felt. What is remarkable about Clarissa is the speed and system with which she has made her start, the intensity with which she lives her brief adulthood, and the intellectual and emotional courage and depth with which she completes her work.

Thus the beginning, middle, and end of Clarissa's Prudence Plot. In it we meet all the required character functions: the protagonist, controlling agent of her own story; the friend, her mirror, coach, critic, and companion; the teacher, who guides her youthful feet; the numerous exemplars of virtues and vices; the judge, the voice of the tradition who evaluates the Self the protagonist presents at the end of her journey. John Bunyan's way with the quintessential seventeenth-century prudence story which is *The Pilgrim's*

Progress both confirms and illuminates some of the features we have been finding in the tradition—and in *Clarissa*. For Christian's journey is built on the Prudence Plot. When the character named Prudence questions him during his stay at the palace Beautiful, the questions are of three kinds: what is your relationship to the self you used to be in your old country? By what means do you strengthen your new self and resist the vices of the old? Why do you want to go to Mt. Zion? These questions, directed at Christian's memory, his understanding, and his foresight, very explicitly examine the executive virtue which keeps him on his progress.

Especially is Bunyan helpful in emphasizing the importance of the contemplation stage of the Prudence Plot. In *The Pilgrim's Progress* as in Richardson, the friend disappears before the end of the protagonist's journey. The story reason is different, Faithful being rewarded for his steadfastness by the premature apotheosis of martyrdom, but the plot reason is the same as in *Clarissa*. Unlike his friend, Christian is obliged by the purposes of the story to live through all the essential plot stages.[15] By the point of Faithful's death at Vanity Fair, however, he has become capable of continuing his journey without his hometown companion. Though for the rest of his trip he is accompanied by Hopeful, his relationship to his fellow traveler and to his own enterprise has begun to change. The nearer Christian comes to Beulah and then the river, the more he engages in the contemplation that will prepare him for the crossing and for his life in the Celestial City. The whole tone of the narrative changes as he himself begins to take intellectual charge, explaining, expounding, deepening his intellectual understanding. This change in Christian's task explains the presence of the tag-along character Ignorance, who trails through a good portion of the last part of the narrative and whose eventually ineffectual simplemindedness is repeatedly contrasted with Christian's increasing doctrinal sophistication. Christian still requires Hopeful's aid in the river; even the greatest of the cardinal virtues is insufficient for completing the Christian's journey. But Bunyan's text spends many pages reminding us that the intellectual work of contemplation is a necessary preparation.

Bunyan also helps us understand Richardson's way with the Lovelace of the Prudence Plot. In addition to the exemplars of human weakness that people Christian's route, there are the various and lurid manifestations of the foul fiend: Apollyon and the monsters, in guises seen and unseen, that tempt, threaten and terrify the pilgrim. These apparitions are Christian additions to the classical virtue tradition, dramatizing the struggle and indirectly giving divine sanction to the rigors and temptations that train the traveler. They infest especially the early and middle stages of the journey, for it is then that Christian is susceptible to terror and trickery, and we are to understand them all as manifestations of Satan the tempter. The disguising, the role-playing, the sudden appearances to which Lovelace is addicted are expressions of this feature of the Christian version of the Prudence Plot. So too is his even more terrifyingly unnatural omnipresence, even in his physical absence, so that Clarissa comes close to being unhinged by her sense of entrapment in an intangible but totally enveloping evil: "Oh Lovelace, you are Satan himself." As with Christian, however, there comes a stage at which Clarissa is no longer menaced in this way because Lovelace is no longer capable of attracting her. Called up by her inevitable human imperfections, exactly corresponding to her vices of excess and defect, he loses his potency as she recognizes him and works to correct her imperfections. As Bunyan shows us, every pilgrim gets his fiends custom-made.

Not all of *Clarissa*'s readers misunderstood the virtue tradition in which Richardson was working. A reader who recognized what he was seeing was one David Graham, who wrote an extended appreciation of the novel as Richardson was in the process of preparing the third edition. Graham's letter discusses the pressures and misinterpretations to which both the author and his heroine were subjected and ends with the character of Clarissa as an exemplar of true Christian excellence:

> Few have discernment enough to reconcile even in Theory, what she joined in Practice; a manly resolution with a virgin delicacy; an unruffled patience with a lively sensibility; and the perseverance of a heart determined to follow the dictates of its own conviction, with that tenderness which made it bleed for the distress of those she was opposing: Very few can conceive how her passions . . . shou'd be blended together in so happy a mixture, as that there shou'd result from them one uniform blaze of virtue, shining forth in its strength: Glorious in her prosperity, still more in her Afflictions, but most of all at the time of death; when possess'd of a hope that smil'd at disappointments; exulting in a Joy, that banish'd the memory of past sorrows; inflamed with love, that cou'd annihilate the sense of human malice, she threw behind her all the comforts, which mankind in those dreadful moments, most closely embraces, and left herself nothing to lean upon but the support of an invisible hand.[16]

This passage strikes off a number of the most important features of the Christian Prudence Plot: the tradition's grounding in character or virtue ethics, its insistence on practice as well as theory, the protagonist's passion as well as mildness and balance, the plot's necessary ending in the contemplation of God. A young student of divinity of a very different sort from the Reverend Mr. Brand, Graham has got the tradition right; we may appropriately leave the last word to him.

7

Three into One: Plotting
and Epistolary Technique

In previous chapters I have focused in turn on Richardson's three received plots—the Tested Woman Plot, the Don Juan Plot, and the Prudence Plot—in order to sketch the inherent logic of each and Richardson's most significant ways with it. But what makes *Clarissa* is their combination, and my focus in this chapter is the integrative technique. Richardson's most powerful effects would be impossible without the plot interactions he is able to pull off. The custom-made temptation of his heroine, for instance. Unlike the standardized and perfunctory seductions faced by most tested women, Clarissa's temptation is masterfully crafted from the stuff of her prudential virtue by the most fluent and astute of professional artificers. Or the emphasis on Clarissa's active morality. Although the rape is deadly, the novel never lets her become passive, never equates her virginity with her virtue or allows what is done to her to take precedence over what she does. Or the novel's open insistence upon the religious foundations of moral authority. The collapse of the human patriarchal structure, though explained, is not disguised. Yet though Clarissa goes to her death knowing that her familial piety has been abused, she believes her family structure to be the humanly flawed representation of a divine and therefore ultimately achievable ideal. The richness with which the novel combines psychological exploration, social critique, and religious affirmation is made possible by its plot work.

Since readers of the preceding chapters have already been connecting up aspects of character and event among these three plots, in this chapter I do not propose to unravel and rewind the novel. My purpose is to probe the relationships in form and technique between its plotting and its epistolary style, and to describe some of the means Richardson inherits or invents for integrating his separate plots. First let us consider the means he does not use. Literary precedent supplied an eighteenth-century writer with two ways of using more than one plot in a single work. One is the interpolated tale of epic or romance, the other the alternating multiple-plot structure of Renaissance drama. In an epic or romance structure, no matter how "novelistic"— in *Don Quixote* or *Tom Jones*, say—the tale takes the reader on a quest or journey focused by the protagonist and his acts. The writer can give us other plots or stories only by stopping the main plot and thrusting those others in. The usual means is the casual or providential encounter on the ship or at the inn during which the fellow-traveler gets to tell his story. It is true that the two plots thus nested together may have some additional connection. This can be a connection of person: Fielding describes the adventures of a woman who might be Tom's mother. It can be a connection of theme: Cervantes' story of El Curioso Impertinente, the husband who cannot believe his exemplary wife's marital faith and puts his friend to test her, is as much about the operation of received fantasy upon the unstable mind as is the story of the knight himself. But the structural connection of such tales with their host plots is minimal: they are cysts, encapsulated within and essentially sealed off from the main organism. *Clarissa* contains faint echoes of the interpolated tale, the most extended being the story of Belton and his Thomasine. But this exemplum is so tightly tied to the moral education of Belford and Lovelace as to be anything but mere interpolation.

The multiple-plotted drama of the Renaissance theater in which actions from primary, secondary, and even tertiary plots are alternately staged was the other possibility Richardson inherited. This technique, which subsequently lost its sense of conviction under the influence of neoclassicism, develops somewhat greater interplot integration than does the interpolated tale. Governed in part by the theatrical need for economy of character and casting, the links among the persons of the separate plots tend to be tighter, so that in *Much Ado About Nothing* Beatrice is Hero's household member, cousin, and friend, and Benedick is Claudio's comrade in arms. The relationship among multiple plots is sometimes very strong: Jacobean playwright Nathan Field's *Amends for Ladies* builds each of its three comic plots around a tested woman—a maid, a wife, and a widow—who engineers a recognition of her virtue and the follies of male possessiveness. Nevertheless the connections, when they extend beyond the opportunistic, are primarily analogical.[1] For example, while in *Much Ado* Benedick challenges Claudio over Hero's slandering, the challenge goes nowhere; the Claudio/Hero plot is unwound by Dogberry and company. *Clarissa* has its incipient secondary plots after this manner, of which the courtship of Anna and Hickman is the most sustained, but not even their story becomes an independent one. Richardson did not intend it to.

The drawback with interpolated tales and alternated plots is that in the absence of structural connections the various plots do not interact. Richardson sought to use the peculiar strengths of both drama and narrative fiction to blend his plots structurally and thus interactively, thereby achieving a more richly lifelike effect and with it more psychological immediacy and greater moral depth. To this end he developed several plot-combining tools, all of them innovative outgrowths of his epistolary style. No one of these tools works schematically or rigidly. Richardson uses them to break down barriers between plots, between the narrative and the dramatic features of his book, between various states of mind. The resultant ebb and flow would, he hoped, have the feel of life, and of course it does. Yet to understand how he did it we have to tolerate categorizing and explaining those tools in isolation. In this chapter I wish first to separate out several of Richardson's plot-integrating techniques, then to discuss their uses in bringing the plots to work upon each other.

The most central of the plot-combining techniques in *Clarissa*, so seemingly inevitable as to be virtually invisible, involves making individual characters essential players in more than one plot. This "character-sharing" technique is matched with its harmonizing opposite, "event-sharing," which causes a given event to operate in more than one plot. In ordinary experience we smudge these two techniques of "character-sharing" and "event-sharing" together, as when we say that people's lives or paths cross. When it is important to make structural distinctions, however, as artists constructing fictions are obliged at least tacitly to do, we have to admit that "people" and their "lives" or "paths" are not precisely the same thing, and we shall see that *Clarissa* is an interesting demonstration of the effects of the technical difference. A third and even more subtle plot-integrating technique involves the combined use of epistolary dialogue and epistolary soliloquy. It is chiefly by means of this third technique, the manipulation of dialogue and soliloquy effects, that Richardson manages to share characters and events coherently among his several plots.

"Character-sharing"—building more than one plot around the same character—is without question the novel's simplest and most central plot-combining device. Throughout the previous six chapters, I have implied our tacit understanding of this technique by arguing for the existence of three different plots, each of which has essentially the same cast of characters.

There are, however, differences of character emphasis among the three plots. In a sense Lovelace has a plot of his own, the Don Juan Plot, which nevertheless requires the presence of women superficially like Clarissa. Clarissa has her own plot, the Prudence Plot, which nevertheless requires the presence of a person who fulfils the function of Lovelace. Each of these plots is focused on its central character; never did two characters so richly imbue their own plots with the force of their personalities and purposes, a force which in both cases carries to the very end of the novel. But Lovelace and Clarissa also share a plot, the Tested Woman Plot, in which both of them are central. It is the meeting ground constituted by this plot that controls the primary shape of the novel.

To say that a character may centrally occupy more than one plot is to revise radically our usual thinking about what constitutes plot. Because our first description and examples of plot structure came from Aristotle on Greek drama, literary criticism historically began with a univocal model which assumes not only that a single work will have a single plot but that an individual character will have a single plot. The first assumption, which was at the root of the neoclassical controversy about dramatic "unity of action," has been repeatedly challenged in both theory and practice. But criticism has never addressed the second assumption so cleanly and self-consciously because that assumption is always subsumed under the first. We simply identify a character with the plot she is in, take it for granted that, if not precisely the same thing, they cannot be separated. How could a character live two different plots at once?

Yet we also take it for granted that actual people do lead complexly multiplotted lives. I do not mean just undercover agents or unfaithful spouses. I mean, for instance, any competent artist who is also a responsible member of a social group: the creative life and the social life are connected in the person of the subject but they are far from tracing the same action. The plot of the writing of *Clarissa* must have been an enormously different thing from the plot of the business life of S. Richardson, printer, yet we know they went on at the same time in the same man. In like fashion the main characters in *Clarissa* lead multiplotted lives. Lovelace sees himself living the Don Juan Plot—it represents his intention for himself. Clarissa sees herself living the Prudence Plot, which is her intention for herself. But brought together, they are forced to recognize that they are also living the Tested Woman Plot. In that plot, Lovelace seeks to deflect Clarissa from her prudential pursuit, and Clarissa seeks to reform Lovelace out of his rake's progress. Neither finally succeeds because however else they may differ they are perfectly matched in a stubborn energy that keeps them on their original life course. But the complexity we perceive in the novel's main characters is in part the complexity which comes from their being essentially caught up in more than one action, a method foreign to both romance and drama because of the expression of interiority it requires.

Like this "character-sharing," the second technique, that of "event-sharing" or bringing a given event into more than one plot, again describes a phenomenon we take for granted in ordinary life. Just as we understand that a single person can live multiple plots—can "lead two lives"—we also know that a given event can be part of different plots because it plays itself out differently for different people. The given conversation or episode may be nothing special to one participant and indelibly, perhaps catastrophically, important to another. Even when all parties agree that an event is significant, how it is significant depends on the plot it is in. Literature makes such distinctions most easily when they can be managed sequentially. Thus we are accustomed to understand that the death of the husband in the arms of grieving young wife and loyal friend may provide both the end of an old love plot and the springing hope of a new one, about which "but that's another story" is often used to delight us with its bittersweet boundary marking. When in *Cyrano de Bergerac* the "death event" turns out to mark neither the end of the old plot nor the opening of a new plot, it is doubly wrenching because it works against that hopeful expectation. This is why in Rostand's play the husband's death is the climax even though he is not one of the protagonists: it is the event that most firmly establishes for us the essential singleness of the work's triangular "frustrated love" plot.

When a key event lies at the heart of several different plots at once, presentation and interpretation are more complex. One way to distinguish the significance of a shared event from one plot to another is to shift the point of view from one character to another, since different people are bound to see the same event differently. But multiple points of view do not of themselves make multiple plots: Clarissa and Anna and Lovelace and Belford all express their opinions about Hickman's courtship, but that does not make the courtship other than a single action. Further, what if the different plots are about the same people? In order to be truly shared, an event needs to be positioned and exploited so as to reveal first one plot structure or gestalt, then another and another. Such positioning and exploitation is something at which Richardson is particularly adept.

Take for instance the rape, an undeniably central event in each of *Clarissa*'s three plots. The rape is viewed differently by the four letter writers who respond most directly to it because of the kind and degree of their involvement. But each also responds differently at different times because the rape has a different purpose in each of the plots. In the Tested Woman Plot it is the key event that both closes the Test and focuses the Trial. It ends the Test because by bringing Lovelace's ultimate weapon to bear it completes Clarissa's education about his nature. It focuses the Trial because it seizes the attention and requires the interpretation of the community. When Anna Howe first hears of the rape, she responds from her perspective in the Tested Woman Plot (L 310, to CH, 5 July, 993), judging harshly and even crudely in a version of the "we told you so" response characteristic of the Harlowes. Because the rape is the premier socially resonant act of this social plot, within this plot both Clarissa and Lovelace must continue to confront its social effects directly. Marriage, prosecution, pregnancy; flight to Pennsylvania or to the Continent; relations with the Montagues and Belford and Clarissa's protectors the Smiths; all these considerations are created by the rape. And if social effects, then psychological ones. Clarissa loses her marriageability, which means her economic and social status. Lovelace loses his independence, the emotional detachment which allows him to casually continue his rake's progress, and becomes subject to social pressure. Both losses have psychological effects that determine their behavior throughout the rest of this plot.

By contrast, in neither the Don Juan Plot nor the Prudence Plot does the rape change the plot's direction. Though it is the rake's ultimate seduction tool, it is impersonal, unsatisfying and ultimately forgettable. When in reading his letters of August and September we have the feeling that Lovelace cannot remember what he has done, we are reading right. As Don Juan he lacks the moral sense or the imagination to feel how the rape affects others' lives. Moreover, because the plot itself is designed to drain human contact of significance, it strings out human interactions until we understand exactly how much they do not matter. From Lovelace's perspective in the Don Juan Plot, the significance of the rape is paradoxically its insignificance; to us it is important only because we keep being astonished at how little Lovelace is affected by it. As Don Juan, Lovelace seizes the fact of Clarissa's growing indifference to him, but he cannot read the rape at all. Not coincidentally, it is the rape that definitively pushes Belford out of his peripheral, increasingly unsatisfying position in the Don Juan Plot and into a central role in the Tested Woman Plot. If he is going to develop a moral, or even a social, response to the rape, he cannot do it as Lovelace's creature.

Because it too is a plot of the life of a single character, the Prudence Plot shares some structural features with the Don Juan Plot. One is that the rape comes to be submerged into the great succession of Clarissa's life events; although unquestionably it is significant, its significance comes from what Clarissa learns gradually to make of it. The rape is one of the most brutal imaginable ways to catapult her into the self-consciousness of adulthood, which she must achieve and live swiftly if she is going to complete her course before our eyes. Not just the violence of Lovelace's attack, or its social destructiveness, but its actual sexual features contribute to this effect of the rape; Lovelace is surely right to intuit that for reasons physical as well as social, sexual contact and especially sexual penetration contributes more profoundly to self-awareness in women than in men. But another trauma might have forced Clarissa's precipitous growth into adulthood, though another trauma would not have meshed so nicely with the other plots. In this plot the trauma itself is not the point, except as trigger: the whole journey is the point. Further, the story of Clarissa's growth in wisdom is not primarily a matter of external happenings. The compelling moments consist of insights, illuminations, heroic efforts of the will. The more strenuously Clarissa lives this inward plot, the more its external event structure flattens out, as it does during the waiting times in March before her flight, in May before her rape, and in August before her death. During each of those stretches Clarissa is processing information about herself and others; during them her understanding of her life is becoming radically complicated and deepened, so that her waiting is a kind of waiting toward, a gathering of forces. To the degree that Clarissa's Prudence Plot is a secular version of the saint's life, it does not much matter what the next events in her life will be. Whatever they are, they will provide raw material for her newly enlarged understanding to work on. As Willa Cather notes in describing the unemphatic event structure in the medieval compilation of saints' lives called *The Golden Legend*, the torments undergone by the saints are "no more dwelt upon than are the trivial incidents of their lives; it is as though all human experience, measured against one supreme spiritual adventure, were of about the same importance."[2] Unlike the Tested Woman Plot with its various stereotyped Test and Trial events, the Prudence Plot, though it has set psychological and moral stages, is relatively indifferent to particular events, which must arise to meet the character of the protagonist as it develops.

To be effective the plot-combining techniques of "character-sharing" and "event-sharing" responsible for the rich structures of *Clarissa* need a performance medium which will do justice to their richness. That medium is letters. The letters of this Richardson novel in particular show an astonishingly wide stylistic range, in part because so many disparate characters are allowed to join the conversation and their particularities are rendered with such liveliness. Behind the liveliness conveyed by the rendering of individual idiosyncrasies is Richardson's deliberate effort to craft a hybrid form—what he called "dramatic narrative"—that would combine the technical strengths of both narrative fiction and drama. In his chapter entitled "The Novel as Drama" Mark Kinkead-Weekes *(Samuel Richardson, Dramatic Novelist)* details how Richardson's writing "to the moment" increases the dramatic vividness of what is basically a narrative form. Given the dramatic origin of so much of Richardson's plot material and the dialogue form in which it is written, I would describe Richardson's matrix as nearly as dramatistic as it is novelistic. Nearly but not quite, since for reasons we will touch on shortly the primary conflicts are rarely rendered directly. Wherever we put the emphasis, however, we know that Richardson was trying to give himself the advantages both of drama's immediateness and of narration's capacity for psychological exploration.

The combination is complicated to achieve. Plays expose and hook together episodes of character interaction as their primary work, attending to psychological issues such as motivation or intention only secondarily. True psychological exploration—probing the relationship between a person's actions and the matrix of habits and intentions that make up personality and character—must be conducted on the stuff of the past, which results in a recursiveness that translates in plot terms into redundancy. But drama has no mechanism for using plot redundancy; as the genre of the ongoing present its dramatic action cannot be stopped to see how the psychological machinery works. By contrast, novels achieve a recursiveness which is not redundant by exploiting the tool of direct or implied narration. The narrative voice provides the means to reflect upon the action without actually replaying it. Psychologically this recursive possibility represents a great gain, but it sacrifices the immediateness of drama in which the point of view is ever and only that of the characters.

The key to Richardson's hybrid form is the fact that a letter has both the immediateness of drama and the recursive possibilities of narrative. Dramatically it is one side of dialogue, which has the characteristic of *immediacy* in both its senses. Thus the letters duplicate the unmediated point of view of a play: the reader receives the language of the writers directly, with no intervening consciousness. Certainly Richardson does not wish to intervene; he wishes—the exasperated tone of his third edition footnotes bears this out—for his readers to take on completely and directly the act of interpretation, so long as their interpretation shall correspond with his. The letters also duplicate dialogue's overpowering presentness in time. In drama, conversation is what establishes dramatic presentness, because a character's language is designed to affect the present state of her interlocutor. So too in the novel's letters, where each letter is an expression of the current state of the writer, designed to speak to its addressee with maximum power at the very moment of reading. Even in the interrupted dialogue of the epistolary form, the sense of presentness in time and the sense of the direct and unimpeded expression of consciousness work together to reinforce and constrain each other. Each character writes not only the present but *her* present. Even when recounting events of the past, of another's past, she is engaged in a performance of her present. And above all, that performance is for another:

> In the very heat of anguish or confession, the letter can never forget that it is turned outwards to another, that its discourse is ineradicably social. Such sociality is not just contingent, a mere matter of its destination; it is the very material condition of its existence. The other to whom the letter is addressed is included within it, an absent recipient present within each phrase. As speech-for-another, the letter must reckon that recipient's likely response into its every gesture. (Eagleton, *The Rape of Clarissa,* 52)

But though the letters are dialogue, for in every case except that of Clarissa's Papers and Meditations they address and are designed to affect another character, and though their first obligation is thus to forward the plot, they are also soliloquies. Soliloquy is performed in the absence of other characters in order to promote self-revelation, even self-analysis. As drama's only recursive mode, the one point at which the playwright signals the abandonment of external "plot action" for the sake of "mind action," soliloquy is received by its audience very differently from dialogue. Because dialogue exists to do plot work, in drama the first concern is its effect on the characters being spoken to, which is why in the theater we often find ourselves watching, not the speaker, but the characters who hear him. The audience receives a piece of dramatic dialogue essentially as another character might receive it; the audience is reactive. By contrast, because soliloquy exists first to do psychological work, the first concern is the speaker's motivations and intentions. In receiving soliloquy, the audience attempts to work in concert with the speaker's mind; the audience is empathetic. Whereas with dialogue the audience plays at being another character, then, with soliloquy the audience plays at being the speaker himself.

In drama the two forms are strongly distinguished: a speech is either soliloquy or dialogue, though dramatists can blur the distinction with the device of eavesdropping. By contrast, a letter is always both dialogue and soliloquy, addressed directly to another but performed in solitude. By writing epistolary drama Richardson can experiment with effects along the entire dialogue/soliloquy continuum. Though the letters are always both forms at once, he can put the emphasis now on one side, now on the other.

The most theatrical dialogue effect is created when a character writes what Kinkead-Weekes calls a "play-book" sequence, as when Lovelace relates the Morden encounter (L 442, 29 Aug., 1278), Clarissa recounts a particularly nasty struggle with Arabella (L 42, [21 March], 192), or Anna Howe stages the dialogue between mother and daughter that reacts to Antony Harlowe's marriage proposal (L 197, 20–21 May, 626). In these cases we have something as close as a letter can get to a standard dramatic scene. The letter-writer does his best to fade from our focal attention; the characters who battle it out before our eyes might as well be playing it out on stage. Deep down we know it is Lovelace, say, who is writing this playlet, that in some sense it is a soliloquy with Lovelace taking all the parts, but as author he is hidden by the Lovelace character who meets the Morden character in Lord M's receiving hall. Both the soliloquy effects and the dialogue with the letter's addressee Belford are disguised behind the pretense to the unmediatedness of drama. A different dialogue effect is created by letters which consist of frank persuasion to the addressee. Clarissa's of 11 March to John Harlowe (L 32.1, 148) passionately attempts to create the impact of the speaking voice as it would be heard in face-to-face appeal. This letter is still technically a soliloquy, for Clarissa writes it while away from her uncle, yet it brings him so close in spirit as almost to give the feel of dramatic monologue, with the addressee physically present and emotionally responsive. Then there are also letters which locate the argumentative or persuasive scene within the letter writer, emphasizing states of mind and playing out internal conflicts and dilemmas. Some of the most agonized are those of Lovelace and Clarissa during their episodes of madness. These are the letters which seem most soliloquy-like, which most frankly seize the opportunity for psychological and moral exploration.

Yet these most intimate and soliloquy-like of the letters paradoxically develop into dialogue. Internal dialogue is a feature of soliloquy because it is in keeping with our antilogistic metaphors for describing psychological states, especially states of stress: we say that we feel embattled or in conflict, are debating with ourselves, are on the horns of a dilemma. The internal dialogue of soliloquy presents this psychomachia dramatically without resorting to the literal presence of the Bad Angel at the left shoulder and the Good Angel at the right. Yet this dialogue within a character has a different relation to dramatic action from the dialogue between characters. Because the internal dialogue works recursively, going back and looping into its ongoing processes, changing itself in the course of enacting itself, conflicting states of minds are allowed to operate on each other with the fervor of opposing dramatic characters but without the irrevocability characteristic of dramatic action. Their work is understood to be provisional and unresolved. What we seem to accept is that in soliloquy what the mind commits it can also withdraw, and no one will be the wiser—except the mind itself.

In *Clarissa* it is the most soliloquy-like letters in which the writers most openly set up an inner conversation among the various states that people their minds, giving themselves the opportunity for this psychological recursiveness. Now in drama the characteristic ending of soliloquy is a decision, a resolution of the internal debate which returns the play to the forward-moving action of dialogue. That is how the dramatist gets back into the play, so to speak. Having debated with himself about Leontes' command to kill Polixenes, Camillo resolves in the interest of a deeper loyalty to flee his king and thereby save the friend—and sure enough, enter Polixenes. But since Richardson is not really writing a play, he is not pressed to end his soliloquies with a decision that will shift his character back into the mainstream of the dramatic action. He has the luxury of soliloquies in which decisions are not reached, or are reached only provisionally, which means that he may use them for extended psychological exploration. The technique is perfectly conscious, both of its uses in portraying character and of the pressure to interpret the plot that it puts on readers. As he complains to Lady Bradshaigh,

Ye world is not enough used to this way of writing, to the moment. It knows not that in the minutiae lie often the unfoldings of the story, as well as of the heart, & judges of an action undecided, as if it were absolutely decided.[3]

Since the process itself is exactly what he wants most to examine, the most soliloquy-like letters are the ones which reveal the most about the operations of judging and deciding. For instance, Richardson explores the idea that sometimes it is wise to resist resolution, to tolerate or even welcome ambiguity and self-doubt. Clarissa achieves her eventual moral understanding in part because she can sustain and use self-doubt. Lovelace never achieves moral understanding in part because self-doubt is what he cannot bear; he never allows his self-probing soliloquies to run for long, characteristically pushing them away from him into the dialogue of a "play-book" scene or of appeals to Belford. By contrast, Clarissa increasingly resorts to the self-probing resources of soliloquy until they become so inward that she ceases to perform them "aloud" at all and the examination of the self goes on in prayer.

We are helped to understand the psychological uses of soliloquy, and its delicate narrative and dramatic balance, by consulting the man who invented or at least named it. In the *Retractationes*, St. Augustine describes a little book he wrote in A.D. 386, the momentous year between his conversion and his baptism. In pursuit of truth about the matters that most concerned him, he says, "I asked myself questions and I replied to myself, as if we were two, reason and I, whereas I was of course just one. As a result I called the book *Soliloquies*."[4] For our purposes the most telling point comes midway through the second section when Augustine finds himself argued into a corner by Reason and realizes with shame that he has espoused a foolish position. Reason, who we must remember is as much Augustine as is Augustine, responds "It's ridiculous to be ashamed. Think of the very reason we have chosen this type of conversation. I want them to be called '*Soliloquies*' because we are talking with ourselves alone." Reason goes on to explain that argument between people, though it may be the best way to get at the truth, has the drawback that people hate to get beaten, so instead of learning they retreat into a "wilful obstinacy" that is perfectly understandable but unproductive nevertheless. The procedure of questioning and answering oneself is far more "peaceful" and "profitable." "So if you have committed yourself too quickly anywhere there is no reason for you to be afraid of retreating and setting yourself free: there's no way out here otherwise" (II, 14; 89). *We; I; You:* without apology Reason mobilizes the paradoxical language resources of conversation with the Self to urge the exploitation of the provisionality which makes soliloquy the perfect device for examining the Self, as Richardson had discovered long before: "Thus foolishly dialogued I with my heart; and yet, all the time, this heart is Pamela."

In *Clarissa* the resources of the dialogue/soliloquy continuum are built right into the plot structures themselves. We can characterize the Prudence Plot, wherever we find it, as by its nature a soliloquy plot: it is because Augustine found himself living a crucial stage in his own Prudence Plot that he wrote his *Soliloquies.* The most concentrated episodes in Clarissa's prudential journey are reflected in her Papers and Meditations, in which soliloquy pure, with Clarissa openly taking all the parts, appears for the only time: "Can you, my dear honoured papa, resolve for ever to reprobate your poor child?—But I am sure you would not, if you knew . . ." (890). Such pure soliloquy is rare because the novel has to be carried out primarily in letters, so the bulk of even its Prudence Plot is expressed in the correspondence between Clarissa and Anna. Since the relationship between the women is that of the *phronemoi* or friends-in-prudence, however, Clarissa writing to Anna is also Clarissa writing to her other self, Clarissa soliloquizing. Paradoxically, the fact that of all the novel's correspondents Clarissa and Miss Howe can most fully engage in genuine converse of mind and soul means that they also carry out the most evenhanded and sustained dialogue the novel has to offer.

The Don Juan Plot parodically simulates the soliloquizing intimacies of the Prudence Plot. Although his histrionic nature forces Don Juan into the public arena of dialogue, he seeks to monopolize all conversation. In *Clarissa*, where this plot too is carried out largely between a single pair of correspondents, Lovelace's letters to Belford are nearly always monopolistic and controlling. Characteristically he puts words into Belford's mouth so he can cajole or laugh them away. A typical formula begins, "Thou saist thou wouldst . . . ," followed by the inevitable turn, the *but* or the bullying ("thou art an awkward fellow") that brings the argument and the words back into his control. The self-conscious *thees* and *thous* Lovelace terms "the Roman style" are the most evident parody of the intimate language of the *phronemoi.* One might expect these pronouns to set up the soliloquy effect of internal dialogue, in which the two minds would work as one, as partners at least in crime. Rather than intimacy, however, the "Roman style" establishes at best a clannishness, a kind of fraternity talk that (like the totally excluding shorthand which by its nature we can never see) does more to seal Lovelace and Belford off from the rest of the world than to bind them to each other. Lovelace's "thou art" and "thou saist," which uses intimacy as a weapon to accuse and subdue, is the opposite of Reason's inclusionary tour of the language of intimacy which binds him to Augustine as expressions of the same mind. In part this is why Lovelace lacks the capacity for inwardness. Because Richardson has so skillfully developed the genuinely intimate dialogue of mutual examination and criticism between the two women, we understand how having practiced with Anna helps Clarissa conduct her solitary self-examination. The dialogue of the friends, almost as trusting and searching as soliloquy, trains for the practices of self-accusation, self-defense and self-judgment that Clarissa's soliloquies involve. By contrast Lovelace cannot sustain and learn from the internal dialogue of soliloquy partly because he has had no such practice with his friend. So much does he hate to be beaten that he has never used Belford's acute and loving concern to help him develop the habit of introspection. At the moments when he most needs the tool of the self-educating internal dialogue, he overbears even himself, bludgeoning and throttling the voice of self-accusation into the submission he demands of all his interlocutors: "There she lies, weltering in her blood! Her death's wound have I given her!" (L 246, 10 June, 848).

Both the Prudence Plot and the Don Juan Plot, then, are positioned at the soliloquy end of the continuum. The Prudence Plot is a soliloquy plot in its essence because its action presses toward the increasing interiority and self-examination of the contemplation stage. The Don Juan Plot parodies a soliloquy plot because its action is directed toward co-opting all voices into the voice of the protagonist. By contrast, the Tested Woman Plot is supremely a dialogue plot. It uses external persuasion and debate first in the Test to threaten or tear apart social connections, then in the Trial to re-form those social relationships. Its major actions exploit the force of dialogue: the heightened voices of seduction, accusation, enforcement, reproach, envy, contempt, and reconciliation are responsible for the most strongly charged moments of the novel. When we run the action of *Clarissa* through our minds, the scenes we resurrect are the agons of temptation, accusation, defense, and judgment: Lovelace and Clarissa confronting each other at the garden gate or in the penknife scene, Clarissa recoiling from the squatting

Solmes, the Harlowes in acrimonious family council, Lovelace springing
out of his disguise at Hampstead, Morden and Lovelace sparring at Lord
M's, Clarissa telling her story at the Smiths', the orgy of familial guilt and
recrimination over her coffin, the somber procession which places the dead
woman at her grandfather's feet. The last of these scenes, virtually word-
less, is a speaking picture nevertheless, an especially poignant exchange in
the familial debate that is the Tested Woman Plot.

So dominating are the dialogic conflicts of this plot that Richardson's
art is devoted to almost never conveying them directly. We hear *of* conflict
and think therefore that we hear it. But whereas in the Prudence Plot and
the Don Juan Plot the "soliloquy" moments of present composition are
psychologically the essential actions, in the Tested Woman Plot by contrast, where Richardson's characters primarily narrate past events to absent
people, the strongest "dialogue" moments come to us through retrospec-
tion. Occasionally the primary agon is directly rendered—in the letters of
July and August between Clarissa and Arabella, for instance—and when it
is, the effect is so tense as to make us grateful we need not endure more.
The most highly confrontational dialogues of the Tested Woman Plot are
dialogues recounted and therefore at one remove, a removal that nevertheless returns us simultaneously to the intimacies of the soliloquizing voice.

Again we have underlined the complexity of the relationship between
Richardson's plot manipulations and his stylistic practices. The intercon-
nected and interparticipatory quality of these techniques, cause as well as
expression of the psychological interconnectedness of the characters in the
novel, is also one cause of the responsiveness, indeed the interpretive hyper-
activity, of readers to the novel. The particular epistolary form that dis-
tributes the story more or less evenly among opposing voices is in part
responsible, for it deprives us of a single narrative authority: "You cannot
have an authorial voice-over if the characters do all the writing," as Terry
Eagleton notes (*The Rape of Clarissa,* 25). Yet such an effect technically
pertains in drama as well, and not just the epic theater to which Eagleton
makes the parallel: you cannot have an authorial voice-over if the characters do all the speaking. So we must note further the degree to which the
urge to interpretation is created by our participation in the very subtle give-
and-take between dialogue and soliloquy effects that Richardson has learned
to exploit in the epistolary form. Not only are the characters "doing all the
writing," not only do their contradictory biases perforce shade and shape
every account of the events, but the characters whose voices we primarily

hear are also writing to expose and scrutinize themselves, so that we are unceasingly called upon to move between our empathetic and our reactive responses.

There is an additional—and I think powerfully explanatory—cause of this reader responsiveness. The very structure of the Tested Woman Plot forces interpretive activity of a distinctive and highly emotional sort. For one thing, we know that Richardson chose a version of the Tested Woman Plot in which the relationship between Test and Trial is morally and psychologically fraught. Since both Clarissa's actions and her reputation are in genuine and contradictory question, since she is both faulty and calumniated, the central action of the novel overtly demands interpretation. The other characters are continually scrambling to assess her behavior, and since readers also are engaged in interpreting this behavior, we find ourselves reading in concert with them. By this means the novel lures us into performing the distinctive authority functions of the Tested Woman Plot. To a remarkable degree, the history of criticism of the novel is a history of the adoption of one or another of those functions by readers themselves. Hence at least in part, I believe, the plurality of readings to which *Clarissa* has been subjected. Hence what Eagleton characterizes as the critical "rape of Clarissa." Hence what Terry Castle sees as the novel's "hermeneutic ambiguity," which I regard as less ambiguity than struggle and ascribe, not to an *absence* of "story" (Castle, *Clarissa's Ciphers*, 40), but on the contrary to the strongly marked workings of the central plot.

So we savor the possibilities of seduction; though shocked at our own connivance, we also glory in Lovelace's schemes. "I have laught at your Lo——e, when at the same time I wished him hang'd," admits Lady Bradshaigh for us all.[5] For we too suffer the provocations of virtue: if readers of *Pamela* can wish that heroine as flawed as themselves,[6] all the more can readers of *Clarissa* long to subdue a character who both seeks and states an excellence which must translate into superiority. So also we accuse and defend—not just the tested woman herself, or her tempter, but her accusers and defenders both inside the novel and beyond it. And as in other forensic enterprises, the testimony of the witnesses becomes part of the text of the trial. Thus we feel the critical compulsion to take on those other readers— the ones who have abused virtue or admired vice and are therefore themselves culpable.

And of course we attempt to judge. The plot itself intends for us to do so. This is the deepest *structural* reason why, as Tom Keymer argues, "it is

never an option simply to sit back and admire the text's ethical indeterminacy"; rather, the novel is so ordered, or dis-ordered, that the reader must
"take on the mantle of the novel's missing judge and strive to order it himself."[7] The novel warns us, however, of what the history of its criticism has
borne out: the function of judgment is both the most crucial and the most
difficult function to perform. It is difficult to the degree that it obliges us to
take account of the whole book of Clarissa's life and the complicated and
subtle purposes for which its parts have been written. It is difficult because
it involves judgment not just of Clarissa herself, but of all parties to the
plot. And that is ultimately what makes the difficulty so intensely personal
and disquieting. The judgment toward which Richardson's radical version
of the Tested Woman Plot pushes us is not remotely magisterial, but empathetic, engaged and self-aware, for it demands that we probe the moral and
psychological roots of our own participation in the action. Clearly the novel
engages our profound longing toward our first myth, our need not just to
tell ourselves that primal story, but to participate in that story, over and
over. The deepest structural reality of the Tested Woman Plot is that the
burden of judgment falls ultimately on those who have caused the plot to be
carried out. To the degree that Richardson's novelistic technique makes us
desire Clarissa's Test and Trial, it makes us complicit, and we are forced to
admit that as readers we too have taken part, and taken parts, in that plot.

Notes

Preface

1. The unusually strong tendency of Richardson critics to write from and about each other rather than the novels has been noted, naturally, by a number of critics including Siobhán Kilfeather, who suggests that this fact may be related not just to the range of interpretations invited by the epistolary mode but to the memorial problems faced by readers trying to find their way around Richardson's huge texts. Thus "it is more convenient for [Richardson's critics], even than for other critics, to rely on the readings of their predecessors" ("The Rise of Richardson Criticism," 254). "Rely on" of course includes spending their time refuting. In *Reading Clarissa: The Struggles of Interpretation,* William Warner ascribes the phenomenon, at least on the part of the "humanist" critics from Diderot and Richardson himself on down, to their desire, serpent-like, to "magnif[y] the value of the Lady," that text they long to approach, attack, and penetrate. Thus they "create the unified textual body they subsequently desire. But to do so they must secretly encourage, and cite at length, the 'false' criticism they claim to abhor" (262). The phenomenon of increasing one's critical stock by treasuring up one's opponents is hardly restricted to the "humanist" critics, as Warner's own book wittingly, even gleefully, demonstrates.

Chapter 1. The Background

1. On 6 April 1772; Hill, ed., *Boswell's Life of Johnson,* II, 175. Not only is the date twenty-four years after Johnson first read the novel, but Boswell is a source which puts Johnson at one remove.
2. "The problem of 'Story' is always at hand in *Clarissa,*" says Terry Castle in *Clarissa's Ciphers* (38), and she admonishes critics that what is needed in studies of the novel is "an investigation of the basic link between 'inside' and 'outside' . . . , between story and shape" (18). Exactly right, I believe, and in a sense (though not in Castle's sense) that basic link is what this book is designed to address.
3. Letter to Richardson, 6 July 1754; cited by Eaves and Kimpel, *Biography,* 203.
4. Ross, introduction to *Clarissa* (20).
5. I agree enthusiastically with Jocelyn Harris's stricture that "any theory about Richardson's creativity that depends upon an assumption of his ignorance will not do" (Harris, "Richardson," 201). On the other hand, many of his richly allusive references are

simply not reliably attributable to a single literary source. For example, the "tennis ball of fortune" language which appears in both *Pamela* and *Clarissa* may indeed be owing to *The Duchess of Malfi* (Harris, "Richardson," 196); as my subsequent chapters show, I regard Webster's play as significantly analogous to and informative about the structure of *Clarissa*. But the metaphor itself is a commonplace from the sixteenth century onward.

6. Slattery, *The Richardson-Stinstra Correspondence*, 26.

7. Ibid., 26–27.

8. In addition to Eaves and Kimpel's *Biography*, see especially Leopold Damrosch, *God's Plot & Man's Stories;* Margaret Anne Doody, *A Natural Passion;* and a more specialized monograph, James Louis Fortuna, *"The Unsearchable Wisdom of God": A Study of Providence in Richardson's "Pamela."* In the course of examining Richardson's purposes and his readers' responses, Tom Keymer's *Richardson's "Clarissa" and the Eighteenth-Century Reader* splendidly situates the novel in its literary and ethical milieu. (Keymer's study, which appeared just as I was finishing the final draft of this book, provides corroboration and expansion of several of the arguments that are central to my discussion of the novel's plots. I have tried to indicate the most helpful of these connections in my notes.)

9. For a discussion of the paper's practice of popular casuistry see G. A. Starr, "From Casuistry to Fiction: The Importance of the *Athenian Mercury*." James Sutherland, *English Literature of the Late Seventeenth Century*, gives an overview of the paper's history and reception (241–42) and supplies the information about Norris's connection with it (227).

10. The second chapter of Tom Keymer's *Richardson's "Clarissa" and the Eighteenth-Century Reader* examines the first two volumes of *Clarissa* in the context of the seventeenth- and eighteenth-century casuistical tradition, the crux provided in that tradition by the issue of paternal authority vs. filial independence, and the way in which Richardson's epistolary form "relays the problem in its full difficulty by communicating it from every angle in a series of letters organized in terms of contending casuistical positions," so that, rather than instructing the reader, it "put[s] the problem to the reader in such a way as to enact the troubling unavailability of resolution" (123).

11. For a summary of the family connection between Bishop Butler and Richardson's friend Catherine Talbot, see Eaves and Kimpel's *Biography*, 357, 360.

12. In addition to an elementary education, Richardson may have had a year's grammar schooling, possibly at the Merchant Taylors' School in 1701–2. See Eaves and Kimpel, *Biography*, 9–11. In *Rhetoric, Romance, and Technology*, Walter Ong describes how from medieval times through the eighteenth century extrafamilial schooling in Latin, characterized by physical punishment, agonistic oratory, and the cult of manliness, served as a rite of passage that removed young males from the company of women and initiated them into (exclusively male) high culture and public life. See chapter 5, "Latin Language Study as a Renaissance Puberty Rite" (113–41), and the overview on 264–70.

13. Richardson was also profoundly influential. Terry Eagleton (*The Rape of Clarissa*, 2) characterizes him as "among the most vitally significant" of the "organic" intellectuals who made the English bourgeois cultural revolution. ("'Organic' intellectual" is Antonio Gramsci's term for "those writers, political leaders and theoreticians who are themselves products of the rising social class rather than remnants of the old.")

14. The bulk of the Richardson correspondence is contained in the standard published sources (Barbauld, Carroll, Slattery; *The Correspondence of Edward Young*) and in the Forster Collection of the National Art Library, Victoria and Albert Museum, which houses the most important unpublished letters.

15. Thus in his letter to Lady Bradshaigh of 5 October 1753, as he was getting *Sir Charles Grandison* through the printing: "What have I lost, by writing so much, and reading so little! Now I have done Writing, if Life be lent me, I must endeavour to recover the Power of Reading: Yet, what will be the End of it, if I do, but to shew me that I ought to have read more, and writt less?" (Carroll, *Selected Letters of Richardson*, 246).

16. Richardson's knowledge of contemporary theater and its dramatic literature is detailed mostly fully by Ira Konigsberg, *Samuel Richardson & the Dramatic Novel*, who describes not just his printing, reading and attending of plays, but his theatrically related friendships. See also A. D. McKillop, *Samuel Richardson: Printer and Novelist*, 139–55. What his dramatic knowledge means to his work is best explored by Mark Kinkead-Weekes, *Samuel Richardson, Dramatic Novelist*.

17. In "Theatrical Conventions in Richardson: Some Observations of a Novelist's Technique," Leo Hughes notes the prevalence of such theatrical gestural language in Richardson. He fails, however, to note the degree to which its use helps Richardson characterize the narrator as well as dramatize the scene. Uncle Antony, to cite an extreme case, mentions gestures primarily in order to caricature female emotions; he displays his own heightened emotion by other means. By contrast, extravagant accounts of extravagant gestures are Lovelace's stock in trade, not just about Clarissa but about everyone from the Smiths and his servant Will to himself.

Chapter 2. The Tested Woman Plot

1. This tradition of obedience to a prohibition, developing as it does into an ethics of refusal, certainly results in the "complicity" William Warner finds at the heart of the "Lady and the Serpent" construct with which he ends his reading of the novel. "Thus the virgin purity of the Lady makes the Serpent's role as violator plausible; the Serpent's attack makes the Lady seem chaste" (*Reading Clarissa*, 261). Unlike Warner, I do not view this "complicity" accusatorily; moreover, by "seem" I would seek to emphasize the idea of demonstration, where Warner insinuates a falsified appearance.

2. Chapters 2 and 3 of Flynn's *Samuel Richardson: A Man of Letters* usefully survey eighteenth-century convention and opinion about the nature and position of women. In *A Natural Passion: A Study of the Novels of Samuel Richardson,* the rich, judicious scholarship of Doody's chapters on pre-Richardsonian novels of love and seduction, on the heroic drama, and on the Virgin Martyr theme provide a helpful background for my thesis in this book.

3. In the terms of the distinction made here, Imogen in Shakespeare's *Cymbeline* is a prime example of a tested woman who feels no desire to be unchaste. By contrast, Bianca in Middleton's *Women Beware Women* is conscious of, and stirred by, the Duke's seductive appeal.

4. Beatrice-Joanna of Middleton's *Changeling* is disobedient and punished; in the anonymous *Edward III* the Countess is simply declared virtuous; Dame Christian Custance of Udall's *Ralph Roister Doister* faces an honest but inaccurate accusation; Shakespeare's Desdemona is the victim of deliberate slander.

5. Webster's Duchess of Malfi is the most powerful example of a tested woman whose trial occurs after her death; *Othello* displays a very swift version of the same plot move.

6. In *The Slandered Woman in Shakespeare*, Joyce Sexton rightly groups these plays as variations of a single type-story, "four tracings of one basic pattern" (11). I of course am situating them within the larger pattern of the Tested Woman Plot.

7. In *Endeavors of Art* (especially chapter 9, "Character," 216–58), Madeleine Doran surveys Renaissance attitudes towards dramatic decorum, attitudes which help account for treatments of class, gender, and motivation. One can summarize Renaissance dramatic practice as being based on a doctrine of types which stemmed from Aristotle's discussion of appropriateness in the depiction of character and was formalized by classical rhetorical advice such as Cicero's list of arguments from the person in *De inventione*.

8. As examples we have, for the tempter seeking possession, Tarquin in *The Rape of Lucrece* (Shakespeare's poem; Heywood's play); for the tempter hoping for a virtuous repulse, Vindice to his sister Castiza in *The Revenger's Tragedy*, probably by Middleton; for the tempter confused about his motives, Angelo in Shakespeare's *Measure for Measure;* for the use of a female bawd, Marina's test in Shakespeare's *Pericles;* for the use of a male bawd, Vindice.

9. An example of the successful seducer who flaunts his possession is Brachiano in Webster's *White Devil;* of the rebuffed tempter turned accuser, Iachimo in *Cymbeline;* of the possessor as accuser, Leontes; of the accuser who attempts to protect the possessor, Aurelio in Ford's *Lady's Trial;* of the accuser who attempts to injure the possessor (by turning him into chief accuser), Iago.

10. An example of the tempter become defender is Adurni in *The Lady's Trial;* of the accuser turned defender, Caraffa in Ford's *Love's Sacrifice.* God does not quite appear as a character in the literal drama, though a divinely inspired accident strikes dead the incestuous tempter of Tourneur's *Atheist's Tragedy* and a dream visitation from Jupiter confirms Imogen's purity and shakes the accusing Posthumus out of his lethargy. In the biblical and saints' tales from which so much of the literal drama takes its impetus, God takes a more active role. Thus He features as chief persuader in various versions of the Constance story, as for instance Chaucer's Man of Law's Tale; in the Susanna story He performs the miracle of opening Daniel's eyes and loosening his tongue in Susanna's defense.

11. We find an at least putatively neutral judge in the Duke of Shakespeare's *Measure for Measure;* the accuser as judge in Leontes of *The Winter's Tale* and Monticelso of *The White Devil;* the defender turned judge in the husband Frankford of Heywood's *Woman Killed with Kindness;* the tempter turned judge in the King of the anonymous *Edward III.*

12. We find male comprehension in *Othello*, expiation in *The Duchess of Malfi*, reconciliation in *Much Ado About Nothing*, a politically united front in Webster's *Appius and Virginia.* We see the wife received back into a marriage in *Cymbeline*, featured as the figurehead of a political campaign in *The Rape of Lucrece*, and, in the form of a calumniated wife/daughter duo, returned from both grave and exile in *The Winter's Tale.* In his monograph entitled *The Rapes of Lucretia*, Ian Donaldson sees this prototypal version of the story as divided between a Lucretia-focused action and a Brutus-focused action and helpfully discusses the range of political and psychological emphases to be found in its various literary treatments.

13. In *The Morphology of the Folktale*, Propp analyzes a large group of (primarily Central European) folktales from which he formulates a set of folktale "rules" or operating procedures. The rules that seem to me most generally significant as well as most salient to the Tested Woman Plot are the following:

A—The morphology of a tale is based on the functions of its characters (19–20).

B—Functions of characters serve as stable, constant elements in a tale, independent of how and by whom they are fulfilled, and the number of these functions is limited (21).

C—The sequence of functions is uniform (22).

D—Functions are defined independently of the characters who fulfill them (66) and may be distributed among characters in a variety of ways (79–83).

E—Motivations ("both the reasons and the aims of personages which cause them to commit various acts"), which are largely responsible for giving individual versions their distinctive coloring, are "the most inconstant and unstable elements of the tale" (75).

F—The overall morphology of a tale consists of one or more "moves," each proceeding from a choice among a stereotyped set of openings through a series of intermediary functions to one of several possible terminal functions (92–96).

14. Changing patterns of accusation, defense, and judgment of the Duchess are part of the history of Webster's sources; see Gunnar Boklund, *The Duchess of Malfi: Sources, Themes, Characters* (1962). Matteo Bandello's *Novelle* (1554), which provides the first account of this real-life horror story, frames the tale with a critique of revenge murders, though it makes no explicit moral commentary on the Duchess herself. But subsequent Renaissance versions, including Webster's main source William Painter (*Second Tome of the Palace of Pleasure*, 1567), increasingly inveigh against the Duchess's actions and character. Webster, of course, both redresses and complicates the balance. Twentieth-century criticism, from as early as E. E. Stoll's case (*John Webster* [1905], 118) that the play is a permutation of Kydian revenge tragedy in which the victim has become hero and her torturers the villains, has to a great extent focused upon the moral, political, sociological, and sexual ramifications of the Duchess's behavior. The most famous disagreement, perhaps, is William Empson's scathing review, "'Mine Eyes Dazzle'" (*Essays in Criticism*, 1964), of Clifford Leech's position in *Webster: "The Duchess of Malfi"* (1963) that Elizabethan audiences would have regarded the Duchess as wanton. Joyce E. Peterson's monograph, *Curs'd Example: The Duchess of Malfi and Commonweal Tragedy* (1978), passes particularly "hard and grievous" judgment on the Duchess. By contrast, D. C. Gunby (*"The Duchess of Malfi:* A Theological Approach," 1970) announces that "to find the positive values which the play offers, we must first consider the character of the Duchess and then her relationship with Bosola. I do not intend to discuss the already exhaustively treated— and it seems to me, peripheral—questions of the Duchess's guilt, or the propriety of the remarriage of widows. It is obvious, after all, where our sympathies are meant to lie: the moral issues are never in doubt" (189).

15. That "blasphemy [will] bring its certain and immediate consequence" of death, a consummation surely to be wished under the circumstances, is the interpretation preferred by Samuel Terrien in his exegesis in *The Interpreter's Bible*, 921.

16. "It is amazing to see how easily Yahweh, quite without reason, had let himself be influenced by one of his sons, by a *doubting thought,* and made unsure of Job's faithfulness. With his touchiness and suspiciousness the mere possibility of doubt was enough to infuriate him and induce that peculiar double-faced behaviour of which he had already given proof in the Garden of Eden, when he pointed out the tree to the First Parents and at the same time forbade them to eat of it. In this way he precipitated the Fall, which he

apparently never intended. Similarly, his faithful servant Job is now to be exposed to a rigorous moral test, quite gratuitously and to no purpose, although Yahweh is convinced of Job's faithfulness and constancy, and could moreover have assured himself beyond all doubt on this point had he taken counsel with his own omniscience" (C. G. Jung, *Answer to Job*, 375).

Chapter 3. Clarissa's Test

1. Of the thirty-nine uses of the word *prudence* (or its variants *prudent, prudently)* to be found in the King James Version of the Bible, including the Old Testament Apocrypha, twenty-nine occur as direct paraphrases of the word *wisdom* itself or in the context of a discussion of the nature of wisdom. Had Richardson wished to search systematically for his scriptural citations and allusions, he could have done so as easily as I, for Alexander Cruden's landmark *Concordance*, still our authority, was first published in 1737.

2. Cicero, *De inventione*, II, lii, 160, 327.

3. Ripa, *Iconologia*, 441–43, my translation. Thomas O. Sloane, whose *Donne, Milton, and the End of Humanist Rhetoric* drew my attention to the Ripa material, situates the Janus figure of Prudence in the context of the Humanist intellectual method of *controversia*. See also his reproduction of the three-faced Titian self-portrait, *Allegory of Prudence* (61).

4. Doody's chapter 7 in *A Natural Passion*, "Holy and Unholy Dying: The Deathbed Theme in *Clarissa*," provides a richly helpful matrix for my comments here. See especially 172–76 on Clarissa's "coffin work" and 185–86 on the antecedents of the coffin emblem of the encircled serpent.

5. In the "Father's House" section of his chapter on the first part of *Clarissa*, Tom Keymer discusses the contemporary religious, political and ethical debate over relations between fathers and children, and the importance of Num. 30:3–5 (footnoted by Richardson himself) in establishing the obligations of the woman living "in her father's house in her youth." Keymer agrees that in terms of the novel's form Clarissa's flight represents her Fall: "Clarissa has transgressed, and in the fullest sense: by disobeying her father's will and leaving her father's house, she has crossed or *passed beyond* its bounds as both a physical and an ethical realm. The rest of the novel will trace her efforts to atone" (*Richardson's "Clarissa" and the Eighteenth-Century Reader*, 107–8).

6. Richardson seems to have been deeply offended by the hypocritical brutalities of social extortion. The abduction and rescue of Harriet Byron introduces the hero of *Sir Charles Grandison* in combat against the extortionary features of the dueling code, under which one man might be forced by the aggression of another both to endanger or sacrifice his life and the well-being of his family, and to risk violating his moral principles by premeditated killing. In both moral and practical terms, the unsought duel was to a gentleman what forced marriage by abduction or rape was to a lady.

Chapter 4. Clarissa's Trial

1. In the introduction to his edition of Rowe's *Tragedy of Jane Shore* (another successful revival of the 1746–47 season), H. W. Pedicord suggests (xx) that Rowe's stage

popularity may have stemmed in part from his dramaturgical astuteness at beefing up and balancing out male roles to provide the maximum histrionic impact for the greatest number of actors. I conjecture further that Rowe may have been especially attracted to "she tragedy," which usually involves some version of the Tested Woman Plot, precisely because the male roles of this plot tend to be so evenly distributed and balanced.

2. "The remarkable histrionic performances given by [David] Garrick as Lothario and [James] Quin as Horatio . . . drew instant recognition from the London audiences; the theatre was crowded night after night" (Scouten, *The London Stage,* 1247). In October 1748, two months before publication of the last volumes of *Clarissa,* Richardson commented to Aaron Hill that he knew Garrick "pretty well." Several kinds of evidence from December 1748—the postscript to *Clarissa,* a letter from Garrick to Richardson, and a detailed explanation of Garrick's activities in a letter from Richardson to Hill—show actor and novelist on well-established good terms. See McKillop, *Samuel Richardson,* 159–62.

3. The schematic clarity with which the plot is laid out is not Rowe's work alone; *The Fair Penitent* is a rewriting and "regularizing" of Philip Massinger and Nathan Field's *Fatal Dowry* (1619). Both Massinger and Field were particularly competent and fluent practitioners of the tested woman play during the decades of its greatest popularity. Massinger's *Virgin Martyr* (1620, written with Thomas Dekker) pulls out all the stops in its presentation of the abused and eventually decapitated Saint Dorothea, whose faith and fortitude convert her Roman persecutors to Christianity, while Field's *Amends for Ladies* (1611) is a seamless triple-plotted comic romp in which the three possible types of tested women—a maid, a wife, and a widow—all bring their menfolk to a recognition of their virtue and the follies of male possessiveness.

4. Florian Stuber draws our attention to the importance of Dr. H., not only the last man to whose authority Clarissa submits, but a "perfectly paternal" figure whose authority is for once fully grounded in professional competence and human benevolence ("On Fathers and Authority in *Clarissa,*" 569–70). That he cannot "cure" Clarissa is part of our evidence that cure is not what she needs.

5. Both Belford and Richardson are explicit on this point, Belford urgently requesting Lovelace to return his letters, Richardson footnoting and explaining the request. Belford to Lovelace: "I shall detain Will no longer than just to beg that you will send me back this packet, and the last. Your memory is so good, that once reading is all you ever give, or need to give, to anything. And who but ourselves can make out our characters, were you inclined to let anybody see what passes between us? If I cannot be obliged, I shall be tempted to withhold what I write, till I have time to take a copy of it.[a]" Richardson's footnote: "[a] It may not be amiss to observe that Mr Belford's solicitude to get back his letters was owing to his desire of fulfilling the lady's wishes that he would furnish Miss Howe with materials to vindicate her memory" (L 452, 1 Sept., 1308). At this point in the novel Richardson is not yet fully committed to Belford's editorship in preference to a joint project with Miss Howe, but he is developing Belford's managerial capacities: Belford's hint about delaying his correspondence by copying if Lovelace does not agree to return the letters is a threat indeed to a correspondent marooned at Uxbridge and increasingly frantic for every scrap of intelligence.

6. In his powerful discussion of the forensic nature of the novel's third installment (*Richardson's "Clarissa" and the Eighteenth-Century Reader,* especially 221–39), Tom Keymer shows that the making of the book is itself a forensic enterprise in which the

epistolary form of the trial, "largely unmediated by counsel," gives the opportunity "to witness directly the sincerity of the parties concerned" (238).

7. Dated Florence, 13 April; enclosed (L 173.1, 561–64) in Clarissa's letter to Miss Howe written in the first week of May. The most persuasive part of Morden's letter, it may be, is his willingness to give Lovelace's charm and talent its due: "for he is really a man of parts and learning.... But you need not be told that a libertine man of sense does infinitely more mischief than a libertine of weak parts is able to do" (563), an effect that Clarissa has already tasted. As to reformation, writes her cousin, "Habit is not soon shook off. Libertines who are libertines in defiance of talents, of superior lights, of conviction, hardly ever reform but by miracle, or by incapacity. Well do I know my own sex" (562).

8. In their introduction to *Samuel Richardson: Tercentenary Essays*, Margaret Anne Doody and Peter Sabor call attention to Richardson's courage as a young businessman ("in his early thirties, with a new family and a great deal to lose") in continuing to print and otherwise support Tory authors under political and legal attack by the Whig consolidation. Other publishers and printers among the "High Flyers" went to jail or lost their presses, and Richardson "cannot have been at all certain during the 1720s that he would escape serious trouble. He courted danger" (2).

9. "Can it then be prudent, or even decent, for a Tradesman to encourage by his very presence, or support by the Effects of his Industry, Diversions so abusive of the Profession by which he lives, and by which not only these Catterpillars themselves, but the whole Nation, is supported?" *The Apprentice's Vade Mecum*, 11.

10. The most sheerly rewarding jibe I have found is a letter from John Cheale, duke of Richmond, 9 February 1748 (FM XVI.1.f.90), correcting Richardson's "egregious Blunder in Heraldry" at calling the "old Viscount's" daughter "Lady Charlotte Harlowe." "A Viscount's Daughter is only Miss before Marriage, and then only Mrs. Harlowe; which I wonder your Brother Booksellers of the genteel Side of Temple-Bar did not inform you of." Cheale's postscript adds "There are other Absurdities in your Book; but depend upon it, that by this I have mentioned, you have highly affronted all the Dukes, Marquisses, and Earls Daughters, in England, Scotland, and Ireland." Note that the postscript, which is by no means completely tongue in cheek, is directed in part at the women with whom by this means he is able to group Richardson and from whom he thereby distances himself.

11. Working from the patriarchal authority rather than the plot structure end of the novel, Florian Stuber reaches a similar conclusion: "Clarissa realizes her own authority gradually, in stages which can be marked by her changing attitude toward her father and the patriarchal authority for which he stands" ("On Fathers and Authority in *Clarissa*," 571).

12. The full title is *Meditations Collected from the Sacred Books: And Adapted to the Different Stages of a Deep Distress: Gloriously surmounted by Patience, Piety, and Resignation. Being those mentioned in the History of Clarissa as drawn up by her for her own Use.* Keymer identifies three copies, one in the Rothschild Collection in Trinity College, Cambridge; one in the Houghton Library, Harvard; and one in the Beinecke Rare Book Room, Yale. *Meditations* was reproduced as vol. 15 of Garland Publishing's facsimile series *Richardsoniana* (New York, 1976; out of print), and is now available as part of vol. 9 of *The Clarissa Project* (New York: AMS, 1990).

13. Determined to argue for Clarissa's "self-neutralization" and self-"removal" after the rape, Terry Castle does a passive-voice bypass of her post-madness activity: "Once Clarissa flees Lovelace and settles in at Mrs. Smith's . . . she is apprised by Anna of more

and more of his iniquities. The 'wilful falshoods, repeated forgeries, and numberless perjuries' are exposed (IV, 138). Her violent antipathy to Lovelace and his associates is the result of enlightenment. But at the same time a kind of hermeneutic malaise, an unwillingness to delve further into the deceitful texts of this world, begins to overtake her" (*Clarissa's Ciphers,* 124). Because such prose drains Clarissa of her initiative, it misrepresents both her character and her actions.

14. This wording, with minor modifications in spelling and punctuation, is that of the edition of the *Book of Common Prayer* established by the Savoy Conference in 1662 and unchanged until the second half of the twentieth century (*A New History of the Book of Common Prayer*). It would therefore have been Richardson's and Clarissa's text.

15. Peter Brooks, *Reading for the Plot: Design and Intention in Narrative*, 28; the Benjamin citation is from "The Storyteller" [*Der Erzähler*], in *Illuminations*, trans. Harry Zohn (New York: Schocken Books, 1969), 94. In *The Rapes of Lucretia*, Ian Donaldson discusses the more narrowly psychological and political issues related to Lucretia's death (see especially 21–25) and devotes a judicious chapter to the Lucretia-related motifs in *Clarissa;* he does not, however, deal with the broader issue of the relation between Clarissa's death and the overall plot shape of the novel.

16. Terry Eagleton notes the importance in Richardson's own life of a community bonded by heart and intellect, not blood or property. "For Richardson, ideology is thicker than blood: his 'family' is one constructed by literary practice, not genetically given. Stretching from his few intimate fellow writers and circle of women friends to his numerous correspondents, it widens to become effectively coextensive with the 'public sphere' of which he is spokesman. Within the extended family of his female coterie, Richardson certainly remains the smugly ensconced patriarch, trading a mildly eroticized banter for an agreeable flattery; there is little doubt that, wittingly or not, he exploits his literary powers to tighten his hold over women. Yet what he thereby fashions as a social form is also a kind of alternative to the patriarchal family, in which what counts is neither 'blood' nor sexual property but acumen and sensibility" (*The Rape of Clarissa,* 13).

Chapter 5. The Don Juan Plot

1. See Montague Summers's introduction to *The Libertine* in *The Complete Works of Thomas Shadwell*, 3, 11–14.

2. In *Le Mythe de Don Juan*, Jean Rousset provides the most interesting and thorough analysis of the structural elements of the Don Juan Plot; my description is based largely on his distinctions and terminology. Leo Weinstein's *The Metamorphoses of Don Juan* summarizes and analyzes the major versions of the story and provides a catalogue of works based on the Don Juan plot. I am indebted, here and throughout this chapter, to them both.

3. H. G. Tan, *La Matière de Don Juan et les genres littéraires*, 52–53, points out the importance of the theme of "la dénonciation de l'hypocrisie" in Molière's version of the Don Juan story.

4. Rousset (*Le Mythe de Don Juan,* 101): "un paladin de l'instantané"; (100): 'L'homme livré au seul présent ne se connaît ni passé ni avenir, comment tiendrait-il ce qu'il a promis? Il ne conçoit pas, au moment où il s'engage, qu'on puisse lui en demander compte plus tard; le futur est un temps qu'il ne sait pas conjuguer, qui échappe à sa compétence, parce qu'il

renvoie au-delà de son désir actual; . . . Et quand ce futur se réalise inopinément dans le présent, l'engagement remonte à un passé déjà tombé dans l'oubli. Don Juan n'a pas plus de mémoire que de prévision" (100).

5. [Thursday, 25 May], Lovelace to Belford—This letter appeared first in the third edition of 1751, though it was summarized by Richardson in editions one and two. Ross, who does not print the letter but does give it a number, argues (16–17) that it was actually written for, but omitted from, the first edition. It appears in the AMS edition as Letter 42, vol. 4 (252–61), and in the Everyman edition as Letter 109, vol. 2 (418–25).

6. *Postscript*, AMS ed., vol. 8 (291–92); Everyman ed., vol. 4 (559–60).

7. Jean Rousset, arguing that the essential Don Juan, the Don Juan of drama, can be characterized as "l'improvisateur contre la permanence" (*Le Mythe de Don Juan,* 95-103), emphasizes his trait of working to the moment rather than to plan, of seizing the target of opportunity: "Don Juan . . . brûle d'impatience, il conquiert à la hâte, il court d'une proie à l'autre; pressé de prendre et de passer, il ne se donne ni le temps ni la peine de projeter à froid, de méditer ses rapts; peu doué pour la prévision et les longues trames, il attaque parce que l'occasion l'entraîne. C'est la rencontre imprévue, c'est la chance de l'instant qui décident pour lui" (96). ("Don Juan . . . burns with impatience, he conquers in haste, he rushes from one prey to another; compelled to hit and run, he devotes neither time nor energy to thinking ahead or deliberating his assaults. Lacking foresight, unequipped by nature for the long haul, he attacks because an opportunity presents itself. The unexpected encounter, the luck of the moment, decides it all"—my translation.)

8. Though beginning from a rather different perspective, Cynthia Griffin Wolff arrives at a similar description of the incoherence of Lovelace's character: "At first the reader may be deluded—believing, with Clarissa, that the disguises merely serve to hide the real Lovelace from our view. As the novel progresses, however, we gradually come to realize that there is no real Lovelace behind the mask, that the mask itself is Lovelace, and that the formlessness of his nature, the very absence of a coherent identity, makes it impossible for him to limit himself by engaging in any social role" (*Samuel Richardson and the Eighteenth-Century Puritan Character,* 105).

9. J. G. Turner, "Lovelace and the Paradoxes of Libertinism," 73–74. Claude Reichler's work is *L'Age libertin* (Paris: Minuit, 1987).

10. Terry Eagleton remarks that Clarissa's most demoralizing double bind is "the truth that it is not so easy to distinguish resistance to power from collusion with it," and he goes on, "Few people are likely to bulk larger in a woman's life than the man who has raped her. . . ." This is why, as I have argued, Clarissa's refusal of the seduction of revenge is so important: "What will finally strike Lovelace impotent . . . is the fact that he cannot secure Clarissa's collusion" (*The Rape of Clarissa,* 82–83).

Chapter 6. Prudence: The Plot of the Purposeful Life

1. Aristotle's treatment of friendship in the *Nicomachean Ethics* is very extensive, encompassing books 8 and 9 and serving as an epitome of the entire ethics. Cicero's treatment in *De officiis* is much briefer and more cursory, but he agrees that although our obligations are owed first to our kin, our moral character is primarily reflected and shaped by friendship: "All needful material assistance is, therefore, due first of all to [kin]; but

intimate relationship of life and living, counsel, conversation, encouragement, comfort, and sometimes even reproof flourish best in friendships. And that friendship is sweetest which is cemented by congeniality of character" (I.xvii.58).

2. In the *Nicomachean Ethics* the importance of habit to the moral character is grounded in definition itself: "Virtue of character results from habit [*ethos*]; hence its name 'ethical', slightly varied from '*ethos*'" (I. ii.1103a16). "It is not unimportant, then, to acquire one sort of habit or another, right from our youth; rather, it is very important, indeed all-important" (I.ii.1103b23). The theme is summarized in X.ix.1179b–1180a, where Aristotle stresses that nature, habits, and teaching are all essential to produce the virtuous person. Among the young, teaching accomplishes nothing unless the soul of the student has been prepared by habit to be receptive to what is good, but adults also need to continue and become habituated to good practices.

3. Phillippa Foot's lead essay in *Virtues and Vices* gives a useful brief overview of the nature and tradition of virtue-based ethics. Alasdair MacIntyre's *After Virtue* describes the post-Renaissance decline of the virtue tradition that eventually devalued *phronesis* to "mere prudence" and that is in part responsible both for the existence of *Clarissa* and for its misreadings.

4. In her first chapter of *Samuel Richardson*, "The Self-Made Saint," Carol Houlihan Flynn describes Richardson's abiding interest in "the possibilities of the created self" (3) and the sources and effects of his moral perfectionism upon his work, especially upon the "saint's life" that is *Clarissa*. Usefully, she recognizes both the ethical and the mystical strains in his work: "[Clarissa's] perfectionism, a softened version of the Puritan progression towards sainthood, comes out of the latitudinarian tradition, an eighteenth-century form of perfectionism that John Passmore [*The Perfectability of Man*, London, 1970] defines as the 'daily practice of morality'. Be ye perfect, gradually." However, the rape "assault[s] her latitudinarian optimism and abruptly, not gradually, forc[es] her to change her notion of herself and her salvation. Purified through her sufferings . . . she emerges a saint in the mystic, not the Pelagian, tradition" (*Samuel Richardson*, 26). Cynthia Griffin Wolff's *Samuel Richardson and the Eighteenth-Century Puritan Character* examines the influence of the Puritan literary forms of the conscience-examining diary and the encomiastic funeral oration on the presentation of Clarissa's personality and social influence.

5. MacIntyre, *After Virtue*, especially chap. 4, "The Predecessor Culture and the Enlightenment Project of Justifying Morality," and chap. 16, "From the Virtues to Virtue and after Virtue."

6. John Norris, *Cursory Reflections upon a Book Call'd An Essay Concerning Human Understanding*, 1699.

7. On 27 April, Miss Howe attempts to make up the sum of money which Clarissa's sister refuses to forward to her: "I send fifty guineas by the bearer, enclosed in single papers in my Norris's *Miscellanies*" (L 148, 512), but Clarissa refuses them in her letter the next day: "Pardon me, my best, my kindest friend, that I return your Norris. In these more promising prospects, I cannot have occasion for your favour" (L 149, 513). Miss Howe regrets: "I am sorry you returned my Norris. But you must be allowed to do as you please" (L 150, 27 April, 514), and reiterates her regret in a further letter of 27 April: "I hope you'll have no cause to repent returning my Norris. It is forthcoming on demand" (L 156, 529). It is this last letter that Lovelace describes to Belford: "The first letter the women met with is dated April 27. . . . She says in it, *I hope you have no cause to repent returning my Norris— It is forthcoming on demand*. Now, what the devil can this mean!—Her Norris forthcoming

on demand!—The devil take me, if I am *out-Norrised!*—If such innocents can allow themselves to plot, to *Norris,* well may I" (L 198, 21 May, 634). Finally, as the Captain Tomlinson action is getting underway, Lovelace to Belford: "But once more I swear, that I will not be *out-Norrised* by a pair of novices. And yet I am very apprehensive, at times, of the consequences of Miss Howe's smuggling scheme" (L 215, [28 May], 691).

8. To emphasize the essentially philosophical character of both Norris's purposes and their realization we may usefully contrast *A Treatise on Christian Prudence. Extracted from Mr. Norris by John Wesley,* a thirty-five-page chapbook that first appeared in 1734 and had a second edition in 1742 when Richardson was getting *Clarissa* underway. In actuality Wesley's tract contains little of the essential Norris beyond the philosopher's name, the general topic, and some of the organization of the second part of the original work, for Wesley is writing, not philosophy, but a brief ethical handbook. Where Norris situates, considers and explains, Wesley defines and exhorts. The very existence of Wesley's hortatory extract, however, emphasizes the general public familiarity with Norris's work, which Wesley presumably enhanced as well as capitalized upon. Wesley's diaries and letters demonstrate his lifelong respect for Norris and his systematic reading of the whole range of Norris's work during the ten years before the publication of his extract. During these years Wesley was a close friend of the London printer Charles Rivington, who several times sat in with Wesley's theological study group at Oxford and who published Wesley's *Prudence* and his 1735 translation of Thomas à Kempis. See V. H. H. Green, *The Young Mr. Wesley,* 274 n. 4; 305–19; 134; and (for the friendship with Rivington) throughout. Rivington in turn was a close personal and professional friend of Richardson's, and his heirs published *Clarissa.* I cannot help wondering whether "Mr. Richardson," the old friend whom Wesley mentions visiting on a trip to London in 1729 (Green, *Young Mr. Wesley,* 129), was our author.

9. *The Practice of Christian Graces or The Whole Duty of Man,* published anonymously in 1658, immensely popular for the next two hundred years, ascribed to a variety of authors, and now generally agreed to have been written by Richard Allestree, suggests as the final ejaculation at the approach of death "Come Lord Jesu, come quickly" (395). We are helped to situate this book in the virtue ethics tradition by knowing its whole title, as above, and by reading "Graces" as intended, to mean "Virtues." The fact that the second, or *Whole Duty,* portion of the title is the one under which it became famous is itself an expression of the shift from a stress on aretic or virtue-based ethics to a stress on deontic or obligation-based ethics well underway by the end of the seventeenth century.

10. For example, in 1639 William Whately provides the definition of prudence as "a virtue by which a man doth worke rightly to happinesse" (*Prototypes,* I.xi. [1640] 102), which, accurately understood, clearly promotes the traditionally strenuous and capacious agenda. By 1899, A. B. Bruce (*Expositor,* 10 July) is capable of this chillingly reductive formulation: "It is better far to have the hero with all his drawbacks than to have nothing in human life that rises above prudentialism, commonplace, and humdrum" (OED).

11. Cynthia Griffin Wolff, *Samuel Richardson and the Eighteenth-Century Puritan Character* (136–41), discusses how Clarissa's prideful, sometimes even petulant, desire for virtuous singularity plays into Lovelace's "test-of-virtue" campaign and details some of the steps by means of which Clarissa begins to reject the dangerous notion that good must depend for its existence upon evil.

12. Translator Terence Irwin's note to 1098a18 on Aristotle's reference to the requirement of a "complete life" for complete virtue is worth reproducing because indicative of the

not always easy distinction in a virtue tradition based on character in action between momentary happiness and the shape of the happy life: "See 1101 a6, 1177b25, *EE* 1219b5, *MM* 1185a5. Complete virtue needs a complete life (which need not, however, be a whole lifetime; see 1101 a6–13) because virtuous activities need time to develop and to express themselves fully. This is especially clear with friendship, 1157a10, 1158a14, and with intelligence [Irwin's translation of *phronesis*, or prudence], 1143b7. Here the enduring character of virtue is important; see notes to 1100b11, 1140b29, 1156b12."

13. See especially *Nicomachean Ethics* X.viii.1177b–78b, in which contemplation (what translator Terence Irwin calls "theoretical study") is described as the most distinctive and elevated activity of the gods, and that of which only man among the animals is capable. To engage in contemplation is to live in a god-like way: "Such a life would be superior to the human level. For someone will live it not in so far as he is a human being, but in so far as he has some divine element in him. And the activity of this divine element is as much superior to the activity expressing the rest of virtue as this element is superior to the compound. Hence if understanding is something divine in comparison with a human being, so also will the life that expresses understanding be divine in comparison to human life" (X.viii.1177b30).

14. In his introduction to *Holy Living*, P. G. Stanwood discusses Taylor's lifelong and un-Anglican rejection of deathbed repentance and his insistence upon conversion to a holy life as the only means to salvation (see especially p. xliii). This position is firmly consonant with Taylor's virtue-based ethics and of course strongly condemnatory of Lovelace's specious hope of expiation by means of an unexpected and violent death.

15. The one exception is the omission of the youthful training stage with its pedagogue figure. This variation of Bunyan's has been typical of *evangelical* Christianity ever since the story of Saul on the road to Damascus. In the evangelical variation, designed for export to those not raised in the tradition, a powerful and sudden conversion serves as substitute.

16. Dated 22 April 1750; FM XV.2.f.83–84.

Chapter 7. Three into One: Plotting and Epistolary Technique

1. Richard Levin's *The Multiple Plot in English Renaissance Drama* makes a lucid and detailed case for the strong analogical relationships among multiple plots. Nearly all the Tested Woman Plays included in his analysis fall under his first two categories of "Direct Contrast" and "Three-Level Hierarchies."

2. James Woodress, *Willa Cather: A Literary Life*, 400. Here Cather is describing the narrative technique of her own saints' life, *Death Comes for the Archbishop*. She also found this compositional style in Puy de Chavannes's frescoes of the life of Ste. Genevieve (Woodress, *Willa Cather,* 399) and, I would presume, in Bunyan, whose *Pilgrim's Progress* she had loved since childhood. In *Death Comes for the Archbishop* Cather is especially adept with two central features of the Prudence Plot: the relationship between the *phronemoi* or virtue-friends, and the stage of contemplation which concludes the plot.

3. On 14 February 1754; Carroll, *Selected Letters of Richardson*, 289.

4. Gerard Watson cites this passage (*Retr.*, 1, 4) in the introduction to his translation of the *Soliloquies* (iv).

5. Lady Bradshaigh to Richardson, 9 October 1750; FM Xl.f.25.

6. See the responses of some of Florian Stuber's young women students ("Teaching *Pamela*," 17).

7. *Richardson's "Clarissa" and the Eighteenth-Century Reader*, 140; 243. Keymer's "missing judge" is the authorial voice, mine in addition, of course, the patriarchal character whose absence controls the plot. Keymer's compelling book grounds its overall argument in his discussion of the forensic characteristics of the novel which leave its interpretation finally, by Richardson's own design, in the hands of his "Sovereign Judges the Readers" (to Lady Bradshaigh, 8 Feb. 1754; Carroll, *Selected Letters of Richardson*, 280; cited by Keymer, *Richardson's "Clarissa,"* 243).

Works Cited

[Allestree, Richard?]. *The Practice of Christian Graces or The Whole Duty of Man*. 1658. Edited by William B. Hawkins. London: William Pickering, 1842.

Aquinas, St. Thomas. *Summa Theologiae*. Gen. ed. Thomas Gilby, O.P. Vol. 36, *Prudence* (2a2ae, 47–56). Translation and apparatus by Thomas Gilby, O.P. Cambridge: Blackfriars, 1974.

Aristotle. *Nicomachean Ethics*. Translated by Terence Irwin. Indianapolis, Ind.: Hackett, 1985.

The Athenian Oracle: being an Entire Collection of All the Valuable Questions and Answers in the Old Athenian Mercuries, . . . 3 vols. 2d ed. London: Andrew Bell, 1704.

———. *A Supplement to the Athenian Oracle:* . . . London: Andrew Bell, 1710.

Augustine, St. *Soliloquies and Immortality of the Soul*. Translation and commentary by Gerard Watson. Warminster, England: Aris and Phillips, 1990.

Barbauld, Anna Letitia. *The Correspondence of Samuel Richardson*. 6 vols. R. Phillips, 1804. Reprint. New York: AMS, 1966.

Boklund, Gunnar. *The Duchess of Malfi: Sources, Themes, Characters*. Cambridge: Harvard University Press, 1962.

Brooks, Peter. *Reading for the Plot: Design and Intention in Narrative*. New York: Knopf, 1984.

Bueler, Lois E. "Role-Splitting and Reintegration: The Tested Woman Plot in Ford." *Studies in English Literature, 1500-1900* 20 (1980): 325–44.

Carroll, John, ed. *Selected Letters of Samuel Richardson*. Oxford: Clarendon Press, 1964.

Castle, Terry. *Clarissa's Ciphers: Meaning and Disruption in Richardson's "Clarissa."* Ithaca, N.Y.: Cornell University Press, 1982.

Cicero, Marcus Tullius. *De inventione*. Translated by H. M. Hubbell. Loeb Classical Library. Cambridge: Harvard University Press, 1960.

———. *De officiis*. Translated by Walter Miller. Loeb Classical Library. Cambridge: Harvard University Press, 1975.

Cruden, Alexander. *Cruden's Complete Concordance to the Old and New Testaments*. London, 1737. Edited by A. D. Adams, C. H. Irwin, and S. A. Waters. Philadelphia: John C. Winston, 1949.

Damrosch, Leopold. *God's Plot & Man's Stories*. Chicago: University of Chicago Press, 1985.

Donaldson, Ian. *The Rapes of Lucretia: A Myth and Its Transformations.* Oxford: Clarendon Press, 1982.

Doody, Margaret Anne. *A Natural Passion: A Study of the Novels of Samuel Richardson.* London: Oxford University Press, 1974.

Doran, Madeleine. *Endeavors of Art: A Study of Form in Elizabethan Drama.* Madison: University of Wisconsin Press, 1954.

Eagleton, Terry. *The Rape of Clarissa: Writing, Sexuality, and Class Struggle in Samuel Richardson.* Oxford: Basil Blackwell, 1982.

Eaves, T. C. Duncan, and Ben D. Kimpel. *Samuel Richardson: A Biography.* Oxford: Clarendon Press, 1971.

Empson, William. "'Mine Eyes Dazzle.'" *Essays in Criticism* 14 (1964): 80–86.

Flynn, Carol Houlihan. *Samuel Richardson: A Man of Letters.* Princeton: Princeton University Press, 1982.

Foot, Phillippa. *Virtues and Vices.* Berkeley and Los Angeles: University of California Press, 1978.

Fortuna, James Louis. *"The Unsearchable Wisdom of God": A Study of Providence in Richardson's "Pamela."* University of Florida Monographs: Humanities, 49. Gainesville: University Presses of Florida, 1980.

Green, V. H. H. *The Young Mr. Wesley: A Study of John Wesley and Oxford.* London: Edward Arnold, 1961.

Gunby, D. C. *"The Duchess of Malfi:* A Theological Approach." In *Mermaid Critical Commentaries: John Webster,* edited by Brian Morris, 181–204. London: Ernest Benn, 1970.

Harris, Jocelyn. "Richardson: Original or Learned Genius?" In *Samuel Richardson: Tercentenary Essays,* edited by Margaret Anne Doody and Peter Sabor, 188–202. Cambridge: Cambridge University Press, 1989.

Hill, George B., ed. *Boswell's Life of Johnson.* Revised by L. F. Powell. 6 vols. Oxford: Clarendon Press, 1934.

Hughes, Leo. "Theatrical Conventions in Richardson: Some Observations on a Novelist's Technique." In *Restoration and Eighteenth-Century Literature,* edited by Carroll Camden, 239–50. Chicago: University of Chicago Press, 1963.

The Interpreter's Bible. Vol. 3. Exegesis on The Book of Job by Samuel Terrien. Nashville, Tenn.: Abingdon Press, 1954.

Jonsen, Albert, and Stephen Toulmin. *The Abuse of Casuistry: A History of Moral Reasoning.* Berkeley and Los Angeles: University of California Press, 1988.

Jung, Carl Gustav. *Answer to Job.* In *Collected Works of C. G. Jung,* vol. 11. 2d ed. Translated by R. F. C. Hull. Princeton: Princeton University Press, 1969.

Keymer, Tom. *Richardson's "Clarissa" and the Eighteenth-Century Reader.* Cambridge: Cambridge University Press, 1992.

———. "Richardson's *Meditations:* Clarissa's *Clarissa.*" In *Samuel Richardson: Tercentenary Essays,* edited by Margaret Anne Doody and Peter Sabor, 89–109. Cambridge: Cambridge University Press, 1989.

Kilfeather, Siobhán. "The Rise of Richardson Criticism." In *Samuel Richardson: Tercentenary Essays,* edited by Margaret Anne Doody and Peter Sabor, 251-66. Cambridge: Cambridge University Press, 1989.

Kinkead-Weekes, Mark. *Samuel Richardson, Dramatic Novelist.* Ithaca, N.Y.: Cornell University Press, 1973.

Konigsberg, Ira. *Samuel Richardson & the Dramatic Novel.* Lexington: University of Kentucky Press, 1968.

Leech, Clifford. *John Webster: "The Duchess of Malfi."* Great Neck, N.Y.: Barron, 1963.

Levin, Richard. *The Multiple Plot in English Renaissance Drama.* Chicago: University of Chicago Press, 1971.

MacIntyre, Alasdair. *After Virtue.* 2d ed. Notre Dame, Ind.: Notre Dame University Press, 1984.

———. *Whose Justice? Which Rationality?* Notre Dame, Ind.: Notre Dame University Press, 1988.

McKillop, Alan Dugald. *Samuel Richardson: Printer and Novelist.* [Hamden, Conn.:] Shoestring Press, 1960. Originally published Chapel Hill: University of North Carolina Press, 1936.

Murdoch, Iris. "On 'God' and 'Good'." In *Revisions: Changing Perspectives in Moral Philosophy*, edited by Stanley Hauerwas and Alasdair MacIntyre, 68–91. Notre Dame, Ind: University of Notre Dame Press, 1983. Originally published in *The Anatomy of Knowledge*, edited by Marjorie Grene. Amherst: University of Massachusetts Press, 1969.

A New History of the Book of Common Prayer. Based on the Work of Francis Procter. Revised and rewritten by Walter Howard Frere. London: Macmillan, 1902.

Norris, John. *A Treatise Concerning Christian Prudence: or The Principles of Practical Wisdom.* London: S. Manship, 1710.

Ong, Walter J. *Rhetoric, Romance, and Technology: Studies in the Interaction of Expression and Culture.* Ithaca, N.Y.: Cornell University Press, 1971.

Ovidius Naso, Publius. *Amores.* I, 8, 43. In *Heroides and Amores*, translated by Grant Showerman. Loeb Classical Library. Cambridge: Harvard University Press, 1914.

Pedicord, H. W., ed. *The Tragedy of Jane Shore*, by Nicholas Rowe. Lincoln: University of Nebraska Press, 1968.

Peterson, Joyce E. *Curs'd Example: The Duchess of Malfi and Commonweal Tragedy.* Columbia: University of Missouri Press, 1978.

Propp, Vladimir. *Morphology of the Folktale.* 1928. 1st ed., translated by Laurence Scott. 2d ed., revised and edited by Louis A. Wagner. Austin: University of Texas Press, 1968.

[Richardson, Samuel.] *The Apprentice's Vade Mecum.* 1734. Introduction by A. D. McKillop. Augustan Reprint Society, pub. nos. 169–70. Los Angeles: William Andrews Clark Memorial Library, UCLA, 1975.

Richardson, Samuel. *Clarissa or The History of a Young Lady.* Edited by Angus Ross. New York: Viking, 1985.

———. *Clarissa; or, The History of a Young Lady: Comprehending the Most Important Concerns of Private Life.* 3d ed. 8 vols. London: S. Richardson, 1751. Reprint, with a new introduction to the AMS edition by Florian Stuber. New York: AMS, 1990.

Ricoeur, Paul. *The Rule of Metaphor.* Translated by Robert Czerny. Toronto: University of Toronto Press, 1977.

Ripa, Cesare. *Iconologia*. Padua, 1611. Facsimile edition. New York: Garland, 1976.

Rousset, Jean. *Le Mythe de Don Juan*. Paris: Armand Colin, 1978.

Rowe, Nicholas. *The Fair Penitent*. Edited by Malcolm Goldstein. Lincoln: University of Nebraska Press, 1969.

Scouten, Arthur, ed. *The London Stage, 1660–1800*. Part 3: *1729–1747*. Carbondale: Southern Illinois University Press, 1961.

Sexton, Joyce. *The Slandered Woman in Shakespeare*. Victoria, B.C.: University of Victoria Press, 1978.

Shadwell, Thomas. *The Complete Works of Thomas Shadwell*, edited by Montague Summers. *The Libertine*, vol. 3, 9–93. 1927. Reprint. New York: Blom, 1968.

Slattery, William C., ed. *The Richardson-Stinstra Correspondence and Stinstra's Prefaces to Clarissa*. Carbondale: Southern Illinois University Press, 1969.

Sloane, Thomas O. *Donne, Milton, and the End of Humanist Rhetoric*. Berkeley and Los Angeles: University of California Press, 1985.

Starr, G. A. "From Casuistry to Fiction: The Importance of the *Athenian Mercury*." *Journal of the History of Ideas* 27 (1968): 17–32.

Stoll, E. E. *John Webster: The Periods of his Work as Determined by his Relations to the Drama of his Day*. 1905. Reprint. New York: Gordian Press, 1967.

Stuber, Florian. "On Fathers and Authority in *Clarissa*." *Studies in English Literature, 1500-1900* 25 (1985): 557–74.

———. "Teaching *Pamela*." In *Samuel Richardson: Tercentenary Essays*, edited by Margaret Anne Doody and Peter Sabor, 8–22. Cambridge: Cambridge University Press, 1989.

Sutherland, James R. *English Literature of the Late Seventeenth Century*. Oxford: Clarendon Press, 1969.

Tan, H. G. *La Matière de Don Juan et les genres littéraires*. Leyden: Presse universitaire de Leyde, 1976.

Taylor, Jeremy. *Holy Living and Holy Dying*. 2 vols. Edited by P. G. Stanwood. Oxford: Clarendon Press, 1989.

Turner, James Grantham. "Lovelace and the Paradoxes of Libertinism." In *Samuel Richardson: Tercentenary Essays*, edited by Margaret Anne Doody and Peter Sabor, 70–88. Cambridge: Cambridge University Press, 1989.

Warner, William Beatty. *Reading Clarissa: The Struggles of Interpretation*. New Haven: Yale University Press, 1979.

Weinstein, Leo. *The Metamorphoses of Don Juan*. Stanford, Calif.: Stanford University Press, 1959.

Wesley, John. *A Treatise Concerning Christian Prudence. Extracted from Mr. Norris by John Wesley*. London, 1734. (I consulted the second edition of 1742.)

Wither, George. *A Collection of Emblemes, Ancient and Moderne*. 1635. Facsimile reprint. Introduction by Rosemary Freeman. Columbia: University of South Carolina Press, 1975.

Wolff, Cynthia Griffin. *Samuel Richardson and the Eighteenth-Century Puritan Character*. Hamden, Conn.: Shoestring Press, 1972.

Woodress, James. *Willa Cather: A Literary Life*. Lincoln: University of Nebraska Press, 1987.

Young, Edward. *The Correspondence of Edward Young, 1683–1765*. Edited by Henry Pettit. Oxford: Clarendon Press, 1971.

Index

Accuser: character function in Tested
  Woman Plot, 30
Adam and Eve, story of: as Tested Woman
  Plot, 23
Amends for Ladies (Nathan Field): as
  multiple-plot drama, 142, 164n. 3
Appius and Virginia (John Webster), 161n.
  12
Apprentice's Vade Mecum, The (Samuel
  Richardson), 81–82
Aquinas, Thomas. *See* Thomas Aquinas,
  Saint
Aretic ethics, 123. *See also* Virtue ethics
Aristotle. See *Nicomachean Ethics*
Atheist's Tragedy, The (Cyril Tourneur),
  161n. 10
Athenian Mercury, The, 16–18; John
  Norris's connection with, 16, 125, 131
Athenian Oracle, The, 17, 18. See also
  Athenian Mercury, The
Augustine, Saint (of Hippo): Norris's
  objection to his definition of Pru-
  dence, 131; *Retractiones,* 152; *Solilo-
  quies,* 152–53
Authority: Test's questioning of, 23
Authority figures, in Tested Woman Plot:
  hierarchical relations among, 23;
  response to woman's choice, 25

Bandello, Matteo, 162n. 14
Beatitude: classical vs. Christian interpretation of, 136–37
Belford assumption of the Defender function toward Clarissa, 77–79; ethical
  retraining of, 98; on the making of the
  book of Clarissa's life, 164n. 5

Benjamin, Walter, 95, 166n. 15
Boklund, Gunnar, 162n. 14
Book of Common Prayer, The, 92–94,
  166n. 14
Bradshaigh, Lady: reaction to Lovelace,
  156; Richardson's letter to, 151–52
Broken Heart, The (John Ford), 21
Brooks, Peter: cites Walter Benjamin, 95,
  166n. 15; on critics' silence regarding
  plot, 12
Bunyan, John, 137–39, 170nn. 2 and 15
Burlador de Sevilla, El (Tirso de Molina),
  100
Butler, Bishop Joseph, 18

Castle, Terry, 71, 156, 158n. 2, 165n. 13
Casuistry: as dramatistic ethics, 17; dra-
  matic spectators as casuists, 20
Cather, Willa, 147, 170n. 2
Changeling, The (Thomas Middleton), 21,
  160n. 4
Character ethics. *See* Virtue ethics
Character functions: in Don Juan Plot,
  101–4; in Propp's analysis of folk-
  tales, 31–32; in Prudence Plot, 15,
  137–38; in Tested Woman Plot, 13,
  29–32, 34–35
Character-sharing: as plot-integrating
  device, 143–45
Chastity, 24–25
Chaucer, Geoffrey: The Man of Law's
  Tale, 161n. 10
Cheale, John, Duke of Richmond, 165n. 10
Cicero: time and the moral character of
  events, 44; virtue ethics, 120, 123,
  167n. 1

Clarissa: her attempt to live prudently, 52–53; as exemplary character in Prudence Plot, 119–21; her hopes for social aid against Lovelace, 62–63; the temptations of virtue, 63–66

Clarissa (Samuel Richardson): exemplars of vice in, 121; its characters' theological ignorance, 94

Clarissa, Don Juan Plot in: 13, 14, 21, 100–116; challenge to Death, 109–10; Clarissa's temptations in light of, 110–13; duel with male relative, 109; Lovelace's atypical staying power, 106–7; Morden as figure of Death, 109–10; problem of existential stasis, 113–16; rape insignificant as plot event, 146–47

Clarissa, integrating plots in: character-sharing, 143–45; event-sharing, 145–48; letters as performance medium, 148–51

Clarissa, Prudence Plot in: 13, 15–18, 117–40; friendship, 121–22; project of the purposeful life, 118; why Clarissa dies, 130–31

Clarissa, Tested Woman Plot in: 13–14, 21, 41–99, 146, 154–57; Heavenly Court and Christian Trinity, 95

Clarissa, Test in: 41–69; Clarissa's exemplary status, 43; Clarissa's flight as Fall, 54–55; effects of novelistic extension of time, 42; examination of moral psychology, 56–58; Lovelace's Testing intentions, 55–60; theme of patriarchal authority, 42–43; rape as end of Test, 68–69

Clarissa, Trial in: 70–99; building the community of friends, 98–99; character functions and patriarchal collapse, 76, 81–84; Clarissa as active agent of, 83, 87; Clarissa's attempt at family reconciliation, 90–92, 95–99; competing versions of the Trial, 71–72; Defender's role, 78–79; discovering and stating the truth, 87–90; disintegration and reintegration of the Self, 83–85; "father's house," 94–95; God

as ultimate Judge, 81, 92–95; Job's language as model for meditations, 86–87; Judge's role, 79–80; male response to woman's behavior, 74–76; Paper II and the Anglican Prayer of Humble Access, 92–94; preparing the book of Clarissa's life, 87; prosecution of Lovelace, 90–92; recognition of the Trial, 70–72, 84–87

Collection of Emblemes, A (George Wither), 44, 51–52; illustrations from, 45–48; contemplation: the final stage of the virtue-based life, 135–37

Courtship: as Lovelace's "plot," 67–69; *Clarissa* not a courtship story, 11–12; Don Juan's perversion of, 105; the Solmes action as, 63–64

Cruden, Alexander, 163n. 1

Cymbeline (William Shakespeare): character functions in, 161nn. 9 and 10; as Tested Woman Play, 27–29, 36–37, 160n. 3; reconciliation in, 161n. 12

Cyrano de Bergerac (Edmond Rostand), 145

Damrosch, Leopold, 159n. 8

Defender: character function in Tested Woman Plot, 30

Dekker, Thomas, 164n. 3

De officiis (Cicero), 120

Dialogue: audience reactive to, 149–50

Dom Juan, ou Le Festin de pierre (Molière), 101, 104, 166n. 3

Donaldson, Ian, 161n. 12, 166n. 15

Don Giovanni (Mozart/Da Ponti), 101, 110–13

Don Juan: attitude toward contract, 103; character of, 102–4; craving for variety, 106–7; incapable of faith in another, 108–9

Don Juan Plot, 100–116; challenge to Death in, 108–10; character functions in, 101; event sequence in, 101–2; identifying features of, 14–15; identity between character and function, 115–16; and libertinage, 102–3; literary history of, 13, 21, 100–101;

parodic of soliloquy plot, 153–54; as structural antitype of Tested Woman Plot, 113–16; temptations of, 110–13

Don Quixote (Miguel de Cervantes Saavedra), use of interpolated tale in, 142

Doody, Margaret Anne, 25, 159n. 8, 160n. 2, 163n. 4; and Peter Sabor, 165, 165n. 8

Doran, Madeleine, 161n. 7

Drama: audience as social/ethical interpreters of, 20–21; stereotyped features in, 19–20

Duchess of Malfi, The (John Webster): as Tested Woman play, 21; bankruptcy of patriarchal authority in, 82–83; critical attitudes toward ethical issues in, 162n. 14; male expiation in, 161n. 12; moral ambiguity of marriage in, 33–34; relation between genre and time in, 28; Trial after Tested Woman's death, 160n. 5; verbal echoes in Richardson, 158n. 5

Dunton, John, 16. See also *Athenian Mercury, The*

Eagleton, Terry, 149, 155, 156, 159n. 13, 166n. 16, 167n. 10

Eaves, T. C. Duncan, and Ben D. Kimpel, 80

Edward III (anonymous), 160n. 4, 161n. 11

Empson, William, 162n. 14

Epistolary form: letters as both dialogue and soliloquy, 149–53

Essay Concerning Human Understanding, An (John Locke), 125

Ethics, legalistic couched as prohibition, 22

Eve, story of: as Tested Woman Plot, 23

Event sequence: in Don Juan Plot, 101–2; in Prudence Plot, 15, 137–39, 147–48; in Tested Woman Plot, 13

Event-sharing as plot-integrating technique, 145–48

Fair Penitent, The (Nicholas Rowe), 19; as rewriting of *The Fatal Dowry*, 164n.

3; Belford's comparison of Calista and Clarissa, 73–74; character functions in, 73; commentary on Clarissa's Trial by means of, 72–74; epilogue to, 20; Lothario as passionate seducer in, 60

Familiar Letters (Samuel Richardson), 17

Fatal Dowry, The (Nathan Field and Phillip Massinger), 164n. 3

Field, Nathan: *Amends for Ladies*, 142, 164n. 3; *The Fatal Dowry*, 164n. 3

Fielding, Sarah: reading *Sir Charles Grandison*, 11

Flynn, Carol Houlihan, 25, 160n. 2, 168n. 4

Foot, Phillippa, 168n. 3

Fortune, James Louis, 159n. 8

Fraud: Cesare Ripa's characterization of, 132; illustration of, 50; Lovelace as Fraud, 132–35

Friendship: Belford and Morden not Clarissa's virtue-friends, 124; classical model of virtue-friendship *(phronesis)*, 121–22; virtue-friends in soliloquy/dialogue, 153

Functions, 13, 29. See also Character functions

Garrick, David, 101, 164n. 2

Genesis, the Book of, 23

Genre: as function of plot timing, 27–29

Gilbey, Thomas, 131

God, the problem of: as character in the Tested Woman Plot, 35–36, 38–40; dialogue between created and Creator, 39–40; God as Judge in *Clarissa*, 92

Golden Legend, The: unemphatic event sequence in, 147–48

Graham, David, 139–40

Green, V. H. H., 169n. 8

Gunby, D. C., 162n. 14

Harlowe, James: his shift from Defender to Accuser, 76–77

Harlowe, Mr.: his abrogation of authority, 54, 80–81

Harlowe family: their response to
   Clarissa's death, 96–97
Harris, Jocelyn, 12, 101, 158n. 5
Hill, Aaron, 19
Holy Living and Holy Dying (Jeremy
   Taylor): beatitude or the practice of
   the presence of God, 136–37; use of
   time, 128–29; virtue ethics, 18. *See
   also* Taylor, Jeremy
Hughes, Leo, 160n. 17

Iconologia (Cesare Ripa): characterization
   of Prudence, 51; characterization of
   Fraud, 132; illustrations, 49–50
Interpolated tale: as device for integrating
   plots, 141–42
Irwin, Terence, 131, 169n. 12

Job, the Book of: absence of the father, 85;
   as Tested Woman Plot, 35–36, 39–40;
   Job's Satan and Lovelace, 55; provo-
   cation of virtue, 36–37
Johnson, Samuel, 11
Jonsen, Albert, and Stephen Toulmin, 17
Judge: character function in the Tested
   Woman Plot, 30; readers as judges in
   the Tested Woman Plot, 156–57
Jung, C. G., 39

Keymer, Tom: "ethical indeterminacy" not
   an option in interpreting *Clarissa*,
   156–57; *Richardson's "Clarissa"
   and the Eighteenth-Century Reader,*
   159nn. 8 and 10, 163n. 5, 164n. 6,
   171n. 7; "Richardson's *Meditations,*"
   86–87
Kilfeather, Siobhán, 158n. 1
Kinkead-Weekes, Mark, 148, 150, 160n.
   16
Konigsberg, Ira, 160n. 16

Lady's Trial, The (John Ford), 161nn. 9
   and 10
Leech, Clifford, 162n. 14
Levin, Richard, 170n. 1
Libertine, The (Thomas Shadwell), 101
Lothario: as antitype of Don Juan, 103; as

tempter in *The Fair Penitent,* 60
Lovelace: as actor and impresario, 19–20,
   59; as Fraud, 132–35; as Tempter in
   the Tested Woman Plot, 53–69; his
   attempt to monopolize character
   functions, 76; his attitudes toward
   women, 53; his dream, 109; his response to Clarissa's death, 97–98; his
   use of rape to force marriage, 67–69
Lovelace in the Don Juan Plot: the issue of
   atheism, 104–6; as Don Juan, 104–5;
   his histrionic flare and moral emptiness, 107; his moral failure as artistic
   failure, 116
Love's Sacrifice (John Ford), 161n. 10

MacIntyre, Alasdair, 136, 168nn. 3 and 5
McKillop, A. D., 160n. 16, 164n. 2
Massinger, Phillip, 164n. 3
Measure for Measure (William
   Shakespeare), 21, 33, 161nn. 8 and 11
Meditations . . . (Samuel Richardson), 86–
   87, 165n. 12. *See also* Kymer, Tom:
   "Richardson's *Meditations*"
Milton, John. *See Paradise Regained*
Miscellanies (John Norris), 125–26. *See
   also* Norris, John
Molière, 101. *See also Dom Juan, ou Le
   Festin de pierre*
Morden: as figure of Death in the Don
   Juan Plot, 109–10; imperfect fit with
   Defender function in the Tested
   Woman Plot, 79
Morphology of the folktale, 31. *See also*
   Propp, Vladimir
Mozart/Da Ponti. *See Don Giovanni*
Much Ado About Nothing (William
   Shakespeare), 27–29, 142, 161n. 12
Multiple-plot drama as a device for inte-
   grating plots, 142–43
Murdoch, Iris, 116

Nicomachean Ethics (Aristotle), 120, 121,
   123, 125, 167n. 1, 168n. 2, 170n. 13;
   classical virtue ethics, 120–21, 123;
   complete life and long life, 169n. 12;
   contemplation, 135–37; friendship,

121–22; translation of *phronesis,* 131; virtue secondary and mediate to happiness, 129

Norris, John: career, 125; nature of fraud, 132; connection with *The Athenian Mercury,* 16; distinction between *actual* and *notional/habitual* understanding, 131–32; *Treatise Concerning Christian Prudence, A,* 125–26; virtue ethics, 18; virtue secondary and mediate to happiness, 129

Obedience: its structure as a moral virtue, 25–26; temptation of virtue of obedience, 63–65

Obligation ethics: in *The Whole Duty of Man,* 169n. 9

Ong, Walter, 159n. 12

Othello (William Shakespeare), 21, 27–29, 33–34, 160nn. 4 and 5; 161 nn. 9 and 12

Painter, William, 162n. 14

Pamela (Samuel Richardson): dialogue in soliloquy, 153; readers' responses to Pamela's virtue, 156; Tested Woman Plot in, 14, 41, 127

Paradise Regained (John Milton), Satan in, 37

Passmore, John, 168n. 4. *See also* Flynn, Carol Houlihan

Pedicord, H. W., 163n. 1

Pericles (William Shakespeare), 161n. 8

Peterson, Joyce E., 162n. 14

Phronemoi, 121, 124, 153. *See also* Friendship

Phronesis, 123, 131. *See also* Prudence

Pilgrim's Progress, The (John Bunyan): the Prudence Plot in, 137–39, 170n. 15, 170n. 2

Plot: three plot structures in *Clarissa,* 12–13

Plot-integrating techniques, standard: the interpolated tale, 141–42; the multiple-plot drama, 142–43

Practical wisdom, 123. *See also* Prudence

Practice of Christian Graces, or The

Whole Duty of Man, The (Richard Allestree?), 169n. 9. See also *Whole Duty of Man, The*

Prayer of Humble Access, The, 92–94. See also *Book of Common Prayer, The*

Prohibition against unchastity, 24; in Tested Woman type-story of Adam and Eve, 23; raises issues of obedience and authority, 22

Propp, Vladimir, regarding character functions in the folktale, 31–32, 161n. 13

Prudence: and Clarissa's coffin emblem, 51–52; and Clarissa's vices of excess and defect, 133–34; and the Tested Woman Plot, 52; as translation of *phronesis* and *prudentia,* 131; changing definitions of, 169n. 10; Clarissa exemplar of, 43–52, 118–21; character of, in *The Pilgrim's Progress,* 138; in relation to time, 44, 51; Ripa's characterization of, 132; synonymous with wisdom, 44–48, 51–52

Prudence Plot: antecedents of, 13; as a soliloquy plot, 153; character functions in, 137–38; ethical and literary features of, 15–16; event sequence in, 137–39; linear time sequence in, 126–28

Prudence Plot in *Clarissa,* 117–40; satanic manifestations in, 138–39; rape submerged into succession of life events, 147–48

Prudentia, 131. *See also* Prudence

Prudenza: Cesare Ripa's characterization of, 41; illustrations, 49

Purcell, Henry: incidental music for *The Libertine,* 101

Ralph Roister Doister (Nicholas Udall), 21, 160n. 4

Rape, in *Clarissa:* as event shared among the plots, 146–48

Rape of Lucrece, The (Thomas Heywood; William Shakespeare), 161 nn. 8 and 12

Reichler, Claude, 107–8, 167n. 9

Retractationes (Saint Augustine), 152
Revenger's Tragedy, The (Thomas
  Middleton?), 161 n. 8
Richardson, Samuel: *The Apprentice's
  Vade Mecum,* 81–82; *Clarissa* and
  the Christian "happy ending," 130–
  31; education and reading, 18; inter-
  est in drama, 18–20; *Meditations . . . ,*
  165 n. 12; youthful interest in ethics,
  16
Ripa, Cesare, *Iconologia:* characterization
  of Prudence, 51; characterization of
  Fraud, 142; illustrations, 49–50
"Roman Style," the: as parody of solilo-
  quizing intimacies of the virtue-
  friends, 153–54
Ross, Angus, 13
Rousset, Jean, 103, 109; 166nn. 2 and 4;
  167n. 7
Rowe, Nicholas, 19, 163 (chap. 4) n. 1;
  Lovelace's reference to, 75. See also
  Fair Penitent, The

Sabor, Peter, and Margaret Anne Doody,
  165 n. 8
Satan: as Tempter in the Book of Job, 36–
  38, 55; as Tempter in *Paradise Re-
  gained,* 37; in *The Pilgrim's
  Progress,* 138–39; Lovelace as Satan,
  134, 139
Scouten, Arthur, 164n. 2
Sexton, Joyce, 161 n. 6
Shadwell, Thomas, 101
Shakespeare: Tested Woman plays, 27–29.
  See also titles of individual plays
Sir Charles Grandison (Samuel
  Richardson), 11, 58, 163n. 6
Sloane, Thomas O., 163n. 3
Soliloquies (Saint Augustine), 152–53
Soliloquy, epistolary form as, 149–53
Stanwood, P. G., 170n. 14
Starr, G. A., 159n. 9
Steele, Richard, 19
Stoll, E. E., 162n. 14
Stuber, Florian, 164n. 4, 165n. 11, 171 n. 6
Summers, Montague, 166n. 1
Sutherland, James, 159n. 9

Tan, G. H., 108, 166n. 3
Taylor, Jeremy, 128, 170n. 14. See also
  Holy Living and Holy Dying
Temptation: in Test stage of Tested
  Woman Plot, 26
Tempter: as character function in Tested
  Woman Plot, 29–30; intentional
  dilemma of, 33; Lovelace as, 53–54
Tender Husband, The (Richard Steele), 19
Terrien, Samuel, 162n. 15
Test: technical use of term, 26
Tested Woman Plot: 13–14; as dialogue
  plot, 154–55; as structural antitype of
  Don Juan Plot, 113–16; character
  functions in, 29–32, 114–15; conflicts
  among authority figures in, 33–34;
  cyclical time scheme in, 126–27;
  duty-based ethics of, 126; literary
  history of, 14–21; moral purpose of
  Test/Trial sequence in, 32–34; two-
  stage event sequence in, 25–29
Tested Woman Plot, Test stage of: choice
  and intention of Tested Woman, 32–
  33; literary variations of, 27; the
  provocation of virtue in, 34–35
Tested Woman Plot, Trial stage of: ambiguities of interpretation in, 32–34;
  audience participation in interpretation of, 34–35, 156–57; for purpose
  of male reconciliation, 26, 28–29;
  literary variations of, 27
Theoria, 135. *See also* Contemplation
Thomas Aquinas, Saint, 123, 129, 131
Tirso de Molina: *El Burlador de Sevilla,*
  100
Tom Jones (Henry Fielding): use of inter-
  polated tale in, 142
*Treatise Concerning Christian Prudence,
  A* (John Norris), 125–26. *See also*
  Norris, John
Toulmin, Stephen, and Albert Jonsen, 17
Trial: technical use of term, 26
Turner, James Grantham, 102, 107–8,
  167n. 9

Virgin Martyr, The (Phillip Massinger and
  Thomas Dekker), 164n. 3

Virtue: the provocation of, 34–40; women's virtue equated to chastity, 24

Virtue ethics as a form of moral psychology, 118; Christian version of, 124–40; contrasted with deontic or duty-based ethics, 126; eighteenth-century decline of the tradition of, 125; happiness as the goal of, 129–31; in complete title of *The Whole Duty of Man,* 169n. 9; Mr. Brand's ignorance of, 124–25; seventeenth-century practice of, 18

Virtue-friends. *See* Friendship; *Phronemoi*

Warner, William, 158n. 1, 160n. 1

Weinstein, Leo, 100, 104, 166n. 2

Wesley, John, 169n. 8

White Devil, The (John Webster), 161nn. 9 and 11

Whole Duty of Man, The (Richard Allestree?), 18, 130, 169n. 9

Will, the: and the problem of knowledge, 58

Winter's Tale, The (William Shakespeare), 21, 27–29, 151, 161nn. 9, 11, and 12

Wisdom, 44. See also *Phronesis;* Practical wisdom; Prudence; *Prudentia*

Wither, George: *A Collection of Emblemes,* 44, 51–52; illustrations from, 45–48

Woman Killed with Kindness, A (Thomas Heywood), 21, 161n. 11

Women as objects of moral tests, 23–25

Women Beware Women (Thomas Middleton), 160n. 3

Wolff, Cynthia Griffin, 167n. 8, 168n. 4, 169n. 11

DATE DUE

7-12-96			
GAYLORD			PRINTED IN U.S.A.